Broadening the Horizons of Chinese History

Broadening the Horizons of Chinese History

Discourses, Syntheses, and Comparisons

Ray Huang

An East Gate Book

M.E. Sharpe
Armonk, New York
London, England

An East Gate Book

Copyright © 1999 by M.E. Sharpe, Inc.

Library of Congress Cataloging-in-Publication Data

Huang, Ray.
[Fang k'uan li shih ti shih chieh. English]
Broadening the horizons of Chinese history : discourses, syntheses, and comparisons / Ray Huang.
p.   cm.
"An East gate book."
Includes bibliographical references and index.
ISBN 0-7656-0347-0 (alk. paper). —
ISBN 0-7656-0348-9 (pbk. : alk. paper)
1. China—History.   2. China—Civilization—Western influences.
I. Title.
DS736.H779713   1999
951—dc21   98-39820
CIP

Printed in the United States of America

The paper used in this publication meets the minimum requirements of American National Standard for Information Sciences— Permanence of Paper for Printed Library Materials, ANSI Z 39.48-1984.

BM (c)   10   9   8   7   6   5   4   3   2   1
BM (p)   10   9   8   7   6   5   4   3   2   1

Contents

Preface

Time changes, and lately at an accelerated pace. The dawn of the present century saw Marconi still toying with transoceanic signals, and the Wright brothers managing to float in the air for no more than several hundred yards. Now, less than a hundred years later, long-distance travel by air is commonplace and FAX machines have become essential to home offices. Circumstances compel historians to work overtime. If we hesitate, chances are that our fresh ideas, even before being proofread, will be overtaken by events.

Some fifteen years ago, when I, for the first time, indicated that the protracted revolution in China is about to come to a fruitful conclusion, I received a mild reprimand from certain critics who felt that I was making a hasty statement. Today I would say that, on balance, the risk stemming from timidity far exceeds that coming out of audaciousness, so far as Chinese history is concerned.

In retrospect, the violent struggle in China in this passing century can be connected to the rapid advancement of technology in the outside world; it exerted an unbearable pressure on that country; overnight she discovered that she had to restructure herself in order to survive. At the conclusion of World War II Theodore White wrote: "China must change or die." The present volume testifies in support of his assertion.

The story can be worked out elaborately or presented summarily. The application of modern technology, in terms of jet liners and FAX machines and so forth, is hinged on an efficient economic workhorse. Capitalism might be an abused word; but, regardless, at this moment it seems that its most prominent feature is not class struggle, but deficit financing. The nation's resources must be utilized to the full to sustain the industrial growth. Based on Western experience, the application of such a system had to be inclusive and exclusive, encompassing both private and public sectors, and through taxation and public debt, especially governmental finance. A prerequisite for the universal dynamism is that the production and distribution instruments in the society must be well coordinated, all components made interchangeable, or else, the nation cannot even be mathematically managed, less to enter into any kind of competition. Traditional China, employing a pool of literati to administer the affairs of millions of peasants, was nowhere close to meeting the requirement.

China has paid a dear price indeed for the changeover. As the dust begins to settle, we realize that doctrinal agitation provides only the locomotion for the revolution; the inner logic of the sequence of events is a different matter; it can only be ascertained afterwards, objectively. I am hereby laying down the proceedings as they occurred, reviewed from various angles. While there are still personal touches in the material, I trust that as a whole it faithfully represents the *fait accompli* of the century: Chinese history has merged with Western civilization.

R.H.
February 22, 1999

Broadening the Horizons of Chinese History

— 1 —

The Structural Approach to Modern Chinese History

In the past several decades I have spent some time examining the financial management of the Ming dynasty. If I must single out one element as its most distinctive feature, I would say that the lack of logistical capacity at the middle echelon of the government was rather astounding. Unlike the Tang and Song, which assigned transportation commissioners to the field, who in turn accumulated material and funds in large geographical areas and disposed of them on broad directives from the imperial court,[1] the Ming system on the whole omitted such an operation.

Under the Ming dynasty the empire's financial resources were broken into numerous small segments. Lateral transactions between the revenue collecting agency and the disbursing agency were kept at the lowest level possible. Often the fiscal responsibility fell on the taxpayers who made the interprovincial deliveries. Likewise, on the Grand Canal the army personnel who operated the grain boats, down to squad leaders and first sergeants, were held responsible by imperial granaries for the last peck of rice in their custody. Thus the nation was thickly covered with short but crisscrossing supply lines. A frontier army post might receive supplies from a score of counties, a county might also make deliveries to dozens of installations.[2] The Ministry of Revenue ceased to be an operating agency; it was an accounting office, undoubtedly the largest in the world by then.

This basic organization should alarm the present-day reader for its negative influence over China's growth and development in modern times. So long as the aforementioned mode of governmental logistics prevailed, the service sector of the national economy had little opportunity to take the first step. Transportation and communication, being delivery vehicles, could not have gone ahead by themselves at a time when the materials and goods were not even packaged for consolidated delivery. Banking and insurance, instruments for commercial transactions, could not have thrived when the potentially largest customer—the government—acted so much in contradiction to commercial practice. The legal service supporting a modern economy of course had no reason to exist when business activities requiring court protection at such a level had not yet come into existence.

Given all this, it must be noted here that private capital in economically advanced societies usually owed its creation to public functions of some kind. From the Italian bankers who handled the papacy remittance to Rome to the Japanese military contractors in service to the *daimyo* lords, the accumulation of wealth was always facilitated by taking governmental offices as clients or by entering into partnership with them. China's fiscal organization under the Ming dynasty, in part reflecting the deliberate design of the dynastic founder, left no such avenue open. It is easy to imagine that when public function managed to carry on without developing the service sector of the economy, the *yamen* officials were least enthusiastic in working on it for private interests, and such service facilities could not have been effectively installed without governmental action, in the form of formal legislation or otherwise.

Indeed, changes did take place during the five centuries following the founding of the Ming. By the sixteenth century, the use of silver for tax payments led to the consolidation of some of the accounts, precipitating the Single Whip Reform. Salt dealers began to appear as an element to be reckoned with, to be followed by the Cohong merchants of the Qing. With the change of dynasty, the Manchus introduced a number of reforms. The most outstanding was the regularization of the collection of melting charges on silver payments ordered by the Yongzheng Emperor. Prototype banks managed by Shansi merchants became prominent after 1800. With the treaty system confirmed in the later part of the nineteenth century, new revenues such as maritime tariffs seemed to overtake the old-fashioned finances, not to mention the inland transit tax instituted during the suppression of the Taiping Rebellion.

But all the additions and revisions enumerated above did not substantially alter the outlook of China during the later imperial period.

The Single Whip Reform did not abandon, to borrow Liang Fangzhong's phraseology, the "Hongwu Model" of governmental finance. The reforms of the early Qing were largely managerial and disciplinary, not institutional and structural. The consolidation of the melting charges, as a recent study points out, had a limited and temporary effect only.[3] Neither the salt dealers, nor the Cohong merchants, nor the Shansi draft bankers had generated enough influence to establish a new trend for China's mercantile capitalization. Nor did the new revenue derived from the treaty system widely effect the complete fiscal changeover of the empire's inland sector. In any case, the bulk of the receipts had been set aside to pay foreign loans and war indemnities. In the absence of a change of the character of governance, the Ministry of Revenue under the Qing differed little from its forerunner under the Ming in keeping accounts of dozens of territorial units. The lack of a central treasury, the scattered receipts of revenue, and lateral transactions at the lower levels for the most part persisted through the Qing until the dawn of the present century.[4]

If I have not assembled sufficient evidence at close range to sustain this broad assertion, logical deduction from the circumstances within a wider context may serve the same purpose. In order to convert the management of China during the late imperial period into a system which we would consider rational today, we must realize, would first have required the establishing of regional treasuries in the provinces by the central government. But the separation of imperial revenue from provincial income would have shattered the monolithic structure of the government and along with it its monolithic administration. To promote commercial income as public policy with government backing would have required a degree of functional specialization which would have divided the bureaucracy, affecting its entire personal management system, including recruitment through literary examinations, training, evaluation, and transfer. Orderly administration could not have been accomplished without strengthening the judiciary branch of the government, whose professionalism would have separated it from the civil service proper. Above all, governmental service with elaboration and proficiency would have significantly increased its cost, which first and foremost had to be paid by the taxpayers, a dominant majority of whom were peasants. To make the system work, therefore, it would have been necessary to elevate their educational level. In sum, those prerequisites would have generally but distantly echoed the demands clamored for by the Hundred Days' Reform, a movement arising only close to the last decade of the Qing dynasty. Yet, despite the loud appeal of the reformers, few of the programs they advocated could have been put into effect. A sober fact remains that even to this day not all the requirements named above have been fulfilled by China.

A modern state differs from traditional China under the Ming and Qing primarily in the fact that its government is an active participant in the works of the national economy. Its influence over the central bank and stock exchange can affect the trend of commerce. Its monetary policy induces or restrains investment and employment. It can float bonds for deficit financing. It can sell public properties to create a deflationary influence. Its taxation, aside from collecting revenue, carries certain regulating power. There are other means of economic interference at its disposal. When these monetary and fiscal tools are perfected, the government can gradually substitute service for governance, thus relaxing the police power hanging over the head of the general population. Needless to say, China under the Ming and Qing never came close to such an eventuality. What makes the reading disturbing is that the fiscal setup did not even show a matrix from which parts of a formative modern state could have emerged.

The originator of the antiquated system was the Hongwu Emperor, the founder of the Ming. His peasant background undoubtedly had something to do with his political philosophy, but there is also evidence that he reacted adversely to the Song experience of Wang Anshi, who had tried without success to partially commercialize the dynasty's fiscal operation.[5] During Hongwu's reign, many large landowners were being persecuted. When things settled down, there was a dominant majority of small self-cultivators throughout the realm. Tax assessment was set at a very low level. In the sixteenth century, when surtaxes already inflated the initial assessment, the most heavily taxed districts of south Zhili registered only about twenty percent of the income from land as tax revenue. In other districts, less than ten percent was the general norm. There were cases when the tax take consisted of less than five percent of the crop yield. Apparently this general pattern was inherited wholesale by the Qing.[6]

Why, then, was there such a large volume of protest against excessive taxation? The answer is that while the general rate of taxation was low, it was horizontally assessed on all taxpayers, on a person who owned five *mou* of land no differently from those who owned five hundred *mou*. The low rate of assessment in fact created a large number of marginal landowners, whose tax delinquency was often pointed to as an example to encourage delay of payment by other taxpayers, which alarmed the officials. Moreover, affluent landowners could detach tax liability from their real estate by buying and selling land. They might pay premium prices for large tracts of land with less tax liability, or conversely, offer small parcels of land for sale at giveaway prices to unload a disproportionally large tax liability. As a rule, the untaxed benefit was not reinvested for production; it became an inducement for several interested parties to live off the same piece of property. The huge population increases from the fifteenth century on, which coincided with a diminishing standard of living, could not have been unrelated to this sequence.

Hongwu's obsession with localized economy was also reflected in the requisitioned services instituted during his reign. Although regular tax payment was low, peasants were obligated, collectively, to answer service calls from the government. Numerous office attendants from the chief clerk down to the doorman were drafted from the general population and remained unpaid. Office stationery, transportation, furniture, utensils, and even building maintenance were provided by the village communities according to elaborate procedures. The most cumbersome features of such levies were later eliminated by substituting them with surcharges overriding the land tax, which provided the basis of the Single Whip Reform. But that came later in the sixteenth century, almost two hundred years after the founding of the Ming. Nor was the reform as broad and sweeping as some scholars wish us to believe.[7] Consequently, the "Hongwu Model" of governmental finance remained in being during the rest of the dynasty and beyond.

What constituted the Hongwu Model of governmental finance? A lack of vision and imagination. Compulsory thriftiness from the viewpoint of a village economist to the point of putting the crude method of production ahead of circulation, distribution, and qualitative growth. And egalitarianism for the short term at the expense of investment for a better future. When the historian applies the present-day perspective to review the records of the sixteenth century, he can hardly agree with the majority opinion of his contemporaries who lament the passing away of the golden age of the Hongwu era (which under the circumstances reflected the state-sponsored orthodoxy anyway), but feels compelled to endorse the view of a handful of independent observers, hitherto unnoticed, that undertaxation which deprives the government of the capability to provide the needed services to the populace does more harm than good in the long run.[8]

Direct taxation on a multitude of small self-cultivators, a feature of the Chinese imperial order, continued through the Ming and Qing. Yet aside from the acts of Hongwu, no large-scale land redistribution was ever executed until the present century. Some historians, using inexact statements in the contemporary sources, built up theories of the concentration of landownership in a few hands during the late Ming. Most of the cases cannot stand serious investigation.[9] For the sheer interest of qualitative growth of the national economy, such concentration, had it taken place, probably would have been better than universal ownership on a small scale. As it happened, tenancy in China during the past five hundred years seems to have maintained a remarkably constant pattern. That is, it occurred atop parcelization of land. Thus large estates, say in excess of two thousand *mou* per household, were rare cases. Even medium holdings from that amount downward to two hundred *mou* do not appear to have been numerous. If they had been, it would have affected tax law and local administration. But the egalitarianism at lower levels did not exclude the situations that peasants and small owners were indebted to one another, held liens against one another's holding, and became part tenants or full tenants. Some empirical data on landholding in the early twentieth century (see appendix) give the impression of a close semblance to the conditions of several hundred years earlier. It leads us to think that taxation and fiscal policies in those several hundred years, treating the nation as a conglomeration of village communities, must have compelled the economy to expand in linear dimensions with few qualitative changes, while at the same time ownership of the modest-sized holdings was rotated, so that the system could perpetuate itself.

For the premodern society of the Ming and Qing, governmental finance in the early years virtually set up a permanent budget that had the effect of an unwritten constitution. For one thing, it defined the functions of the civil service and settled the disposition of the military. This we shall spell out in the following paragraphs. For another, it provided a general ceiling on the land tax, the revenue from which always tended to remain inelastic. Not only did after-tax income from the landed properties help to determine land price, tenancy conditions, farm wage, and local interest rates, it itself was also interlocked with these factors after the tax law was in effect for some time. The key to understanding this is that farm surplus, if any, lacked external outlets for investment, while at the same time the small cultivators had no other place to borrow except from their next door neighbors. In this way farm income, after the initial government take, had been claimed by too many interested parties to leave room for readjustment.[10]

Significantly, a general tax increase on a permanent basis was never declared by the Ming or Qing. The military supplies ordered by the former in the early seventeenth century to meet the Manchurian crisis, declared to be temporary, were apportioned through the provinces, where the regional authorities decided the internal rates. It was not that the imperial government wished to relax its centralized control, but that the Ministry of Revenue was not confident of the feasibility of a horizontal increase. Yet, as it happened, after the surcharges were ordered, one-third of the counties across the empire accumulated tax arrearages in excess of half the revenue due to the central government. Among them more than one hundred counties delivered nothing at all.[11] This is a case that can be described as one of the fiscal machinery being too fragile to sustain the overload.

After the Manchu takeover, most of these increases became permanent, despite official announcement to the contrary.[12] How it was done has never been clear; but it seems that military campaigns during the early Qing and the compilation of *Comprehensive Books on Taxation (Fuyi quanshu)* provided opportunities to absorb the levies into the tax ledger. Aside from those exceptions, tax increases were always made *ad hoc*, informally and locally. They could not be drastic because budgetary expansion in certain quarters would have led to imbalances in their relationship with corresponding offices. Thus the increases contributed little to the general finance. Toward the end of the Qing dynasty, state income from land showed no appreciable increase from the receipts of its early years, although by then the population had expanded by at least two and a half times.[13] Land survey for tax revision as a rule failed in the face of local obstruction, despite the fact that it was ordered under the Ming during the Zhang Juzheng era and under the Qing during the reign of Kangxi.[14] Circumstances surrounding those cases suggest that there were physical difficulties in implementing the plans, after so many small parcels of land had been exposed to so many complexities within the rural economy for so long.

The efficiency of the government, of course, could not be separated from the appropriation, both having been determined by tax income. If we look carefully at the contemporary records, we will notice that every office was understaffed by modern standards, the functionaries underpaid, and the funds either insufficient or barely sufficient for office maintenance. Many modern scholars have uncovered evidence of official embezzlement and off-schedule collections. But not enough has been said about the inadequate budgeting which perpetuated the old-fashioned polity.

An alert observer cannot fail but see the passive management of the Chinese local government in the later imperial period running over the long stretch of five hundred years.[15] Aside from exercising authority over tax collection and maintenance of law and order, the local magistrate represented no more than a goodwill office of the imperial court, profuse with ceremonial functions vis-à-vis the conglomeration of village communities. The legal system best reflected the arch-conservatism of this long period. The *Ming Code* was an imitation of the code of the Tang, which in turn followed the *Nine-Chapter Law* of the Han. The *Qing Code* stuck with the same pattern. Thus despite minor modifications and accretion of substatutes, China's written law over the past five hundred years, during which time the Western world made most of its advances, carried on a tradition of two millennia.

Jurisprudence of this mold took for granted that the imperial order personified the cosmic spirit on earth. Legal enforcement of Confucian morals therefore had the sanction of Natural Law. When translated into reality, human relationships, complicated as they were, could be summed up as self-evident in that the educated elite guided the unlettered, the male preceded the female, and the elder generation took a superior position over the younger. Graded kinship was moreover clarified by the differentiated degrees of mourning, a social institution that had state backing since the B.C. era. Broadly speaking, the function of the law code was to apply penalty to nonconformity against this body of precepts.[16] An ideal situation would have been that laws never need be enforced, or good conduct of the citizenry was assured by the semi-private offices of social hierarchy and kinship hierarchy. This atmosphere stymied any interest in developing the civil law.

I must admit, at this point, that in a long-term review of institutional history, the causes and effects can often be found interchangeable. While the small budget restricted the function of the government, the simplified governance aligned with a strict social discipline also demanded less funding. But since my objective is to survey the salient features of a state and society at large, the mutual influence between institutions serves my purpose just as well. From the above interlocked situation we can sense that a literary bureaucracy could benefit from it. Most posts within the civil service had been rendered identical. The overall design avoided complicated technical commitment. Beforehand, the economic issues arising from regional particularity had either been minimized or brushed aside. The officials, with their mental homogeneity and uniformity instilled by the standard classical education, could work diligently for more cultural coherence. A high degree of political centralism was feasible because administration had been made easier by the fact that the lower end, rather than the most advanced sector, had been selected as the natural criterion.

The arrangement also facilitated the civil service examination. Since the bureaucrats were recruited to perform a general function, the scope of the examination could be narrowed down and its content diluted and simplified, even though procedurally, it might appear to be more elaborate than ever.[17] But for this stability and equilibrium the Chinese have to pay a heavy price. The examination as an institution, as it is recognized today, provided most locomotion for upward social mobility, as the successful candidates were expected to become prominent, and, in due course, provide themselves with suitable family assets. This is to reap economic benefit through a noneconomic process. On the other hand, there was no mechanism, economic or otherwise, to prevent downward mobility.[18] Apparently, the social milieu put the accumulation of capital in disfavor. Consciously and unconsciously, state institutions fostered family estates of modest size changing hands. Fortunes of more substantial capitalization and more entrepreneurial design remained rare exceptions. As such, none of them left any significant mark in history as their Japanese counterparts did. It was not that their wealth failed to attract public admiration; but rather, they had no compelling function to perform in a society the public affairs of which were so deeply entrenched behind the village economy. Isolated, their success only made them more vulnerable; one slip could constitute a fatal failure. More often, though, the large fortunes were squandered away by descendants who did not know what to do with them.[19]

The "government-supervision and merchant-operation" (*guandu shangban*) enterprises of the late nineteenth century did little to alter the situation. In retrospect, their success relied on immunity and governmental protection rendered to those firms to compensate for all the disadvantages suffered by the mercantile interests, to fend off bureaucratic abuse and harassment, social prejudice, and legal incapacity; in addition to assistance beyond the ordinary scope. In other words, the public component, almost the left hand of the government, had to counter the works of its right hand. In the end it was the right hand that prevailed in its usual way.

Until very recently, groups of Chinese historians were trying to advance the theory that during the late Ming, a "sprouting of capitalism" took place in China. The thesis is built on a substantial number of entries, albeit scattered, about the introduction of commercial crops, the rise of handicrafts, and the influx of farm labor into the cities.[20] As I see it, the enumerated evidence has tumbled under its own weight because of a lack of organization. This is to say that exceptional and uncoordinated economic activities never by themselves appear as a system; much less do these carry a society, dominate its politics, and influence its thought.

According to French historian Fernand Braudel, neither Marx nor Adam Smith ever used the word "capitalism." The term in its present-day usage seems to have been started by Louis Blanc in the nineteenth century and further publicized by Werner Sombart in the early twentieth century.[21] English historian Sir George N. Clark has this to say: "The use of the word 'capitalism' as a name for the modern economic system was, I believe, invented in the middle of nineteenth century by socialists, and it meant a state of society in which the predominant power is that of the owners of capital."[22]

The sense of an organization induces us to think that in order to establish a modern economic system, there must be a wide extension of credit so that unused capital can go through the process of private borrowing to reach its maximum circulation. Entrepreneurs must furthermore hire managers on an impersonal basis, so that the scope of administration extends beyond their own supervisory power and that of their family circles. Likewise, technical support, including transportation, communication, insurance, legal services, etc., must be jointly utilized by various firms so that the extent of business transactions goes beyond the limit of separate operations. In this way a network of multilateral relationships is established, to be distinguished from strands of bilateral relationships. But the success of the three underlying conditions—i.e., wide extension of credit, impersonal management, and pooling of service facilities—depends on trust, and trust can never go very far without court protection. Everything has to be legally binding.

When capitalism takes hold in economically advanced nations, it marks the gradual application of commercial laws to the entire population. Not only family relations and inheritance must be bound by modern usage, but also, matters of fraud and deceit, embezzlement, mortgage, bankruptcy, etc., have to be treated in accordance with mercantile practice. If not, a lower level infrastructure cannot be built up on a broad basis to foster the business empires and networks.

Venice became the vanguard of this new system, in the same manner that the entire republic functioned like a business corporation. When the Dutch Republic came to the forefront, the federal constitution permitted the province of Holland, the most developed area, to continue its advancement instead of being dragged down by the territories still under dominant rural influence. When England completed the Glorious Revolution in 1689 to enter into the capitalist epoch *par excellence,* the judiciary made the readjustment. The King's Bench began to handle cases involving merchants according to mercantile practice.[23]

China under the Ming and Qing was neither inclined nor capable of taking such a plunge. There was too wide a distance between a society governed by patriarchal authority and one based on property rights that had been derived from municipal franchise. To cite certain economic impulses to be a sprouting of something which is beyond their character and purpose can be grossly misleading.

An American author had this to say about the founding of the Ming dynasty: "First came epidemic diseases, flood, famine, and population loss in the 1340s, then empirewide civil insurrection in the 1350s. Out of this crucible there rose by 1368 one of the largest, most centralized, and most despotic of the many dynastic regimes of China's history. It took another half century for that regime to evolve a stable institutional pattern, but that pattern, once established, sustained Chinese civilization down to the fall of the last dynasty in 1912. In some subtle ways, its influence continues to the present day."[24]

Imperial Chinese authority always seems to be centralized and despotic to Westerners, as there is no political entity in the experience of the entire Western world which has been so successful in ignoring regional particularity in its natural endowment to create a cultural cohesion over a large geographical area. But the above author's view on the Ming dynasty's enduring influence is well taken. And in today's perspective, this influence deserves to be examined just as readily for its negative effect as for its positiveness.

Chinese history, because of the magnitude that it encompasses, often creates illusory impressions with self-contradictory pictures when events are separated from the main context. On the founding of a dynasty and immediately after, there was usually a sudden burst of energy, which might or might not correspond to the constitution of the dynasty. The Ming and Qing are no exceptions. On the early Ming, the same American author said:

> A huge new capital city materializes almost in the middle of no-where, at imperial command. Ports and frontiers are thrown open to external trade one day, and slammed shut the next. Entire sectors of economic activity are fostered or stifled at the imperial wish. Vast armies march in and out of Mongolia and Vietnam. Gigantic fleets sail as far as East Africa. And it all works as if at the conscious twist of a hand on a faucet—or is shut down, at an opposite turn of the same hand on the same faucet.

This flurry of activity was supported mainly with off-schedule taxation and requisition.[25] The Chinese may have been the first to discover that at the founding of a dynasty, wartime mobilization can provide a temporary substitute for organizational logic, to compensate, at least for a while, for weak and ineffective state institutions, and that military efforts allow the empire to perform a few things extra. But the unusual exertion in no way contributes to the health or rationality of its fiscal system. On the contrary, when retrenchment sets in, the dismantlement as a rule takes down more than what is called for, as the above passage so aptly infers.

The Yongle Emperor might well have been more talented than his descendant the Wanli Emperor. Or, in a similar manner, the Qianlong Emperor seemed to be more resourceful than the Daoguang Emperor. But anyone making comparisons between those monarchs and the military exploits in their reigns should not consciously put aside the state institutions and social milieu behind them. The Ming military establishment, the *weisuo* system, was an imitation of a similar institution of the Mongols.[26] The system itself was used in turn by the Manchu banners. The overall objective of those institutions was to separate the military population from the general population, so that while the former retained its martial spirit, the latter would never be disturbed by wartime mobilization. The dynastic potency of the early Ming and early Qing stemmed mainly from the freshness of this arrangement. The lack of continual and renewed economic maintenance, however, quickly made them inoperative. In analyzing the cause of failure to provide the service support, one may have to take every item mentioned in this chapter into consideration.

In a broad and general sense, state institutions of the Ming and Qing could not make the dynasties adaptable to modern technology. In the Western experience, science and technology thrive on a robust economy which makes a great extent of division of labor possible, and which encourages regional specialization. In sum, the society as a whole takes advantage of natural imbalance and reaps benefits from the mutual competition of those diversified elements until they complement one another, even though in the process another state of imbalance on a higher level emerges. The key to the success is incessant activity. Against this trend, Ming and Qing society can be said to have been organized by a magnificent peasant who was obsessed with the traditional concept of equilibrium at the lowest level. The maneuver created an artificial balance beforehand.

We have read enough about the Sino-Japanese War of 1894–95, during which China's Beiyang Fleet engaged the Japanese navy in a crescent formation; at the crucial moment no one was sure whether it was under orders of the admiral, the British adviser, or the captain of the flagship, and ammunition was critically short for the guns in the main turrets. After the Battle of the Yellow Sea, the Japanese were able to take the fortress of Weihaiwei, then turn the coast defense guns against the Chinese warships seeking refuge in the harbor. We have also read enough about the Opium War of 1840–42, when Manchu bannermen used traditional weapons to face the modern armament and steamships of the British. From Arthur Waley's translation we have further learned that when the Chinese forces attempted to retake Ningbo, the commanding general was ninety miles away from the battle scene; that many staff officers of his had no military training at all; that ten days before the attack they held an essay contest to see who could write the best victory report in advance. During the operation the troops ran directly into mine fields.[27] These failures and mismanagement don't shock me, because in my own research of the

Liaodong Campaign of 1619[28] I came across details of how a Chinese general abandoned his firearms to engage the Manchu forces, how the attacking columns, dividing themselves on an arc of a hundred fifty miles, allowed Nurhaci's army to decimate them one after another, and how when the firearms were deployed, they were so ineffective that the Manchu cavalry dared to charge in close formations, which led to the complete collapse of the expedition.

What do the above three cases have in common? Poor generalship and poor admiralship, convincing as they are, do not provide all the answers. Nor does inadequate logistics. Armed forces are supposed to be the limbs of a nation; as such they have to be linked with the body, to put it figuratively, by bone structure, blood vessels, sinews and muscles, and the nerve system. This is a different way to say that in order to make an army and navy effective, not only the flow of personnel and equipment must be ever-ready and constant, but military technology and military thinking have also to correspond organically with the level of the society behind them. In the above cases the armed forces were actually foreign bodies in an all-out gamble of the empire, be it Ming or Qing. Yang Hao's army, before being routed by Nurhaci, was supported by an emergency tax increase over all the provinces except Guizhou.[29] Silver bullion was extracted from its circulating area for delivery to a remote frontier region. During the Opium War Yijing, the commanding general, set up four quartermasters' offices in two provinces to receive imperial remittances, which were either divided into four equal parts or delivered in a lump sum at one place. The accounts never tallied.[30] The Sino-Japanese War is sometimes referred to as Li Hongzhang's war.[31]

These are by no means arbitrarily selected cases. Each campaign marked a turning point of the empire. Yet even centuries apart, the pattern persisted; whether the supreme authority rested with a Chinese emperor or an alien ruler made no difference. Financial management best illustrated the organizational order. If loose connections recurred in times of crisis, it was because under ordinary conditions such connections did not exist. When the military blundered repeatedly so as to violate the basics and act against common sense, more likely the civil leadership directing it had been out of step. For the historian, a blank charge of corruption and incompetence against the individuals involved in the cases, justified or not, is not enough. He must reach back over several hundred years to the incident to visualize that if there was anything which was fundamentally wrong, it was structural and constitutional: China had to react to emergency situations with numbers that lacked quality control.

Indeed, my sketch is short and cursory. But the distinctive features of the Ming-Qing Empire—including its tax system, the land tenure under its management, the function of its local government, the classical education it patronized, the social values it promoted, the ceremonies it sponsored, the civil service examinations it regularly held and the social mobility that resulted from them, its jurisprudence and its armament, and, above all, its fiscal administration which penetrated through all these compartments and activities—persistently show a polity that on examination is nothing for which a close parallel can be found in the Western world. Its introversive and noncompetitive position, which have made the above closeknit pattern possible, makes it exceptional even in the Chinese tradition handed down by the Han, Tang, and Song. It was during the centuries when the Western nations busied themselves with the modernization process which united ownership and employment and tied public affairs with private interests (called capitalism, see above) that China was left alone to work out its own system, politically centralized, economically self-sufficient with numerous village cells, and culturally coherent enough to minimize regional differences. When in the nineteenth century the two civilizations clashed, the first to be exposed was the structural weakness of the Chinese Empire.

Some historians habitually call pre-Republican China feudal. But a conglomeration of village communities under an imperial cloak had little in common with a system where the political authority never relinquished its residual ownership of land. Compared with China's amorphous situation, the feudal system had an obvious advantage in that its power structure maintained an economic interest within the nation's production means. In Tokugawa Japan, the fief holder was also a large landowner. After the Meiji Restoration, the imperial government could follow the practice of the feudal barons to impose a land tax up to fifty percent of the yield, and for decades to come this revenue remained the major item of governmental income.[32] It is doubtful that the new government could proceed to create credit by issuing bonds and currency confidently with this financial mainstay as an assurance.

Further back in history, it is general knowledge that England created the national debt as an institution with the establishment of the Bank of

England in 1694. The shareholders loaned the government one million two hundred thousand pounds to start the latter's career in deficit financing. Less mentioned is that two years earlier, in 1692, the first unified land tax, doing away with tax farmers, had delivered two million pounds of its proceeds to the Exchequer.[33] In comparison, China's revolution in 1911 was a fruitless event. An antiquated monarchy was done away with. But as for source of revenue, the vanquished empire left next to nothing for its successors to exploit. The land tax was such a tattered patchwork that few could make sense of it, let alone derive from it revenue for national reconstruction. Its yield was so low that in most cases it was only adequate to support local government of the traditional type. (Yet the warlords in Sichuan are said to have collected payments for twenty years in advance.) When the national government was established in Nanjing, it simply disclaimed it.[34] For a large agricultural country, its inability to derive governmental income from agrarian sources must be an exceptional case. It would be most difficult to discount it as a factor responsible for the instability of the early years of the Republican era, when every major political crisis started with questions on finance, usually concerning the power to borrow overseas.

Yet, this was not the kind of constitutional problem that could be corrected by a better phrased and better thought out document. Pre-Republican China, as I have described it in my publications elsewhere, is like a submarine sandwich. The long piece of bread on the top resembles the literary bureaucracy, large but undifferentiated. The bottom piece simulates the peasantry, also lacking firm organization. The *baojia,* an improvised chain of command, could transmit simple orders only. The cultural links, represented by social values which placed the educated elite over the unlettered, the male over the female, and the older over the young, had lost much of their validity. Under any circumstances the circulation between the top layer and the bottom layer had depended entirely upon the civil service examination. Since the termination of the examinations in 1905, the superstructure of the nation was no longer in any effective way maintaining contact with the governed.

If within the agrarian population the landholding pattern had been clear and simple, or even if ownership had been concentrated in a few hands, the restructuring would have been an easier matter. But they were not. Apparently, the parcelization of land, peasant indebtedness, varying tenancy rates from place to place, and mortgage and usury in minute scales had been going on for centuries (see appendix). Customary rights associated with those practices were usually overseen by clan leaders and village heads, rarely attracting the attention of even the local officials.[35] If they had not been, the rural economy could not hold on and food production would be in jeopardy. Nevertheless, as it was, the lower strata of the nation, hundreds of millions of people, remained unreachable by the modern form of government on the top. As another measure of the latter's limited influence, before the war with Japan that started in 1937, the national government, deriving income mainly from commercial sources, compiled an annual budget of 1.251 billion *yuan*,[36] or at the three to one ratio equivalent to US$417 million, a sum woefully inadequate to keep pace with what it wished to accomplish.

What does all this mean? What is this chapter getting at?

Modern Chinese history, involving waves of mass movement, cannot be treated piecemeal. The cause-and-effect relationship applicable to the major events runs away from the short chronological order that we are familiar with in our own narrow disciplinary confines. Confronted with the unprecedented upheavals in China, we are more than ever being pressed to produce a synthesis that brings the events up-to-date. In view of this demand, I hereby propose:

1. That the base line of modern Chinese history be rolled back five hundred years to include the Ming dynasty. The longer time span enables us to see through the origins of China's dilemma in recent years. This vision also brings to the fore a number of interlocked issues.

2. That a structural renewal be recognized as the main theme of China's struggle in the past hundred years. While no precedent to this Herculean task can be found in the history books, we may visualize a certain anatomical semblance between China's case and that of England in the seventeenth century. At the settlement of the Glorious Revolution in 1689, England achieved a restitution of the superstructure (parliamentary supremacy, ceremonial monarchy, de facto separation of church and state, a prototype cabinet, and the two-party system), a reorganization of the infrastructure (gradual elimination of the copy hold, more integrated landholding, and more clarified tenure), and a restrengthening of the institutional links between the two (the bill of rights, the acceptance of equity, and commercial practice by the

common law courts). The proceedings and motivations of the two countries, unfolding centuries apart, may differ enormously. Nevertheless, the overall theme of a thorough restructuring to render the nation mathematically manageable and therefore to convert an organizational order based on an agrarian setting into one of commercial usage is prominent in both cases. This should do better than the tired abstract polemics on capitalism rising over feudalism.

3. That a "macro history" based on the aforementioned approach be worked out through consensus if possible but through individual effort if necessary. China in the 1980s differs drastically from what it was in the 1920s. What has been achieved, and why? These vital questions have not yet been answered. Historians are required to lengthen and widen their vision in order to inform the reader what changes are transient and what are of permanent value.

4. That courses of study be introduced at the college level to include macro history. The approach, emphasizing inductive method and synthetic process, has to differ from the normal analytical study typical of the doctoral dissertation format. This does not mean, however, that the latter should be discontinued. The study of micro history may need to be checked with macro history. Its findings may in turn feed back into the broader and more general studies.

I can anticipate the frowns of some of our colleagues for the boldness of my proposal and my rashness. But that is not what concerns me. We are facing a most unusual situation. World affairs are moving so fast that politicians, strategists, businessmen, and even tourists are currently acting without the benefit of our wisdom. I am afraid that if we continue to remain irresolute, we may risk the possibility of never being read at all.

Appendix

Quotations on Land Tenure
Before or at Mid-Twentieth Century

"Some of this privately owned land, which is held in large amounts by single landowners and leased to farmers, constitutes one of China's important problems, though the magnitude of this is sometimes overestimated. Somewhat less than three-fourths of the farm land is owned by the farmer himself and over one-fourth is rented. Ownership is more prevalent in the Wheat Region where seven-eighths is owned in comparison with three-fifths owned in the Rice Region." "The proportion of farmers who are in different categories of land tenure is another measure of the extent of tenancy. Over one-half of the farmers are owners, less than one-third part owners, and 17 percent are tenants. In the Wheat Region over three-fourths of the farmers are owners, while in the Rice Region less than two-fifths are owners. Tenant farmers in the Rice Region constitute one-fourth of the farmers, while over one-third of the farmers are part owners.The largest proportion of each class of tenure for the various areas is 80 percent for owners in the Winter Wheat-Kaoliang Area, 53 percent for part owners in the Rice-Tea Area, and 43 percent for tenants in the Szechuan Rice Area. In some localities all the farmers are owners, in others all are part owners, and in still others, all are tenants."

> —John Lossing Buck, *Land Utilization in China*
> (Shanghai, 1937), pp. 192–193. (A study of
> 16,786 farms in 168 locales and 38,258
> families in 22 provinces of China,
> 1929–1933.)

The Land Situation in the Border Areas . . .

"Roughly speaking, more than 60 percent of the land belonged to landlords and less than 40 percent to the peasants. In the Kiangsi sector, landownership was most concentrated in Suichuan County, where about 80 percent of the land belonged to landlords. Yunghsin came next with about 70 percent. In Wanan, Ningkang, and Lienhua there were more owner-peasants, but the landlords still owned the bulk of the land, i.e., about 60 percent of the total, while the peasants owned only 40 percent. In the Hunan sector, about 70 percent of this land in both Chaling and Linghsien belonged to the landlords."

> —Mao Zedong, *The Struggle in the Chingkang Mountains*
> (originally dated November 25, 1928. Reprinted in the
> *Selected Works* of the same author).

"Ten years ago there were two or three families each of whom had as much as 80 to 90 *mou,* and five or six families who had from 50 to 60 *mou.* In the last decade all these families have either broken into small units or else been forced to sell their land because of losses inflicted by bandits or because of the extravagance of their children. At present, perhaps no family has a holding greater than 40 *mou.*"

—Martin C. Yang, *A Chinese Village* (Columbia University Press, 1945), describing Taitou Village, close to Qingdao in Shandong. (A *mou* is approximately one-sixth of an acre.)

"Over 92 percent of the families owned some land, over 96 percent farmed some land. The average farm-owning family had four plots of ground with an area of 21.9 *mou.* The average farm-operating family farmed 21.2 *mou.* The per capita average for the *hsien* (county) was 3.6 *mou.* The largest family holding was 660 acres. But only 132 families, 0.2 percent, owned as much as 50 acres and only 9.0 percent as much as 50 *mou.*"

—Sidney D. Gamble, *Ting Hsien: A North China Rural Community* (Stanford University Press, 1954), p. 11. (Dingxian was in Hebei Province.)

" . . . In the whole *pao* (containing 854 persons) there are 1,535 *tan* of rice land. Of this, 1,137 *tan,* or roughly 75 percent, are farmed by full tenants. Only 398 *tan* are farmed by men who own all or part of their land."

—Doak Barnett, *China on the Eve of Communist Takeover* (New York, 1963), p. 120. Describing a community in Baxian, just outside the city of Chongqing, Sichuan Province. (A *tan* is the normal produce of about 107.4 liters in dry measurement.)

" . . . Measured against the local norm, those possessing over 30 *mou* constituted the landlord class. Those who possessed 20 to 30 *mou* or operated a farm of over 30 *mou* of owned or rented land were rich peasants." (pp. 40–41).

    " . . . There were five families, A, B, C, D, and E, who were large landowners by village standards though pitifully small by Western criteria. The land possession of those families in 1948–1949 totaled

310 *mou* and was distributed as shown in the accompanying tabulation. [It shows the largest owner had 120 *mou,* or about 20 acres.] These 310 *mou* constituted 25.8 percent of the village's total cultivated land, but the five families made up only 2.18 percent of the village's families . . . " (pp. 43–44).

—C.K. Yang, *A Chinese Village in Early Communist Transition* (MIT Press, 1959). Describing a village near Canton, Guangdong Province.

" . . . On the eve of land revolution the landlords and the rich peasants together made up about seven percent of the population and owned directly 164 acres, or 18 percent of the land. Through religious and clan associations they controlled another 114 acres bringing the total land under their control to 278 acres, or 31 percent." (p. 28).

" . . . The heart of Ching-ho's 'empire' (the holdings of the largest landlord) consisted of 23 acres of fertile land." (p. 29).

—William Hinton, *Fanshen: A Documentary of Revolution in a Chinese Village* (New York, 1966). Describing a village in Lucheng County, Shanxi Province.

Notes

Source: Proceedings of the Second International Conference on Sinology, Academia Sinica, Taipei, Taiwan, Republic of China, 1989.

1. For the function of the transportation commissioner under the Song, see *Song shi* (Beijing Zhonghua shuju, punctuated ed.), vol. 12, ch. 167, pp. 3963–3965. This is not to be confused with a Ming official assuming the same title. The latter, a salt administrator, had very limited authority.

2. A good example is provided by Shen Bang in *Wanshu zaji* (Beijing, 1961 reprint), pp. 49–50.

3. For the nature of the Qing reforms, see Frederic Wakeman Jr., *The Great Enterprise: The Manchu Reconstruction of Imperial order in Seventeenth-Century China* (University of California Press, 1985), vol. 1, pp. 454–465; vol. 2, pp. 706–7, 852, 856, 909–10. For the limited and temporary effect of Yongzheng's reform with the melting charge see Madeline Zelin, *The Magistrate's Tael: Rationalizing Fiscal Reform in Eighteenth-Century Ch'ing China* (University of California Press, 1984), pp. 264–66.

4. Ch'en Gonglu, *Zhongguo jindaishi* (Taipei, 1965 rev. ed.), pp. 238–39, 665–66, 687–89; E-tu Zen Sun, "The Board of Revenue in Nineteenth Century China," *Harvard Journal of Asiatic Studies* 24 (1962–1963), pp. 175–228.

5. *Ming shilu: Taizu shilu* (Taipei, 1962 reprint), pp. 2141, 2681–2682.

6. Ray Huang, *Taxation and Governmental Finance in Sixteenth-Century Ming China* (Cambridge University Press, 1974), pp. 170–74.

7. Ibid., pp. 118–22.

8. Ibid., pp. 186–88.

9. Ibid., p. 157.

10. Ibid., pp. 159–62.

11. *Chongzhen cunshi suchao* (Beijing, 1934 reprint), vol. 2, pp. 72–89.

12. This can be observed from annual statistics in *Qing shilu.* See Ray Huang, "Fiscal Administration during the Ming Dyansty," in *Chinese Government in Ming Times: Seven Studies,* ed. by Charles O. Hucker (Columbia University Press, 1969), pp. 121–22. Additional evidence appears in note 7, Huang, *Taxation and Governmental Finance,* p. 365.

13. Yeh-chien Wang, "The Fiscal Importance of the Land Tax during the Qing Period," *Journal of Asian Studies* 30: 4 (1971), p. 342. The same theme is restated in the same author's *Land Tax in Imperial China, 1750–1911* (Harvard University Press, 1973).

14. Gensho Nishimura, "Shinsho no tochi jiryo ni tsuite," *Toyoshi Kenyū,* 23: 3 (December 1974), pp. 424–64.

15. Those features can be seen in T'ung-tsu Ch'ü, *Local Government in China under the Ch'ing* (Harvard University Press, 1962).

16. T'ung-tsu Ch'ü, *Law and Society in Traditional China* (Paris and The Hague, 1961). Derk Bodde and Clarence Morris, *Law in Imperial China: Exemplified by 190 Ch'ing Dynasty Cases* (Harvard University Press, 1967), pp. 76–112.

17. Teng Ssu-yü, *Zhongguo kaoshi zhidushi* (Taipei, 1967), p. 73.

18. Ping-ti Ho, *The Ladder of Success in Imperial China* (Columbia University Press, 1962), pp. 262–66.

19. Ping-ti Ho, "The Salt Merchants of Yangchu: A Study of Commercial Capitalism in Eighteenth Century China," *Harvard Journal of Asiatic Studies* 17: 1–2 (1964).

20. A fairly recent survey is provided by Jin Shi, "Zhongguo zibenzhuyi mengya lilunde pingjie," *The Chinese Intellectual* 2: 4 (summer 1986), pp. 3–45.

21. Fernand Braudel, *Civilization and Capitalism, 15th-18th Century,* vol. 2, *The Wheels of Commerce,* trans. by Sian Reynolds (New York, 1982), p. 237.

22. Clark, *The Seventeenth Century,* 2nd ed. (New York, 1947), p. 11.

23. Theodore Plucknett, *A Concise History of the Common Law,* 5th ed. (London, 1956), pp. 245–48.

24. John Dardess, "Review of Edward Dreyer's *Early Ming China,*" in *Ming Studies* 15 (fall 1982), p. 9.

25. See Huang, "Administrative Statistics," in *Explorations in the History of Science and Technology,* for explanation.

26. Romeyn Taylor, "Yuan Origins of the Wei-so System," in Hucker, *Chinese Government in Ming Times,* pp. 23–40.

27. Arthur Waley, *The Opium War Through Chinese Eyes,* paperback ed. (Stanford University Press, 1968), pp. 158–85.

28. Ray Huang, "The Liaotung Campaign in 1619," *Oriens Extremus* 28: 1 (1981), pp. 30–54.

29. *Ming shilu: Shenzong shilu* (Taipei, 1966 reprint), pp. 10862–10865.

30. Waley, *The Opium War*, p. 179.

31. John L. Rawlinson, *China's Struggle for Naval Development: 1839–1895* (Harvard University Press, 1967), pp. 131–32, 138–39, 142, 184.

32. John K. Fairbank, Edwin O. Reischauer, and Albert M. Craig, *East Asia: The Modern Transformation* (Boston, 1965), pp. 235–36.

33. J.S. Bromley, ed., *Cambridge Modern History,* vol. 6 (Cambridge University Press, 1970), pp. 285–86.

34. Fairbank et al., *East Asia: The Modern Transformation,* p. 100.

35. Martin C. Yang has provided some interesting illustrations. See Yang, *A Chinese Village: Taitou, Shantung Province* (Columbia University Press, 1945).

36. Arthur N. Young, *China's Nation-Building Effort 1927–1937: The Financial and Economic Record* (Hoover Institution Press, 1971), pp. 433–39.

— 2 —

The History of
the Ming Dynasty and
Today's World

After several decades of hard and intense work by scholars in and out of China, the history of the Ming Dynasty is no longer an immature field. This situation I have not hesitated to take advantage of. Benefiting from the wide circulation of reprinted source material and the appearance of a large number of monographs and articles on the period, my small book, *1587, A Year of No Significance,* tries to present a profile of the dynasty in its late stage. The compilation is made possible by the voluminous data on hand, which would not have been so readily available even a short time ago.

True, there is no limit to the depth of factual details that historians may endeavor to unearth. At this point, however, we can at least claim that a general picture of Chinese society in the late sixteenth century is within our power to present.

With a slight touch of crudeness, we can even assert that the society in description is a submarine sandwich. The long piece of bread on the top is the literary bureaucracy and the long piece of bread on the bottom is the peasantry, both enormous and undifferentiated. Simplicity and uniformity being its structural features, this traditional organization is fostered by a legal code that gives deference to the imperial patentee over the commoner, the male over the female, and the aged over the young. The link between the top and the bottom, provided by the civil service examinations, affirms those principles. While successful in warding off all the possible complexities, such a social order from today's viewpoint can never escape the criticism of being obsolete and uninspiring.

But others may challenge us: Is this a fair observation? Have not the observers, dissatisfied with conditions in the twentieth century, tended to see their shadows in the sixteenth? If the old society must be renewed, how far should the reconstruction go?

Will not the reform necessitate a total negation of Chinese civilization altogether, or, if the history of the Ming Dynasty appears to be a negative influence, will not a correction be possible by simply reversing its most vital features?

Historians are supposed to supply answers to these questions.

Another complication requiring our attention is that in the past score of years the records of the Ming Dynasty have been greatly abused by a number of writers. Chinese authors are accustomed to latent and subtle comments. Characters of the sixteenth century, together with their deeds and backgrounds, exaggerated and distorted, have been utilized as political tools. Admittedly, we have averted such manipulation, which makes political capital out of scholarship, but how can we clear ourselves of the suspicion of similar misapplications?

The history of the Ming Dynasty alone does not empower us to clarify the situation. A better way to establish confidence is to test our findings with facts and developments lying beyond our field of speciality. Mutual consistency between the two should be on firm ground to testify for the reliability of the conclusions drawn. In our study of the Ming Dynasty, experience has convinced us that answers to big questions are not always to be found within. On the other hand, there are historical events that occurred elsewhere the significance of which becomes more readily perceptible to us than to other specialists. This article proposes to go out of the way to establish such connections. The self-imposed boundaries of scholarly specialization, after all, are no more than a device for collegiate division of labor. They have never been set up to encourage parochialism and justify accountabilities.

The following is the preliminary result of an attempt in that direction.

First, while criticizing the characters of the Ming Dynasty, we must keep in mind that the Ming empire itself was a product of the terrain and climate of the Asian continent.

At a quick glance, two prominent features of the Ming Dynasty demand our recognition. In the area of political organization, there was a preponderant concentration of power at the center. In the more than 1,100 counties, all the magistrates were appointed and removed by the court of Peking. The districts were not empowered to decide on matters of budget and taxation, which were controlled by the imperial government. In the area of social organization, the substitution of an ethical code for law was evident. The reliance on doctrinal cohesion to maintain communal order exceeded the extent reached by any other dynasty in Chinese history.

In part due to the perceptive narrowness of the Ming people, the aforementioned setup nevertheless had to be considered a result of circumstances. In its formative years, the Chinese civilization had been influenced by the contributing factors of the Yellow River region, the land of the loess. It is generally understood that the river, running through a vast area where the fine and porous soil accounts for the large silt content in its current, has a constant tendency to clog its own course and cause dikes to break and enormous inundations to occur. The problem cannot be dealt with locally. This predicament has a historical origin that can be traced at least to the Spring and Autumn Period (722–481 B.C.). In 652 B.C. Duke Huan of Qi convened his league of principalities at Kuiqiu. A mutual pledge by the participating states is recorded in the various sources as "not to execute improper dikes," "not to hinder the water flow," and "not to clog the ravines." In the *Book of Mencius,* water control is mentioned no less than eleven times. On one occasion, the Second Sage said to Bai Gui: "Yu took the Four Seas as a receptacle [of the overflowing water]. Now you instead take the adjacent states as receptacles. . . . Flood is one of the things that humane administrators dread. Sir, you are just too much." The stone inscriptions of his own achievements erected by the First Emperor of the Qin are reproduced in *The Records of History.* One of the meritorious deeds that the Great Unifier credited to himself was the "neutralization of the barriers that obstructed water flows." These are evidence that China's political unification, achieved in the B.C. era, had come under the pressing demand for a coordinated effort in dealing with the flood problem which, over and above other technical considerations, has remained in force for the past two thousand years.

A second factor compelling China to proceed to an early national unification and to follow it with political centralization was the effect of monsoon rain on agriculture. The summer monsoon in China comes from the direction of the Philippine Sea. It by itself does not give rain. The moisture in the air current depends upon winds blowing from west to east and north-east, lifting it to an altitude to be cooled; only then does rain come down from condensation. This climatic arrangement subjects agricultural crops of the nation to the synchronization of two sets of variables. When the two kinds of currents miss each other, drought sets in. When they repeatedly converge over a specific area, flood and inundation are the inevitable result. It is not uncommon for lack of rain and too much rain simultaneously to victimize two or more parts of China. Only an enormous empire in control of vast resources can deal with the situation. The requirement imposed by the power of nature was at first felt, too, during the B.C. era. In *Zuo zhuan* we read many stories about wars between the principalities during times of natural disaster. The "Food and Money Monograph" of the *Han shu* states: "Hunger or a good harvest is up to the grace of Heaven." Yao Shanyu, working from the summaries of *Tushu jicheng* and other sources, calls our attention to the fact that in the 2,117 years under study, 1,621 floods and 1,392 droughts caused damage serious enough to be reported by the imperial courts. Such conditions induced Mencius repeatedly to use such expressions as "the old and the young turning to the gutters" and "looking out for clouds in time of great drought" to justify his position. Egalitarianism at the low level, a doctrine of Mencius which was subscribed to by Ming officials, could not be separated from the environmental conditions in the background.

Further ruling out the possibility of a decentralized China was the potential threat of the nomads. The traditional line of defense that China erected along the steppeland, customarily referred to as the "Great Wall," was by no means fixed. It moved back and forth, yet never too far away from the "15-inch isohyet line." That is to say, the territories north and west of the Great Wall, having an annual rainfall of less than fifteen inches and therefore inadequate for cultivation, remained a grazing ground for the nomads. In times of bad weather and in periods of China's disunity, these nomads have a natural tendency to execute large-scale invasions. This is a problem whose cause is so deeply rooted in geography that the Chinese have not been able to solve it merely through military offensives. Long-term experience has commanded them to put the regional and local government under a strong center, allowing national defense to dictate to them a degree of homogeneity and uniformity in order to survive.

These factors have exercised a depressing effect on China's cultural development in the modern era. An often-cited maxim of the Chinese is that "in order to fend off external pressure, internal pacification comes first." But either internal or external, the gigantic effort implies a focus on quantity rather than on quality. The demand for homogeneity and uniformity forestalls higher efficiencies in technology and economy, for progress in these two areas usually comes from uneven situations.

The pattern established in the Ming Dynasty, with emphasis on political centralization and the reliance on the social effect of traditional ethics to attain balance over its wide realm at the expense of regional particularities, can be seen from the evolution of the civil service examination. The open examination as an institution was initiated by the Sui and became regularized during the Tang; by then the areas for contest included classical literature, mathematics, and law. During the Song current issues gained currency, but poetry and annotations of classics were not neglected. It was during the Ming that the form of examination became more important than the substance, and about the middle of the dynasty, the "eight-legged essay" turned out to be central. Teng Ssu-yü, an expert on the subject, summarized the historical development as follows: "In the course of time the content of the examination became progressively shortened and simplified, while its procedures grew more elaborate."[2] This process reflected the fact that the civil service itself had turned into one undifferentiated element. Unable to handle any pluralistic situation, naturally it would not encourage the growth of a plural society.

Yet, in tracing the ultimate causes of this development, we note the fearsome effect of terrain and climate. Today, some 341 years after the fall of the Ming, the effect of those factors may be less compelling, yet it has by no means vanished.

Second, the Ming Dynasty had a strong contractive character, in contrast to the expansive character of the Tang and Song.

Professor Ch'ien Mu, in his *An Outline of Chinese History,* cites the Tang as "a political power unlimitedly emancipating itself, while its governmental organization was also under a boundless expansion."[3] In reality, this expansive character was at least to an extent carried on by the Song.

As a succeeding dynasty of the Sui, Northern Qi, Northern Zhou, and the Tuoba Wei, the Tang carried on and refined a distinctive tradition, the organizational principle which was much influenced by the *Rituals of the Zhou.* The institutions that it took over from its predecessors, such as the "three chiefs," the "equalization of landholding," and the "*fubing,*" are noted for their schematic designs. Such a system took effect when the landholding of the population, and along with it taxation and conscription, was proclaimed to follow an ideal mathematical formula. The scheme was enforced in as large an area as was feasible. But whenever and wherever the formula conflicted with local reality, deviations were allowed and compromises were accepted. The main purpose was to derive maximum benefit from the geometrically balanced scheme as an administrative device, not to reshape the contours of the earth.[4] Its applications could not be extended indefinitely. With the An Lushan Rebellion of 755, such a scheme could no longer remain in effect. Thereafter decentralization took over. Regional strongmen gaining control over taxation and organizing private armies became the order of the day, a situation essentially not different from that of Japan's premodern era.

We cannot take the position that an effective regional government had to be less desirable than a central government that was corrupt and lacking in substance. But traditional historians, accustomed to bureaucratic management, were deeply disturbed by the absence of a legitimate imperial court functioning as the patron of public morals. The real loss occurred in the area of defense. Lacking a strong center, during the ensuing period of Five Dynasties and Ten Kingdoms, the semi-sinicized state of the Liao organized by the Khitans took possession of the sixteen northern prefectures, including today's Beijing, thus opening the door for nomadic incursions. The situation continued with the alien dynasties of the Xi-Xia, Jin, and Yuan. Not until the founding of the Ming, more than four hundred years later, did China regain its territorial integrity.

It would be impossible to make an item-by-item comparison of the Ming with the preceding four hundred years. But the northern Song stood in sharp contrast to the style and management of the later dynasty. Moreover, during the Song, Wang Anshi's reform further marked a high point of its history, unsurpassed by other deeds. For reasons to be explained below, the retrograding and contracting dispositions of the Ming could be taken as a long-term reaction to the failure of the Wang Anshi experiment. In fact, students of the Ming Dynasty can benefit from the case. If they scrutinize the case at some length and seriously probe the cause of the Song's inability to achieve a breakthrough despite its highly developed national economy, they may discover that the history of the Ming Dynasty has been rendered easier to comprehend through the analysis. The penetrating power derived from the comparison can in turn enable them to understand better why, during the Ming and early Qing, Western Europe managed to overtake China in practically every sphere of activity.

With fewer words, the situation may be preliminarily assessed from the observation that, in modern times, a nation's monetary management carries an all-inclusive character, similar to the monopolistic tendency of large businesses. The circulation of money must prevail over politics and law and penetrate into intellectual and social life to make its effect felt within the four corners. China during the Song and the Ming was not ready for such an all-out operation. What actually happened may be summarized as follows.

As mentioned, the Song followed the expansion initiated by the Tang. The evolution of the taxation system from the three-component package of *zu yong tiao* to the semi-annual delivery of *liang shui* appeared to be a major reform on the surface. Yet, the shift actually did no more than to bow to reality after the previous legislation was found to be inoperative. Nor was the *liang shui* a uniform system effectively enforced by the central government. Behind the scenes, the tax procedure and power of collection had slipped into the hands of provincial authorities. Regional military leaders collected taxes to finance their own armed forces. In consequence, their office became inheritable. But, as happened in Japan's early modern era, administrative fragmentation did not necessarily hinder economic expansion. The interregnum of the Five Dynasties, for altogether fifty-four years, did not cause a disturbance of any great extent. The unification of the Song marked a takeover of control of the armed forces and taxation power from the provincial strongmen.[5] No thorough revamping of the society was contemplated.

The dynastic founder, Zhao Kuangyin, being an army general, ascended the throne as a result of a coup engineered by his subordinates. He and his dynasty seemed to have the potential to endow China with a new outlook. The national capital was settled at Kaifeng, a commercial metropolis. Refraining from land redistribution as the basis of structuring the new dynasty, the Song promoted commerce, making headway in constructing ships, minting money, opening mines, collecting commercial taxes, and installing government monopolies. Military manpower was procured through recruitment instead of conscription, continuing a trend established during the Five Dynasties.

The new dynasty did away with a great many of the abstract intonations characteristic of China's imperial courts. The emperors were personally involved in manufacturing weapons, establishing military depots, and even combat. They separated themselves from the rulers of the orthodox tradition who took up rituals profusely and busily engaged in plots and machinations to secure the throne and to terminate rivals while paying lip service to benevolence and righteousness.

The early Song emperors also set a goal for themselves to recover the traditional Chinese territory, which called for elimination of the Xi-Xia, established by the Tibetans, and the Liao, established by the Khitans. For this purpose, an eye was set on the productive power of the South, which was thought to be sufficient to carry out the task. Economic mobilization therefore became a national concern.

But this effort backfired. Not only did they fail to expel the Khitans, even the Tibetans were able to inflict heavy losses on the Song army, sinking Chinese morale and causing great humiliation. In the 1060s, with Wang Anshi's "New Laws," it was hoped that the army could be strengthened after a reorganization of taxation and government finances. Again, the outcome was unexpected. As soon as the new laws were proclaimed, their impracticalities were exposed. Yet, it would be difficult to rescind the laws immediately. Thereafter fluctuations plagued the reigns of Shenzong, Zhenzong, and Huizong and, in between, the regency of Empress Dowager Gao. Wang Anshi was dismissed and recalled, before he was cashiered the second time. Sima Guang was appointed to replace the leadership of the reformers. Zhang Chun was banished, and Cai Jing took charge. One group of courtiers was labeled partisans; another, evil counsel. The controversy fulfilled the narrative, "while the Song statesmen were deadlocked with their polemics, the Jin army crossed the Yellow River." The partisan bickering nevertheless continued until the collapse of the Northern Song.

From today's perspective, the Wang Anshi affair is basically a technical problem, not a moral problem.[6] In the background, financial management in traditional China relied on a low-level land tax broadly and horizontally applied to a huge pool of small self-cultivators. In the absence of an independent judiciary, there was no guarantee that the operation would be just or even precise in individual cases. The watchdogs or censorial officials would, it was hoped, make the management more or less correspond to general expectation. This was why governmental operation targeted itself for moral approval. Modern management, on the other hand, would conduct itself according to a strictly businesslike manner. Due process must hold property rights inviolable on every count. Whenever a precedent served as a guideline, deviation from it in the name of morals should not be allowed, unless the change effected a reversal of policy which was legally justifiable. Furthermore, the respect for property rights was not limited to government functionaries alone; it was extended to the population at large.

The centralization of financial matters of the Northern Song attained a modern outlook. Wang Anshi's reform went a step further; it had the tendency to commercialize the entire fiscal operation. If his scheme carried, the central government would have gathered around itself the business of a holding company, even though a commercial firm was the last thing it intended to turn into. For one thing, the enormous scale of the business would have necessitated civil support. Private business would be enlisted to provide the needed depth, to carry out lateral transactions, and to bring the effect of the monetary management to the grass roots. That being the case, statutes governing business corporations, bankruptcy, inheritance, and so forth had to attain a measure of modern outlook in tune with the civil law. This would have implied a revolution that would have touched upon bureaucratic structure, dominant thought, and social custom in addition to jurisprudence. Indeed, such implications would have been beyond China's capacity in the eleventh century.

With those factors in mind, we can no longer give Wang Anshi approval or disapproval merely because his economic thought disagrees with our own thinking or not. A more meaningful test is to see how his maneuvers fit into the social structure of his day. A score sheet can be worked out from the classical sources.

His *fang tian fa*, which was supposed to provide a graded land tax according to soil productivity, was not in effect twenty years after its proclamation, as the land survey, even in the vicinity of Kaifeng, ran into technical difficulties. The *mian yi fa*, intending to commute labor service of the monetary payment, was held by his critics as to enforce the circulation of money in the rural areas. The *shi yi fa*, which authorized the government to engage in trade, was not utilized to stimulate wholesale business, but to turn office functionaries into retailers, some of them peddling fruit and ice blocks in the streets. And the *qing miao fa*, effecting a government loan to peasants during the planting season, could not be carried out in an orderly manner due to the lack of institutional supervision. There were no banks to handle the funds and no court proceedings to oversee the rights and liabilities of borrowers. The prevailing method was for parcels of money to be handed out to groups of peasants, regardless of whether they had applied for a loan, and then to hold them mutually responsible. One man's delinquency thus encumbered all others in the group. Once the law was put into effect, every county was assessed a quota of interest. There were districts that did not provide the funds as principal. With no money loaned out, the alleged "interest" was collected from the population as a surtax.[7]

In brief, the Song Dynasty projected the advanced sectors of the national economy as the basis of its monetary management. But the bottom structure of the village communities could not measure up to the standard. The office apparatus serving Wang Anshi at the intermediate level could not be modernized. The ensuing bureaucratic practice led to falsification of data in appalling proportions. The *Song shi* indicates that during the period of the new laws, there were nine methods by which the government could compulsorily purchase food from the population. In an official document, Sima Guang disclosed that troops numbering several hundred thousand could be "phantom figures."[8] This state of affairs continued during the Southern Song period. By then, the accounts handled by the district financial officers, referred to as *jing zhi qian* and *ban zhang qian,* appeared neither as a budget nor as a cash ledger. It was unclear whether tax collection should follow fixed rates or be assigned to farmers in lump sums. The issue of negotiable notes, without effective auditing, caused currency inflation on a grand scale. In contrast, the less developed states in the North that were in contest with the Song, leaning on their crude economy and seemingly more backward methods, fared better in delivering the needed personnel and equipment to the battlefields.

When the Mongol Yuan Dynasty took over, it found no solution to bridge the gap. A *modus operandi* was reached by separating the administration of the North from that of the South. Drastic tax reductions were authorized to court public support, although the policy was hardly substantiated. Failure to develop a workable system was a major reason for the political instability under the Yuan.[9]

The founding of the Ming in 1368 marked a gigantic step backward in Chinese history. The extrovert disposition of the Tang and Song was replaced by a mood of introversion. The competitive stance of the two previous eras gave way to a noncompetitive outlook. Zhu Yuanzhang, the dynastic founder, at one time explicitly stated: "Shenzong of the Song commissioned Wang Anshi to handle financial affairs. When evil characters made inroads, whatever was under heaven was disturbed. This we should take as a monition." His instructions to the Ministry of Revenue labeled Sang Hongyang of the Han and Yang Yan of the Tang two able administrators who had widened state revenue by introducing commercial practices to their offices, as immoral opportunists. A public proclamation of his in part reads: "Our tax income has been settled. Surplus will come from thrifty management. Our aim is to reduce the service obligation of the population, so that farmers lose no time working on the fields and women lose no time weaving. [Our policy to] promote the basics [of production] to the prejudice of ill-sorted jobs will turn the indolent hands to work on land. When producers are hard at work and consumers are few, abundance comes as a natural result."[10]

This conservative approach to economy, with a long historical standing, was put into practice by deeds. During his reign by implication and machination, Zhu Yuanzhang seized the opportunity of four criminal cases ranging from treason and larceny to falsification of fiscal records to persecute his own bureaucrats and the regional and local officials. According to the Monograph on Penalty of the *Ming shi*, "most households of the middle class and above were ruined." In 1397, there were still 14,341 households across the empire that owned 700 *mou* of land (approximately 120 acres) or more. A list of them was presented to the sovereign himself.[11]

Under decrees of the dynastic founder, merchants and their family members were not allowed to wear silk. All imperial subjects were forbidden to take to the sea. The entire troop of office clerks, runners, and attendants was drafted from the population and remained unpaid. Utensils and stationery for public use, along with bows and arrows, were requisitioned from village communities. To protect the farming population from the disturbance of mobilization, a system of hereditary military households was organized, to follow a similar institution of the Yuan. The dynasty proscribed the use of precious metals in business transactions, yet it refrained from minting bronze coins. When the paper currency printed in quantity fell into disuse, there was a shortage of money. While government functionaries of the Tang and Song engaged in manufacturing and transit of goods, the Ministry of Revenue of the Ming remained nothing more than a large accounting office.

The lack of positiveness of the Ming approach was apparent. The dynasty installed centralized power which was used to promote the most advanced sectors of the national economy. Instead, it compelled them to maintain pace with the backward sectors, to assure the stability of the empire. We cannot, of course, deny the sanity of Zhu Yuan-zhang for the odd position he took, after the bad experience of the Tang and Song, on top of his own strong feelings against Wang Anshi's reform. Nevertheless, it is all too obvious that his historical perspective ran against the world trend. An additional note must be inserted here that, contrary to the description of a number of writers, the Ming Dynasty in no way qualifies as a "feudal society." A major feature of feudalism is the fragmentation of authority.[12] The Ming never relaxed its centralization of power; it even took a contracting and retrograding position economically.

The story of Zhu Yuanzhang reminds us of the three geographical and climatic conditions conducive to China's political centralization. In Wu Han's biography of the Ming Dynasty founder, the opening paragraph starts with the drought, locusts, and epidemic that hit the Huai River region in 1344. These natural disasters provided Zhu with an opportunity for empire-building. Water control reemerges in the story; in the background during the waning years of the Yuan, Jia Lu gathered a large number of workers near Huanglinggang for the resti-tution of the Yellow River. Inadequately cared for, the workers re-volted, fueling the general disturbance that led to the subsequent change of dynasties. The racial relationship between the Mongols on one side and the native Chinese on the other also contributed to the peasant rebellion. But whatever the immediate cause, the event flashes back to us the historical theme that the nomads' cavalry organization compelled the Chinese to take a similar position in arriving at a unitary structure, politically. Even though not explicitly stated, the principle that geography determines history runs through the entire length of the twenty-four dynastic histories of China. In this perspective, Zhu Yuan-zhang's despotism is not surprising.

But today, the Chinese can no longer be bound by the theme that their destiny has been prearranged by geography. The monolithic structure of a unified empire, built on the premise of egalitarianism at the lower levels true to such Mencian doctrines as "the general popula-tion should be kept away from cold and hunger" and "those above seventy should eat meat," has proved untenable since the Opium War.

Nor could Chinese culture keep pace with world civilization, should the Chinese insist on maintaining their traditional organization which disallowed variety, a lesson they learned from the May Fourth Movement. This awakening induces us, especially students of Ming history, to look into the story of the economic growth and expansion of Western Europe, which is my next point of emphasis.

Third, the "modernization" of Western Europe, including the Renaissance, the Reformation, the formation of so-called capitalism, and the breakthrough in science and technology, took place within the time span of the Ming, from the late fourteenth to the mid-seventeenth century. A comparison with the contemporary West therefore gives the history of the Ming Dynasty a new sense of relevance.

In the summer of 1972, I went to England to assist Dr. Joseph Needham in collecting data for his monumental *Science and Civilisation in China*. Subsequently I stayed in Cambridge for a year. At our first meeting, Dr. Needham reminded me that as far as he saw it, the aforementioned four events were interlocked with one another. To this day I am taken by his insight.[13]

The mature stage of division of labor in Western Europe and America encourages scholars to take disciplinary approaches to social studies, to categorize one phase of human activity as "economic" and another as "social." But the same collegial division of labor may work less satisfactorily with large-scale historical themes. For example, *shi huo* (food and money) is a commonly used phrase in Chinese historiography. Does it stand for economic thought, or planning and regulation of the government, or social problems overlapping with economy and politics? No simple answer will suffice. Our own purpose, moreover, is to investigate why China's unitary structure cannot adequately transform itself into a plural society. If the analyst should adopt a refracted vision beforehand, to see plurality prior to a general survey, it is all too easy for him to confuse the effects with the causes. Recognizing the mutual influence of the four events (or four aspects of a larger event), Dr. Needham has pointed to the direction of an interdisciplinary approach.

The reason to precede capitalism with the word "so-called" is that to this day the term lacks a generally accepted definition. Many scholars and authors, before coming to the substance of the subject, have already clouded their vision with the judgment of good and evil. A fact that has often escaped general recognition is that the term "capitalism" was only occasionally mentioned in the nineteenth century, and it begins to appear frequently only in the present century.[14] Unable to avoid it, we propose to accept Sir George Clark's view that capitalism marks an organization and a movement. We further decide that only under the following three conditions can capitalism go forward and make headway. (1) Wide extension of credit on private ownership, so that idled capital is fully utilized. (2) Impersonal management, so that the supervising power of business goes beyond the capability of the entrepreneurs themselves. And (3) pooling of service facilities, such as transportation and communication, so that the sphere of operation exceeds the logistical capacity of individual firms. The key to the growth potential of all three components is trust, which cannot be sustained without court protection. The law extends its jurisdiction over private matters because they are deemed inseparable from public interest. The fact that such a connection is given general recognition indicates the support by political philosophy, at least unhampered by religion. All this points out that the whole movement and the entire organization involve many aspects of public life. They are intellectual and legal, no less than economic and social. The emergence of capitalism is not merely a change of mode of production or a sudden thrust of capitalist spirit.

This interpretation, stressing organizational technicality in its many facets, brings capitalism back closer to Adam Smith's idea, expressed in *Wealth of Nations,* that the "system of commerce" is superior to the "system of agriculture" in "enriching the people."

From this viewpoint we see the pioneer of capitalism in the city-states of Italy, among them Venice being the most prominent. The autonomy of those states was attained during the contest for power between the empire and the papacy. As neither maintained firm control over the peninsula, those cities managed to remain virtually independent. Venice, located on the sea, was little affected by its continental possession. On the whole it was a "city without territory." The salt water in the city made manufacture impractical. Its nobles were converted into a plutocracy. The labor problem was solved by periodic admission of migrating workers. The ecclesiastic prohibition of usury was simply ignored. Without an organized group as a challenger, the violation was not brought under fire. In this way the entire city made up the state, and the state differed little from a trading company. All commercial laws instantly became civil laws, and the merchant fleet became inseparable from the navy. Venice's defeat of Genoa in 1380, a dozen years after the founding of the Ming Dynasty in China, confirmed its position as a major sea power. Organizational simplicity had a great deal to do with its ascendancy. The drawback was that without a production base, its hegemony was not so durable. The occupation of Constantinople by the Turks and the navigation of the Cape by the Portuguese, taking place during the reigns of Jingtai, Tianshun, Chenghua, and Hongzhi in Ming China, sealed the fate of Venice. Yet, in the sixteenth century, a high point of the Renaissance, the city continued to shine with its cultural brilliance. It maintained a leading position in trade. Only toward the end of the century was that passed to Holland.

What we usually refer to as Holland is actually Koninkrijk der Nederlanden, historically known as the United Netherlands or the Dutch Republic. Holland was only one of its seven provinces (now eleven). When this nation became independent in the early seventeenth century, the province of Holland had two-thirds of its population and contributed three-fourths of its finances. Agitated by the Reformation and the resistance to the Spanish Inquisition, the Dutch organized their first national state. But internal unevenness remained a serious problem. With the port of Amsterdam, Holland fared well as an industrial and commercial vanguard. Yet several provinces and the agrarian communities within them retained a medieval outlook of different shades. To place them under a unitary court system would be unworkable. A solution was found in federation, effecting the retention of jurisdiction over local affairs by the towns and provinces. The Dutch Republic thus became the first modern state so deliberately structured,with a two-tier government to absorb the internal diversities. At first, Holland even asserted that it had full power to enter into diplomatic relations with other nations without federal approval. The navy of the Netherlands was made up of five separate admiralty colleges.[15] Even though the entire nation accepted Calvinism, the interpretation of the doctrine of predestination led to a splitting movement. The Reformed church continued to exclude usurers from communion; universities withheld degrees from them. After much agitation by the theological faculty at Utrecht, the states of Holland and Friesland finally settled the issue by declaring that the church had no concern with questions of banking. Maurice of Nassau, the stadtholder, was supposed to have declared: "I don't know whether predestination is green or blue."[16] In the long run, under intense competition abroad and rapid development at home, the Netherlands overcame its many internal difficulties.

To connect the story to our topic, we note that the Dutch declared independence in 1581, the ninth year of Wanli.

Following the Netherlands, England became the next foremost capitalist nation. With Scotland, the United Kingdom had an acreage about five to six times that of the Netherlands. A small country by today's standards, before the eighteenth century it was considered to be fairly large. Moreover, it had a large agricultural base.

Rarely brought up nowadays, England had been subject to maneuvers by economically more advanced nations before it structured its own commercial organization. For instance, at one time its banking business was in the hands of the Italians. Later, the Dutch monopolized its insurance business. The Italian district in London was called Lombard Street, and its residents were entitled to extraterritoriality. As wool remained the staple of British export, the Italians financed its production by making advances to growers. With the stock they controlled its overseas market as well.

For the entire seventeenth century, England appeared to be a troubled country. At first the king clashed with Parliament, taxation being the main issue. The situation was complicated by religious uncertainty. A dispute arose on judicial matters. And atop all this, the conduct of foreign affairs further intensified ill feelings and mutual distrust. The nation went through the dissolution of Parliament, civil war, regicide, an experiment with commonwealth, protectorate, and restoration. It also witnessed political assassinations, pamphleteering, persecution of religious nonconformists, secret pacts with foreign powers, and foreign bribery of the king. With a population rising from four to six million, the nation demonstrated an ungovernable character not fundamentally different from that of China in a good portion of the present century. Naturally, the story is open to a variety of interpretations. Historian Maurice Ashley even goes on to introduce new themes to refute the old ones that he himself had laid down earlier. The events described also happened during the time span of the Ming Dynasty. The year that Cromwell defeated King Charles I at Marston Moor (1644) was the same year that the Chongzhen Emperor hanged himself, to mark the downfall of the dynasty.

An urgent message I wish to deliver to Chinese readers is that in parallel with the macro history of China, the history of England must be reviewed with the Glorious Revolution of 1688–89 as a major milestone. Before that date, England was mathematically unmanageable.

The laws were divided. Three or four different kinds of law courts appeared. The common law, a legacy of the medieval period, observed tradition to such an extent that whatever had not been done earlier could not be done later. Its application could be effective in upholding *seizin* (possession) of landed properties but became uncertain in sustaining the claim to ownership. It lacked adequate causes to handle inheritance of chattels. Its provisions for mortgage ignored the fact that the mortgagor in the new era needed the cash yet also the possession of the land under cultivation. Under the jurisdiction of the common law, rents were difficult to adjust upward in relation to the value of money, if possible at all. It determined that agricultural products could only change hands at designated local markets, usually established centuries ago. Matters concerning corporation, bankruptcy, and managerial defrauding were largely hanging in the air. In brief, the legal concept was anchored in the stability of agrarian communities under the feudal rule, unprepared for the changing circumstances. In the early seventeenth century, corresponding to the reigns of Wanli and Tianqi in China, the inflow of Spanish bullion from the New World caused steep rises of prices in Europe. The effect of international war and foreign trade began to be felt even in England's hinterland. Now landowners were anxious to secure their holdings, and merchants were adamant to pay the extra assessment, at a time when the king found no easy way to raise funds to meet the higher cost of armament. The impoverished farmers and city dwellers found their livelihood threatened, their emotions fanned by the preaching of the new sectarians. The contest between royal prerogative and parliamentary supremacy prompted both sides to appeal to the practice of the Middle Ages; yet in reality the current development had run beyond the realm of past experience. After their military triumph, the Cromwellians could not fare any better. What happened was that the social structure was still awaiting reorganization. Short of that, government policies were unable to reach the bottom layer of the village communities.

After 1689, the unsettled conditions began to give way. The disturbance that had shaken the nation for half a century gradually died out, including even the religious controversies. A major development in the background was that after the prolonged struggle and rehabilitation, land tenure began to show a degree of regularity. Swept away were the worst absurdities: that owners were unable to identify their estates in the fields, that the chief tenants could not be located, and that some of the cultivators were unsure whether they were owners or tenants to be evicted. Indeed, the reform was by no means thorough; the process of clearing the lingering effect of feudal land tenure still had some distance to go. But the uniform land tax of 1692 was able to do away with tax farmers and to centralize the revenue at the Exchequer, giving evidence that field holdings as a whole had been rationalized and integrated.[17] The situation caused Professor Tawney to comment, rather humorously, that foreclosure cost less by war than by court proceedings.

The admission of equity to the common law courts showed another step toward the era of a breakthrough. Equity itself is not statutory law, but a principle of justice in fair dealing originally amounting to "king's conscience." Some of the principles were derived from Roman law. Its administration had been limited to the prerogative courts. As the common law was so far from reality, the stopgap device provided some relief. Starting from the denial of precedents, soon the equity application also accumulated a body of precedents of its own. This paved the way for the merger of the two systems. In 1689 John Holt became chief justice of King's Bench; he decided that the courts should treat litigations involving merchants in accordance with mercantile practice.[18] The effect was far-reaching. With the merger of legal practices and integration of land tenure, the interflow of capital was possible. Thereafter, agriculture became consonant with industries and commerce. The distance between the hinterland and coastal cities was shortened. In this way, the three conditions that characterize the operation of capitalism became applicable to the United Kingdom. The entry of England into the capitalist era was unprecedented in world history; never before had a nation with a fairly large agrarian base managed to install monetary management to administer its realm as a whole, as if it were a city-state, and under which private interests began to be infused with public interests. This accomplishment enabled Britain to assume a leadership role in world affairs for several centuries. The length and purpose of this article, however, do not allow us to elaborate on the negative influence of capitalism.

The above survey points out that the formation of capitalism is not a conscious effort, as starting from a plan and a timetable. Its spread from smaller nations to larger nations, from states surrounded by water to those with land bases, and from countries unhampered by agriculture to those with an agrarian background nevertheless follows a pattern. With the expansion of international trade, internal and external pressure exerted upon each nation calls for a reorganization. The demand for a mathematically manageable situation compels it to make readjustments within the feasibility of its geography and history. The proceedings extend to social, jurisprudential, intellectual, and religious aspects.

The history of Europe reassures us that the prime mover in the reorganization is trade, not industry. In 1694, the Bank of England was established. It became an important instrument of capitalism.[19] Chronologically, it fell into the reign of Kangxi in the Chinese court. On the other hand, the Industrial Revolution in England gathered force only in the early nineteenth century, already the reigns of Jiaqing and Daoguang, approaching the late Qing.

On the record, the formation of capitalism has established an irreversible trend. So far no nation has turned back the movement toward the extension of credit, impersonal management, and pooling of service facilities once it is set up in an integrated manner. Socialism can be regarded as a variation: technically it works with an identical business structure based on trust. It differs only in that ownership is modified; the sphere of action of private property is somewhat restricted.

This leaf of history should give students of the Ming Dynasty something to think about. China is a continental country. During the Ming, the tradition of a centralized political power remained formidable. International trade could hardly pressure it enough to cause it to yield its ancient structure and social customs. The war against *wokou* (Japanese pirates) during the reign of Jiaqing demonstrated that the massive agrarian economy still had sufficient strength to fend off a rising new commercial organization. In the era of Wanli, Chinese forces maintained contact with the Portuguese and clashed with the newly arrived Spaniards. The encounter was not always in China's favor. There could be little doubt, however, that the defenders were comfortably in control in holding their cultural frontier. More than two hundred years had to lapse before this balance was broken, when the capitalist countries of the West, riding on their Industrial Revolution, arrived with steamships and modern weapons. By then the difficulties of launching a cross-ocean expedition had been overcome by technology, and the numerical inferiority of the invaders was more than made up by a solid organization. The Chinese had to yield. Their introverted and noncompetitive position dating back to the Ming Dynasty was no longer tenable. The imbalance accounted for the aggressive acts of the Western imperialist powers.

Our emphasis on the conservative and backward character of the Ming Dynasty links it with this discomfiture. If the long-term consequence should be disregarded, indeed the historian could present the era on a much more cheerful note. Over its span of 276 years, no internal rebellion was ever started by a Ming military commander. For the scholar-gentry, having passed the civil service examinations, to maintain a middle class lifestyle was an effortless matter. The carefree leisure could be enviable. For this reason, the mellowness of many essays written by Ming writers is often admired. But such aloofness, too remote from our life and pursuits, is not of vital interest to us.

There is the other fallacy of compulsorily linking the period with current themes. Since the formation of capitalism in the West coincides with its time span, it is all too easy for writers to portray a "budding capitalism" in Ming China, as has been done by a considerable number of historians. Without presenting capitalism as an organization and a movement, their collection of data repeats the story that many smart people during the period amassed large fortunes. True or false, such tales lead nowhere, as no sequel can be built up.

Fourth, in the vision of macro history, the Qing easily copied its predecessor but brought forth few breakthrough innovations. Accordingly, in our study of modern China, often we may find the roots of its many problems in the Ming Dynasty.

The collapse of the Ming was caused by fiscal insolvency. In 1632, across the empire 340 counties accumulated tax arrears of 50 percent or more. Among them, 134 counties had not delivered any proceeds at all.[20] It was not so much that the level of taxation itself had been excessive; it happened that when the surtaxes for military supplies were assessed, the situation could no longer be handled technically. Fundamentally, the Ming had started by using commodities in kind instead of silver as its basis for fiscal management. Tax rates were low; expenditures were few. The self-supporting element of the hereditary military households also absorbed some of the outlays. But in the late sixteenth century, local conditions in wide areas differed drastically from what they had been. At this time, even the centralized power in the capital was unable to introduce sweeping changes. Both the "junyao method" and the "single-whip reform" featured spot readjustments initiated by provincial authorities, with precautions not to alter the outward form of the centralized system and not to break the backbone of the poorest taxpayers. As a remedy the move was feeble.

The limited amount of silver in circulation across the empire presented another problem. As shown in Zhang Juzheng's fiscal retrenchment in the late sixteenth century, when the treasuries still held some twelve million ounces of silver from circulation, the deflationary influence had already caused a wide drop in food prices. The Manchurian war in the early seventeenth century brought a new kind of dilemma. At that time silver was circulated in the South. An extraction of a considerable amount from that region to defray expenses in the extreme North, a frontier area where a money economy had yet to be developed, was to work against the mechanics of economy before the military campaign began. From the report by Xiong Tingpi, we can see that in the midst of material shortages, the inflow of silver into Manchuria only fanned the prices.[21] Censorial officials also revealed that a large amount of bullion thus delivered, without contributing to the war effort, was shipped back by the generals who received it, in the original parcels. The banditry in the northwest burdened the fiscal administration even more, as now the demand for military supplies spread to another area.

The internal problem of the bureaucracy also worsened. It had started from the Wanli emperor's suspension of morning office, the Tianqi emperor's delegation of power to the so-called eunuch dictator Wei Zhongxian, and the Chongzhen emperor's impetuous personal rule. The combined effect of abuses accumulated to a general decline of morale, which progressed to such a stage that there was no public consensus as to what was right and what was wrong. The deterioration of the quality of local government was marked.

The Manchus subsequently remedied the situation. Some residents in North China were relocated, so that the vacated farmland could be made homesteads of the newly arrived Bannermen. The displaced families were victimized, but the measure enabled the Banners to replace the defunct Wei-Suo System, thus substantially reducing the cost of maintaining a recruited army. The campaigns against the "former and later feudatories" (a trio of Ming pretenders to the throne and three former Ming generals) called for enormous amounts of military supplies. But the funds, circulated in South China, did not directly counter the working of the national economy. The revocation of the privileges of the Ming imperial clansmen and rank-purchasers relieved the empire of numerous sinecures; the evil influence of these groups on the local government was also removed. Luckily, the continuous inflow of silver from overseas, coinciding with the founding of the new dynasty, solved its monetary problem. Modeling themselves after the sage-like kings in Chinese history, the early Manchu emperors provided a reinvigorated leadership. They would not hesitate to exercise the intimidating power of conquerors over the conquered. The order to shave the front pate was enforced with the threat of the death penalty. Literary inquisition came in waves. Yet they knew how to court the support of the scholar gentry class. The project of compiling the history of the Ming Dynasty engaged their service. Veteran Ming scholars were nominated for academic distinction. The combination of these measures worked, as they were delivered at the vital points within a simple organizational structure. In 1661 the Kangxi Emperor gave tax delinquents in the Yangzi Delta a severe punishment. Along with it, the compilation of regional and local fiscal records went on in earnest. The steps led to China's resurgence in the late seventeenth century.

The Manchu takeover, however, basically featured disciplinary and technical touches only; they were not institutional or organizational renewals. Under the Qing, the positions of ministers and vice-ministers were doubled to accommodate Chinese and Manchu officeholders in equal number. At the direction of Kangxi, the quota of the *ding*, or able-bodied males, was permanently frozen as of the record of 1711, which made it possible later to merge the poll tax and the land tax. The Yongzhen Emperor ordered that the collection of melting charges on payments made in silver be institutionalized, the proceeds being distributed as supplementary salary to officials in charge to "nourish their honesty."[22] He also organized the Grand Council, with a handful of top bureaucrats who could meet the sovereign regularly, so that matters requiring the attention of the throne could be dispatched speedily. These several items exhausted the list of major institutional innovations of the Qing.

The new dynasty, with a larger population, an extended territory, and a higher level of production, could not separate itself substantially from the pattern established by its predecessor. The same four books and five classics provided the spiritual guidance to its bureaucracy. The same set of principles, stressing status, sex, and age differentiation, tightened its social order. The civil service examinations continued to function as an institutional link between the governing and the governed. During the Opium War the Daoguang emperor's instructions to Lin Zexu more than ever upheld the principle that truth descended from top to bottom, which could not be disputed. The report of Jiying to the emperor, identical in spirit with the memorial to the throne later submitted by Woren in opposition to the opening up of an interpreters' college, reaffirmed the traditional introverted and non-competitive position. This attitude linked the Ming and the Qing. Nor could there be a great deal of difference between and among the followers of the doctrine, be they Chinese, Manchu, or Mongol. The cultural characteristic was a historical product of long standing; it had nothing to do with the heredity of any racial stock.

Can we, therefore, connect the history of China's republican era to the history of the Ming Dynasty, bypassing the Qing altogether? No proposal as such is advocated by us. There are, of course, particularities in the history of the Qing Dynasty deserving special attention. For example, the Cohang trade in Canton did not exist under the Ming. The relationship of the Qing Dynasty with the minority groups on the frontier is another topic of current interest. The draft banks of Shansi, prominent from the eighteenth century onward, made their imprint on China's monetary history. As suggested in an opening paragraph of this chapter, there is no limit to the investigating depth of a competent historian. It is not impossible that certain neglected clues within the span of 267 years under the Qing, one day brought to light, may compel us to revise our understanding of China's past to a significant extent.

But from our current point of view, we have to say that the periodication of Chinese history marks the Qin and Han as one segment, the Sui, Tang, and Song as another, and the Ming and Qing as the third. The baseline of many topics on contemporary China may have to be pushed back for several centuries; only then will the view against a distant background clarify matters. We have already brought up the metaphor of a submarine sandwich. The unsophisticated social structure based on the status, sex, and age differentiation, more a product of the Ming than anything else, provides us with an anchorage from which to see things differently. For instance, once again the Opium War may be brought up. The xenophobia of Daoguang and Jiying, ludicrous as it seems to us, is not completely illogical against their background. The historical justification was that China's unsophisticated organization could not make room to accommodate a new Western system, especially after a compromise had already been made, authorizing the thirteen Cohang to maintain business contacts with the foreigners. If this were not enough, the Treaty of Nanjing appears to be a more convincing argument. It demonstrated that once the door was open, it brought not only discomfiture and humiliation to the Chinese, but also made their traditional system truly unworkable in the long run. Along the same lines, we can now realize that the fatal weakness that led to the defeat of the Taiping Tianguo did not come from the indecisiveness of Lin Fengxiang's northern expedition, nor was it a direct result of Yang Xiuqing's sorcery, but, more significantly, the freedom of conscience championed by the Taiping had no relevance to the social structure of a submarine sandwich. The abuse of the alien ideology only played into the hands of Zeng Guofan, who seized the occasion and excuse to restore the social order built up from the status, sex, and age differentiation. This same unsophisticated social structure explains the hopeless situation of the Hundred Days Reform organized by Kang Youwei and Liang Qichao. Talking extravagantly about financing his program by floating domestic bonds, Kang did not measure his goal with his own starting point. The approach was utopian. That is to say, the grasp of the history of the Ming Dynasty equips us with a penetrating vision to see things from a technical angle. The principal figures' virtue or lack of it, along with their personal gains and losses, is of less concern to us.

The benefit of such an approach is that in teaching history, the repetitious material can be abridged, once it is recognized that the causes of various events have a common origin. In writing history, we can rid ourselves of the bad habit of turning up the volume of rancorous denunciations simply because the events do not please us. Instead, we can present it straightforwardly and unemotionally: The traditional society does not meet the requirement of a modern state. In 1905, China terminated the civil service examinations; the link between the nation's superstructure and infrastructure was thus permanently cut. Yet the land tax ledger of many locales continued to follow Ming records.[23] The failure of the constitutional movement during the early republican era could not be a surprise, since the state in anticipation and the society in being were two different things. Law becomes operative only because there is a social compulsion in its backing. Politicians of the early republican period, being foreign bodies to the society, could not change its destiny. The door was now open for warlordism, an inevitable consequence from today's point of view. China's agrarian economy was beset with problems of landlordism and usury. Both were contracted at the bottom in minute scales and both were immune from governmental intervention. Nor could the principles of status, sex, and age differences be revitalized as the basis of a new social order. The only alternative left was private military power, which alone managed to effect some measure of control over a period of anarchy. But such a private military power could not remain effective when it was extended over several provinces.

This summary is an overview of China around the period of the May Fourth Movement, prior to the Nationalist revolution. In a word: The country was not mathematically manageable.

Conclusion

The Ming, being China's last indigenous dynasty, was less affected by external affairs. It had a strong native character. In our study we have found that it often exercises decisive influences over the interpretation of contemporary events. If we compare it with the expansive Tang and Song, to be followed by the Qing and the republican era, further link it with pertinent geographical and climatic background factors, and finally wrap up the proceedings by contrasting it to the development of capitalism in Western Europe, we arrive at a pattern of traditional Chinese design, with the center, front, rear, left, and right in a linkage. The check and double check of the mutual consistency of the interrelated areas give us the assurance that we have not deceived ourselves by making lopsided observations. To handle the history of the Ming Dynasty in this way, we are not picking up episodic occurrences from the past, nor making satirical critiques by exploiting their incidental resemblance to current affairs. We are not shackled by any ideological frame, thus making conclusions before assessing the facts.

The result of the study is part of macro history, which links causes and effects in longer time spans. Their relationship, affirming the long-term rationality of history, dwarfs petty concerns and even individual merit.

On the last point our approach is likely to invite criticism. It seems that the historian has no standpoint of his own. In narrating the events he seems to be unconcerned with character and personal virtues. What is going to happen is bound to happen. Ethics and morals do not count. This, however, is not the message of the present writer.

In the closing decades of the twentieth century, the greatest difficulty encountered by historians is not the lack of a moral standard, but too many of them. The danger of their clash looms large. Morality,

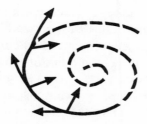

after all, is by itself abstract. Its realization takes hold of individual characters and personal deeds. On account of the fluid situation that we are in, it is necessary constantly to readjust our criteria to suit. A most obvious example is the egalitarianism at the lower level preached by Mencius. Although it maintained much moral appeal into the early part of the present century, today it no longer stands as an inspiring platform. The goodness toward one's fellow men that underlies the doctrine is one thing; to enforce it unthinkingly with brute force is another.

In the above diagram, the solid portion of the curve represents human history. The skyward arrows stand for moral aspirations; but human history does not follow their courses. Evidently, even if all members of the society had been sage-like characters, their combined deeds still would not have been perfect. Under the circumstances, the inward arrows show man's inner weakness, his unintentional errors, and the bad situation that he inherits from the past. Unlike the *lixue* thinkers of the Song and Ming who wished to suppress "human desires" in favor of "heavenly principles," we would rather bow to Christian humility to acknowledge that "original sin" is inevitable. History is the result of the merger of good and bad, or *yin* and *yang*. It absorbs the faults of man, yet it still enables him to progress.

It is impossible for us to remove all that was done in the past. What we call a "fresh start" cannot be literally true in the light of macro history. While each important event happens only once, the new generation nevertheless has to pick up the pieces left by its predecessor. The new segment of life inevitably incorporates some legacy of the old. It is predestined. The relay activates the concept of *karma*.

A search for the meaning of life in connection with the major events of mankind leads us close to religion. Yet, in the present case we have not set out for theological constructions. Only after exiting from the history of the Ming Dynasty are we brought immediately to the general history of China. Furthermore, circumstances compel us to link our experience with the history of the Western world, all within the timely relevance of the late twentieth century. Pondering the relationship, we have on our way caught up with a point of philosophical speculation that tightens up our synthesis.

It may be called historicism. Viewing history as a continuous process, we find that after technically evaluating the deeds of Wang Anshi, Zhu Yuanzhang, and Kang Youwei it is needless to lay severe moral condemnations on them or on historical figures of similar stature. Undoubtedly, each carries his own sense of morals. Particular to his own time and circumstances, it cannot stand for the universal morality in the interest of natural law. This realization more than ever convinces us that morals, constituting an absolute quality, stand as the highest ideal of mankind. Handling historiography as technicians, we should postpone their convocation as long as possible, because once they are cited a verdict must be given and a compromise can no longer be reached. In macro history, we would rather let the long-term rationality of history be the arbiter.

What is the good of macro history? Its larger frame of reference provides more room for accommodation. It absorbs various moral standards, outdates them, disarms them, neutralizes them, transcends them, and renders them parts of the material that paves the path of the future of mankind. Its magnanimity comes from its broadness. At this point the reader is reminded that for Confucians, forgiveness follows loyalty. For Daoists, even being and nonbeing are the same substances assuming different names. If the historian keeps such a majestic vision in handling his craft, he should never feel worried that morality has escaped his attention.

Similar to astronomy, macro history takes time as its fourth dimension. It implies that while historical discoveries are incessantly made, so are historical interpretations. The recorded history of mankind is only several thousand years old, a small segment of time in the span of the universe. When we use this short curve to gauge the true meaning of life and Creation, a great deal of speculation is involved. The unrecorded portions of our destiny, shown on the diagram in dotted lines, suggest *noumena* in Immanuel Kant's world. We can only assume their existence. The true nature of "things in themselves" defies clarification.

It is not our purpose to indulge in empty talk. In the context of China today, the aforementioned philosophy of history endows us with double-edged wisdom in handling contemporary events. On one side it reminds us that whatever we do, we cannot completely detach ourselves from the footsteps of our predecessors. Even revolutionaries cannot tread on air. There are, at the time of writing, a number of young people who wish that China could instantly transform itself into another United States. On the whole they have confused "freedom" with "liberty." In the Western world the latter has grown out of municipal franchise. With that in its grasp, the United States has further benefited from the experience of Britain, thus having its agriculture remain consonant with industry and commerce since its inception. Still, the country has undergone various kinds of struggle of its own, culminating in a civil war that lasted for four years. Another unusual situation is that it developed in a virtually empty space, a fact that was more than ever confirmed by the Homestead Act of 1862. That legislation authorized each household that had worked on public land for five years to purchase 160 acres of it at a nominal price. The freedom of American citizens is derived from the protection and guarantee by law of their particular economic interests and social life under a well-developed economy in which the division of labor and exchange of services and goods have been ramified. This cannot be copied in toto by another country of a different background, not to mention that for all the favorable conditions it has on its side, the United States still has to carry the burden of its problems.

On the other hand, there are older men such as ourselves who, with the fanciful dreams of our youthful years already dashed, insist that the younger generation should carry on the fruitless struggle, to the extent of taking the Soviet Union as a model. The unworkable plan is held as the "inevitable stage of development in the history of mankind." This approach is even more disturbing in light of the fact outlined above, that Chinese history developed from a different matrix than that of tsarist Russia, and in the light of macro history many measures taken by the Soviet Union since the October Revolution are no more than improvisations arising from a mathematically unmanageable situation, which makes imitation foolish.

The dotted portions of the spiral, preliminary and unsubstantiated, carry the message of Thomas Jefferson: "early belongs to the living." As historians, the utmost role of a prophet that we can assume is to suggest that the unfolding of history involves certain regularities. Yet, how exactly the events may occur involves many surprises. The main reason is that the timing of major trends, even to a certain extent predictable, cannot be programmed by us. It could further be upset by minor incidents. All this should make life aesthetically interesting. To the next generation may we declare: Pandora's Box has not been emptied; hope is still yours.

Notes

Source: Chinese Studies in History XIX:4 (summer 1986).

1. Yao Shanyu, "The Chronological and Seasonal Distribution of Floods and Drought in Chinese History," *Harvard Journal of Asiatic Studies* 6 (1941–42), pp. 273–312; Yao, "Flood and Drought Data in T'u-shu Chi-ch'eng," Harvard Journal of Asiatic Studies 8 (1944–45), pp. 214–26.

2. Teng Ssu-yü, *Zhongguo kaoshi zhidushi* (Taipei, 1967), p. 73.

3. Ch'ien Mu, *Guoshi dagang*, 10th ed. (Taipei, 1966), 1:312.

4. Both the *juntian* and *zuyongtiao* represented schematic legislation to be flexibly applied to actual cases. For this reason, Denis C. Twitchett refers to it in his *Financial Administration under the T'ang Dynasty* (Cambridge, 1963) to reflect only "theory and general policy pronouncements," even though the work, using the "Food and Money Monograph" of the *Jiu Tangshu* as a starting point, makes use of a large collection of source materials. For a glimpse of how the statute was locally applied, see Han Guopan, *Sui-Tang de juntian zhidu* (Shanghai, 1964).

5. Wang Gungwu, *Structure of Power in North China during the Five Dynasties* (Kuala Lumpur, 1963), and Sudo Yoshiyoki, "Godai no setsudoshi no shihai taisei," *Shigaku zasshi* : 61, 4 (1952), pp. 1–41; 61: 6 (1952), pp. 20–38. The contribution to regional development by the provincial regimes during the Five Dynasties period can sometimes be found in local gazetteers.

6. James T.C. Liu, in *Reform in Sung China: Wang An-shih (1021–1086) and His New Policies* (Cambridge, Mass., 1959), criticizes Wang's policy as "neither clearly nor firmly built upon a well-defined social basis" (p. 115). But he does not bring up the technical aspects of the problem.

7. See *Song shi,* punctuated ed. (Beijing, 1976), vol. 13, ch. 127, p. 4200; ch. 128, p. 4244; ch. 129, p. 4281; ch. 130, p. 4304; ch. 139, p. 4549; vol. 29, ch. 312, p. 10227; vol. 31, ch. 338, p. 10810; ch. 344, p. 10927, p. 10930.

8. Ibid., vol. 13, ch. 175, p. 4243; vol. 14, ch. 190, p. 4708.

9. The separation of the administration of South China from North China is mentioned in the "Food and Money Monograph" of the *Yuan shi*. On taxation, the text reads: "The revenue derived from interior prefectures included a poll tax and a land tax, which followed the system of *zuyongtiao* of the Tang. The revenue derived from the south of the Yangzi included a summer tax and an autumn tax, which followed the two-tax system under the Tang." See *Yuan shi*, punctuated ed. (Beijing, 1976), vol. 8, ch. 93, p. 2357. A study of the fiscal administration

under the Mongol period in considerable depth is Herbert Franz Schurmann, *Economic Structure of the Yuan Dynasty* (Cambridge, Mass., 1956). The effect of regional administration separating the North from the South by the Yuan lingered on, and to an extent it affected the tax administration under the Ming. See the various studies by Yamane Yukio, such as "Mindai Kahoku ni okeru ekiho no tokushitsu," in *Shimizu hakase tsuito kinen Mindaishi ronso* (Tokyo, 1962), pp. 221–50.

10. *Ming shilu: Taizu*, reprint (Taipei, 1962), pp. 2131, 2681–82 (ch. 135, 14th year of Hongwu, 1st lunar month, *dingwei;* ch. 177, 19th year of Hongwu, 3d lunar month, *wuwu*).

11. Ibid., p. 3643 (ch. 252, 30th year of Hongwu, 4th lunar month, *guizi*).

12. See Derk Bodde, "Feudalism in China," in *Feudalism in History,* ed. Rushton Coulborn (Princeton, 1956), pp. 49–92. Note that Bodde maintains that feudalism happened only in the late Zhou. During the Wei-Qin Nanbeichao period there were feudal elements, but not feudalism as a system. An argument that Ming society was not feudal is provided by the present writer in "Administrative Statistics in Ming *T'ai-tsung Shih-lu,"* printed in *Explorations in the History of Science and Technology in China* (Shanghai, 1982), pp. 115–30.

13. But the present essay does not fall into the scope of any collaboration; I alone am responsible for the opinions expressed.

14. It seems that the term "capitalism" was first used by Louis Blanc in the nineteenth century. In the early twentieth century it was used by Werner Sombart. Marx, while referring to the "capitalist era" and the "capitalist mode of production," never used the word "capitalism." See Fernand Braudel, *Civilization and Capitalism: 15th-18th Century*, vol. 2: *The Wheels of Commerce*, trans. Sian Reynolds (New York, 1982), p. 237. Sir George Clark writes: "The use of the word 'capitalism' as a name for the modern economic system was, I believe, invented in the middle of the nineteenth century by socialists." See Clark, *The Seventeenth Century*, 2d ed. (New York, 1947), p. 11.

15. Clark, *The Seventeenth Century,* pp. 36, 55, 119. Herbert H. Rowen, ed., *The Low Countries in Early Modern Times* (New York, 1972), pp. 191–97.

16. Rowen, *The Low Countries,* p. 116.

17. For the connection between landed properties and civil war in England during the seventeenth century, two important pieces of literature should be examined by all students of history. They are: R.H. Tawney, "The Rise of the Gentry, 1558–1640," *Economic History Review* 11 (1941), pp. 1–38, and H.R. Trevor-Roper, "The Gentry, 1540–1640," *Economic Review Supplement* 1 (1953). The background of the controversy is provided by Lawrence Stone, *The Causes of the English Revolution* (London, 1972), pp. 26–31. For the anomalies of property rights during the period see Joan Thirsk, ed., *The Agrarian History of England and Wales,* vol. 4: *1500–1640* (Cambridge, 1967), pp. 280–85. For the land tax of 1692 see J.S. Bromley, ed., *Cambridge Modern History*, vol. 6 (Cambridge, 1970), pp. 285–86. But until the early eighteenth century, there were still cases of the lingering effect of feudal land tenure that had to be eliminated. See G.W. Southgate, *English Economic History* (London, 1970), p. 108, and G.E. Mingan, *The Gentry: The Rise and Fall of a Ruling Class* (London, 1975), p. 173.

18. About the relationship between equity and common law, a quick clarification can be accomplished by referring to the basic references on the subject, such

as Theodore Plucknett, *A Concise History of the Common Law*, 5th ed. (London, 1956), and Edward Jenks, *The Book of English Law*, reprint (Athens, Ohio, 1967). The development after the Glorious Revolution is presented by Plucknett on pp. 245–58 and 664. Also refer to George N. Clark, *The Wealth of England from 1496 to 1760* (London, 1946), p. 114.

19. For the establishment of the Bank of England and its early success in utilizing credit on continental Europe during Marlborough's war against France, see John Giuseppi, *The Bank of England: A History from Its Foundation in 1694* (Chicago, 1966), and R.D. Richards, *The Early History of Banking in England* (New York, 1965). For the subsequent credit inflation, see Phyllis Deane and W.A. Cole, *British Economic Growth: 1688–1959,* 2d ed. (Cambridge, 1969), and P.G.M. Dickson, *The Financial Revolution of England: A Study of Development of Public Credit* (London, 1967).

Note that Marx commented on the organization of the bank as "As with the stroke of an enchanter's wand, it endows barren money with the power of breeding and thus turns it into capital, without the necessity of exposing itself to the troubles and risks inseparable from its employment or even in usury." John Kenneth Galbraith has no better appraisal of the bank: "It is, in all respects, to money as St. Peter's is to faith." See *Money: Whence It Came, Where It Went* (Boston, 1975), p. 30.

20. *Chongzhen cunshi suchao,* reprint (Beijing, 1934), ch. 2, pp. 72–89.

21. Cheng Kaihu, ed., *Zhou-Liao shihua* (1620 ed.), ch. 44, p. 24.

22. On this subject a new monograph is provided by Madeleine Zelin, *The Magistrate's Tael: Rationalizing Fiscal Reform in Eighteenth Century Ch'ing China* (Berkeley, 1984).

23. An example is provided by Sidney D. Gamble, *Ting-hsien: A North China Rural Community* (Stanford, 1954), p. 170. The mathematically unmanageable situation is cited on pp. 166–67.

3

The Rise of Capitalism
in Venice, the Dutch Republic,
and England:
A Chronological Approach

In 1972, at Dr. Joseph Needham's invitation, I took my family to Cambridge, England. A year's residence was devoted to gathering data for his monumental work, *Science and Civilisation in China.* My portion of work fell under the heading of volume VII, section 48, which embodied the question of why modern science originated in Western Europe, not China. In his previous writing, Dr. Needham had suggested that between 1450 and 1600, China's science and technology still ran abreast of that of the West. Only after its breakthrough at that time did Western Europe begin to outdistance China. I had maintained contact with Dr. Needham by mail since 1967. Therefore, with the correspondence of the past five years, I had a general perception of his historiography when I met him in person. By 1972, the draft of my own book, *Taxation and Governmental Finance in Sixteenth-Century Ming China,* had been completed. It emboldened me to say that I was not entirely unfamiliar with the basics of the Chinese society and the Chinese economy during the period in question. Yet, how to apply my understanding to Dr. Needham's work was by no means a simple matter.

We could at this point, as some critics did, charge Dr. Needham for having asked a question that was too buoyant and diffuse. But the criticism could also be tossed back to the critics. Many of them had produced books and monographs without a synthetic focus. Anyone could take up a petty topic and play with this endless analysis. Obscure

57

and inconsequential subjects best fit the dissertation format. Frontal and lateral connections with other evidences in print or not could be disregarded. Under the circumstances, the pieces did not add up.

The situation compelled us to proceed from our own synthesis. On the China side, there was no alternative but to take the *Twenty-four Dynastic Histories* as a primary source. To scan the entire series would be too burdensome, hardly profitable for the labor invested. As of today, the most economical and readable edition is the punctuated imprint published by the Zhonghua Shuju. It comes to 76,815 pages bound in 233 volumes. If a scholar sets his mind to study fifty pages a day, it will take more than four years to complete the first reading. For the beginner, another point to be watched is that these dynastic histories were compiled over millennia; they differ in phraseology and diction. Included in the volumes are astronomical and geographical data and commendable deeds of filial sons and chaste women—entries that might not be of interest to the present student of history at all. Furthermore, it would be utterly impractical to prepare one's own card index.

We decided to work through the "Food and Money Monographs" (sometimes referred to as "Economic Monographs") of these dynastic histories. Twelve of them are found in the series. Besides, the "Essay on Equity and Standards" and "The Collected Biographies of Prominent Merchants" in the *Shiji*, with a similar content, could be counted as an extra. Of the dozen, six have already been treated by modern scholars, appearing in either annotated translations or explanatory summaries (the Han by Swann, Jin by Lien-sheng Yang, Sui by Balazs, Tang by Twitchett, Yuan by Schurmann, and Ming by Sei Wada). This collection offers an excellent guide for the investigator. If one starts from the five books plus Yang's article, traces back to the originals, extends the reading to the identical monographs of the other dynasties, follows the context to review a good portion of the *Dynastic Histories* themselves, and compares notes with the publications of current writers, including general history, dynastic summaries, and topical expositions, one can feel assured that the maximum effort has been made. He has done enough preparation to be compared favorably with any other individual under present circumstances.

Actually, the unmanageable situation of the source materials on the West is not substantially different. We also had to chart our own course. The second time I saw Dr. Needham, he took me for a walk along the banks of the Cam River. On the way he told me that, as he saw it, the Renaissance, Reformation, development of capitalism, and breakthrough in modern science and technology came to Western Europe as a package. One thing led to another, mutually. To this day I respect the insight of this observation. An obvious piece of evidence is that modern banks started in Italy during the fourteenth century, then spread to Northern Europe, covering areas of today's Netherlands and West Germany in the sixteenth century. Roughly, the timetable came in order with the Italian Renaissance, Trans-Alpine Renaissance, and English Renaissance. With the "package" concept, Dr. Needham's thesis was settled with a general direction. We could at this time say that between the fourteenth and seventeenth centuries, Western Europe experienced a drastic transformation, affecting its thought, arts, architecture, religion, economy, and social organization, those factors being interlinked. Together they made the situation irreversible, and thereafter Europe could never again revert to the conditions of the Middle Ages. It would make the change of dynasty in China relatively minor in scope. But what we laid down remained a very coarse concept. A great distance still existed between this concept and what we would like to accomplish—that is, to pin down why the two sides, Western Europe and China, differ so much, exactly what the differences are, and whether there is a fundamental cause behind them or not.

In 1974, my sabbatical provided a chance for another visit to Europe, this time with a short continental tour. Thereafter I spent some time in Dr. Needham's library. As he directed, I went through his collection of books on capitalism. Since we had decided that Europe had undergone a transformation that was large in scope, occupied a fairly long period, and remained irreversible in its consequences, it was clear that the formation of capitalism should be counted as one phase of this polyhedron. By nature, the topic is closely related to economy, the bannerhead of volume VII, section 48 of *SCC*. The latter is more synonymous with the "food and money" concept established by the classical Chinese writers. (By food, they really meant agriculture; and by money, commerce.)[1] The reading of the materials on the two sides, with so many overlapping interests, should have by this time yielded simple and direct answers to our questions. But that was not the case. After Dr. Needham's collection, I extended my browsing to the University Library. I frequented several bookstores, all neighbors of Gonville and Caius College (of which Needham was then Master). I was looking for new titles. The search widened my vision. But nowhere could we find adequate explanations that might enable us to build up a theoretical foundation for section 48.

In the summer of 1975, I was in Cambridge for the third time. When again no clear perspective was opened up, a sense of anxiety began to set in.

In Maurice Dobb's work, *Studies in the Development of Capitalism*, he mentions that literature on the subject can be divided into three categories. One group of writers stresses the change of production relations. When capitalism prevails, the worker sells his labor power as a commodity. He no longer has any claim to the goods produced. (Following general practice, we can refer to these writers as Marxists.) Another group gives emphasis to capitalist spirit. (We can also say that although Max Weber positively supports the spirit, R.H. Tawney raises serious questions along with his support, and Werner Sombart feels scornful about it. They all fall into this category.) One more group focuses its attention on the transition from a natural economy to a money economy. Capitalism empowers the wholesaler to intervene in the retail trade and in production. (We can also say that all those who do not belong to the above two categories have tendencies to fall into this third category.)

The proponents are many; their theories vary. Why can't we find a single author whose work we can endorse and adopt?

In this connection, we may follow economic historian Joseph Schumpeter, who makes it clear that with his craft every historian tries to rationalize the past in the interest of the present. The above specialists either approve of capitalism or disapprove of it, either appreciate capitalism in certain respects or denounce it for specific reasons, or are insiders who live with Western civilization. We, on the other side, strive to maintain an independent view from the outside. The difference in viewpoint affects the gathering of data no less than the programming of their synthesis.

Another example is French historian Fernand Braudel, admired by both Joseph Needham and myself. Professor Braudel promoted "total history" along with several others, Marc Bloch for one, who died a martyr in World War II. Braudel was not politically colored. The source material at his command, overwhelmingly rich, is sufficient to make us conscious of our own inadequacy. Yet in his voluminous writing Braudel carries an impression that capitalism is a settled matter, in numerous cases its ingredients being rooted in various countries.

We feel, however, that in world history capitalism still represents a current movement with plenty of vigor. Moreover, it is heralded by oceanic nations, and it carries certain organizational principles diametrically different from those that have a strong continental background. When Braudel sorts out certain commercial and business practices of China and those of other countries and attaches them to the chapters discussing things European for comparison, he moves far away from us because of our different sense of timing. A simple illustration may clarify the point: In the history of the formation of capitalism, a merchant who possessed one thousand ounces of silver as capital under the Wanli era in Ming China differed greatly from another merchant in possession of the same amount of capital in Holland during the same period. The different social structures on the two sides had put themselves in different stages of maturity so far as exchange or money economy was concerned.

As we all know, on the topic of the formation of capitalism, Marx's writing exerts a great amount of influence on those who followed him. Today when we read *The Communist Manifesto*, we are still under the impression that in Europe capitalism follows closely the collapse of feudalism. In reality, the two events are centuries apart. St. Albans is a village on the north side of London. At present, as part of the urban district, it is connected to the metropolitan area. Centuries ago it was a manor. After the Black Death, the population in the area drastically decreased. The villeins seized the opportunity to destroy the manor rolls and emancipate themselves. This incident, which took place during the mid-fourteenth century, or in the closing years of the Yuan Dynasty in China, is generally regarded as a substantiation of the end of manorialism, centuries after the decline of feudalism in England.

There is another episode that took place in a small town called St. Neots, about twenty miles due west of Cambridge on the Ouse River. In the early years of Elizabeth I, a local squire spent some money leveling the ground and railing in an area as a marketplace. He encouraged the farmers nearby to trade their produce there and levied a toll for using the facility. As business grew, no one even challenged him as to whether he owned the land or had been licensed to operate the market, since this was still an era of uncertainty. The enterprising squire, after reaping considerable profit, leased his business to another person. Only during the next generation did someone bring up a lawsuit against the operator of the marketplace, calling the collection of a toll on that spot illegal, as there was no such precedent. The source, however, does not elaborate on the outcome of the legal dispute.[2] But we do know that similar incidents took place at that time. What happened was that the custom requiring commodities to be sold at fair prices, in public, and at the historically designated marketplaces had been shaken, yet the replacement of open markets by private marketing and the introduction of urban finance into such transactions, barely started, had not grown into a general trend. Feeling curious about the aforementioned affair, one time Dr. Needham drove me to the banks of the Ouse River to locate the site. The incident is timed to be somewhere between the Longqing and Wanli eras in China during the Ming Dynasty, more than two hundred years after the burning of the records at St. Albans. The two places are no more than fifty miles apart. One of the events indicates the collapse of the feudal system some time ago; the other signals the oncoming capitalism still in the distant future. With such a long time lag, we can imagine that the formation of capitalism involves a large number of factors and goes through rather complicated procedures. Marxist scholars, in their effort to oversimplify history, provide few useful guides. A number of Chinese writers under their influence tend to underline specific economic developments in China. Without examining whether there has been an organization or a movement behind those economic activities, they laboriously work out a theory of the "sprouting of capitalism." The purpose is to shorten further the duration of the formation, to the extent of conferring the title of "pre-adult" on a child.

We feel that the "geist" concept of capitalism may even lead us to more abstractions and uncertainties. Numerous entries can be found in the history of Chinese thought that seem to be comparable with the thoughts of thinkers elsewhere, hundreds or even thousands of years apart, if we should disregard the mutual relations between ideas and social structures. An example is that Yang Zhu's doctrine of unconditioned self-interest could be held as the world's earliest proponent of individualism and materialism—an approach we have no intention of following.

When we appear to be so ready to find fault with others, will not our own special position be attacked? To be realistic, we are aware that criticism is inevitable. But this article has started with an explanation that we became interested in capitalism because of its relation to the development (or, more precisely, the undevelopment) of science and technology in China. There was no preconceived idea as to whether capitalism is good or bad. Taking a Chinese position, we were on the side of "nonexistence" to review something that existed. Numerous scholars, living with the subject matter over decades, take a number of things for granted, things that would, however, appear to be peculiar and unusual to us. As a whole, we feel that their interpretations of capitalism are much too localized and narrow. This is not a claim that we have more wits or a higher moral standard that enables us to challenge the authorities.

As it happened in the summer of 1975, Dr. Needham gave a round of lectures in Canada. Upon his return to England, he was still suffering from jet lag. I nevertheless went to see him and advised him that from the material available on capitalism, we could not find an adequate explanation directly applicable to China's development or undevelopment of science and technology. One way out was to follow the sources cited in the publications, return to a fuller historical context, and in that way produce our own vision of the formation of capitalism in Europe. At a glance, the proposal delayed our objective of concluding volume VII, section 48 of *Science and Civilisation in China* further. I counted myself as knowing the author well enough to put forth the suggestion. Joseph Needham was endowed with a sense of humor. He can be childlike. When our son Jefferson was little, Needham often bent low enough to run his index finger on Jeff's nose several times and allowed my son to reciprocate the treatment on him. But he can also terrify those close to him with his seriousness at work. Self-trained and strictly disciplined since childhood, he not only insists that each of his books be kept in a definite place, but also demands that his own limbs and muscles provide the maximum efficiency to his study. His eyes and ears not to be diverted to other matters, he banishes joking altogether during the working hours. Time is absolutely valuable to him. More than once I heard him say, "I wish there would be another fifty years!"

On the other hand, when a problem has not found a proper solution, Dr. Needham can be stubbornly pertinacious. Sometimes he will tie a knot with his handkerchief, not to be untied unless the question finds an answer. As for the suggestion that I had just brought to him, the point is that it had involved him personally for some time. Maurice Dobb, mentioned earlier, is a friend of his. Mark Elvin, now teaching at Oxford and author of a book on the same topic, was recognized by Needham for his prodigiousness when he was still a student in Cambridge. Their exchange of notes is still on file in the library. By the time of our talk, Perry Anderson had published his *Lineages of Absolute State,* in which he mentioned Needham more than once. All these connections have something to do with volume VII, section 48, the importance of which must hold a high position in his mind. On this occasion our conference did not last very long. But Dr. Needham fully supported my proposal for an all-out withdrawal and regrouping in order to start the research anew. After my return to the United States, he continued to send me books on the subject.

But because of this reversal, the two supporting foundations that had sponsored this portion of the project became unreceptive to our request for further financial assistance. They had shown interest in our joint article. Now, upon hearing that to study science and technology in China we had to extend our coverage to legal proceedings and land tenure in England, they could not help but regard the idea as absurd. Moreover, the competitive proposal had to be referred to specialists for opinion. Some of them never understood our difficulty. They reacted in this way: As Sinologists you are eminently qualified to perform within your sphere of speciality. But now, to step out from the area in which you can do well to venture into something else, you have completely altered the situation, and that is not something we can routinely approve. We further explained that our purpose was to rearrange the existing material, and to produce a conclusion that would appear to be direct, simple, and practical enough to suit the style of *Science and Civilisation in China.* It was not to start from mining our iron ore, rolling our own steel plates, and manufacturing our own machinery. In the background Dr. Needham had published articles discussing English history. As an undergraduate and graduate student at the University of Michigan, I too had taken sixteen courses on or related to modern European history. Within Gonville and Caius College, there were a number of specialists we could consult. There was also Professor Joan Robinson, an economist of world renown, whose office was only a short distance from Dr. Needham's and who had read some of our drafts and commented upon them. Those arguments should refute the notion that we were embarking on an unsound adventure with the odds against us. But the persuasion failed to carry. Meanwhile I received a fellowship from the John Simon Guggenheim Foundation to work on a book that presented a profile of society during the later stage of the Ming Dynasty, which subsequently appeared as *1587, A Year of No*

Significance. So, for the forthcoming year and a half, aside from teaching, I was engaged in my own project. In the summer of 1977, Dr. Needham, accompanied by Dr. Gwei-djen Lu, honored us by staying with us for a night during his lecture trip to the United States. Our unfinished work was briefly mentioned. But that part of the research was on the whole sidetracked.

Our work relied upon constant contact. In Cambridge, we held weekly meetings. Even matters of phraseology and bibliography were decided either on walks or over cups of tea. It would be impractical to continue with the Atlantic Ocean between us.

In a book of his, Professor Braudel mentions that after numerous disputes over it, the term "capitalism" has never been settled with a definition by consensus. It seems that Louis Blanc might be the first who threw in the word with the present meaning; that would date it to 1850. Marx for one did not include it in his vocabulary. (Marx, of course, referred to the "capitalists," the "capitalist era," and the "capitalist mode of production.") Wide circulation of the term occurred only in the present century. Some writers believe that such a word, full of political implications and repeatedly abused, should be banished forever by "scholars with self-respect." Braudel himself believes that the suggestion, although not put forth without reason, would leave a large hole in history, unnamed and unfilled.

In 1975 we had not yet had the opportunity to read this passage. But some time before, our attention had been drawn to the works of Sir George N. Clark, in which there is the statement: "The use of the word 'capitalism' as a name for the modern economic system was, I believe, invented in the middle of the nineteenth century by socialists, and it meant a state of society in which the predominant power is that of the wonders of capital."[3] With all this, our problem—that the term capitalism lacked a settled definition, that it could not be avoided, yet another author's writing was totally acceptable to us—remained unsolved. Before I left England, I composed a short passage, based on a statement published earlier jointly by Dr. Needham and myself: "Modern commercial practice stresses the active utilization of capital. Unused funds must go through the process of private borrowing to reach its widest circulation. The entrepreneurs must furthermore hire managers so that the scope of administration extends beyond the personal supervision of the owners. Likewise, technical supports including transportation,

communication, etc., should be jointly utilized by the various enterprises, so that the extent of business transaction goes beyond the limit
when those supports are operated separately by individual firms."

In sum, the wide extension of credit, impersonal management, and
pooling of service facilities place the focus on commercial capital. Its
large-scale expansion in Europe preceded industrial capital. Even
Marx and Engels in *The Communist Manifesto* gave international trade
a prominent place in "the capitalist era."

What my paragraph does not explicitly point out is that the development of the aforementioned three conditions hinges on trust, which
must be sanctioned by law. Not only is court protection required, but
the exercise of police power must also foster the arrangements in private contracts that give rise to the three conditions. Those prerequisites
implicitly cast a shadow of the state into the foreground. In discussing
the formation of capitalism, many Chinese and Japanese writers ignore
the business protection by statutory and customary law. In doing so
they create an impression that capitalism could be made up by merchants alone. This approach deprives them of an opportunity to visualize one of the fundamental differences between the history of modern
China and that of modern Europe.

Our interpretation is not to undervalue the influence of thought. So
long as capitalism appears as an "ism," it must have its ideological
basis. Yet "the spirit of capitalism" has to manifest itself with events
and deeds. As suggested, the government spends its manpower and
financial resources to enforce the agreements contracted by private
parties. It is an indication of a change of social norms. In the background, public opinion begins to hold that the trust embodied in the
private agreements affects not only the interests of the contracting
parties, but public welfare and security as well. For this reason, Max
Weber can, while enunciating the spirit of capitalism, dwell on saying
that making money is not evil but good. Under this spirit, the accumulation of wealth is no longer a means to reach something else, but an
end in itself. Nor should the amassing of a fortune be stopped at a
traditional "satisfying level," but the more the better.

Weber far from neglects social organization. When enumerating the
features of capitalism, he includes the separation of business from the
household, of corporate property from personal property in front of the
law, rational bookkeeping, and the relation between money and credit.
On the circulation of capital, he says: "For six pounds a year [paid as

interest], you may have the use of one hundred pounds, provided that you are a man of known prudence and honesty." He goes on to stress the importance of law. Law must not only be precise, but also be thoroughly practical. "Among those of undoubted importance are the rational structure of law and administration. Modern rational capitalism has need, not only of the technical means of production, but of a calculable legal system and of administration of formal rules." He took one more step to sound the warning: "Administration of law also follows the law of economy, cumbersome and unenforceable laws become defunct."[4]

Those conditions do not differ substantially from the prerequisites of our drafted paragraph. Why must the cumbersome and unenforceable laws become defunct? A law is practical because it has social compulsion in its backing. Generally speaking, in eight or nine cases out of ten, the persons concerned are already inclined to act according to the statute, which provision is regarded to be either legal or equitable. An important point is that the legislation in general coincides with the daily habit of the population. Only in certain specially situated cases, such as one or two out of ten, are court decisions required to clarify the uncertainty. If not, or even if there is the extreme that every case demands an inquiry by the court, the dispatch of judiciary police, the serving of subpoenas, and handing out injunctions, there must be a dislocation between state institutions and social reality. If the dislocated conditions persist, the nation will be engulfed in a civil war.

Puritan literature is the basis of Weber's writing. Puritanism, in turn, is a historical product of England in the sixteenth and seventeenth centuries. From Weber's work, it can be observed that under the general topic of capitalism, thought is closely linked with religion, jurisprudence, and economy. We have expressed our uneasiness when the topic of capitalism is approached with thought alone. It will be a completely different matter when the history of thought is reviewed with the necessary links. We can even gain a new field of view on capitalism, if in an integrated manner the works of the great thinkers of the sixteenth and seventeenth centuries are examined as a coherent whole. More than ever, it may enable us to see capitalism as an organization and a movement.

In this view Machiavelli, Hobbes, and Locke have made considerable contributions to the formation of capitalism. Even though we cannot say that they are capitalist thinkers, their materialism, individualism, and historicism reflect the surge of ideas in the sixteenth and seventeenth centuries, which, having run through the Renaissance, Reformation, and the formation of national states, finally crystallized at the labor theory of value. Their inconsistencies on the surface can be put aside; there is a general direction in their way of thinking.

Machiavelli is the one who has introduced materialism in its most uncompromising manner. In human history, only those elements that exist count. A factor that cannot survive the running of history, although praised for its virtue, is in the end distracting and illusory. Hobbes believes in the evil nature of man, which cannot be distorted or dressed up with goodness. Since self-preservation is man's nature, there is no basis to denounce the exercising of this inborn function as a violation of Natural Law. Locke rectifies Hobbes's pessimism. He believes that the natural rights of man can still be preserved through a social contract; absolutism is not inevitable. But his concept of self-interest is no different from that of Hobbes. He also brings up the labor theory of value. God gives all the material things in the world to mankind, collectively. Individuals mix their labor with portions of this gift, and that part of the natural endowment noted for a man's labor becomes his personal property. Since all this is consistent with the natural rights of man, it should not be subject to the arbitration and encroachment by a medieval moral standard or royal prerogative.

As outside observers, we can feel amazed by the enormous scope of this thought system, even though in the survey we have to condense each giant's lifetime work into two or three sentences. Regardless, here Natural Law is mentioned; so is man's nature; so is the true meaning of political life; and behind them, following very closely, is the principle of the inviolability of property rights. The publications of these three writers stretched over close to two hundred years; yet a sense of linear progression persisted. All this demonstrates that capitalism did not come up as a short-term impulse—no similar movement in the history of Chinese thought can stand as its rival. Needless to say, Yang Zhu's doctrine of self-interest, which came up abruptly and then disappeared altogether, cannot be compared. Recently, many Chinese authors have sorted out from the sources of the late Ming and early Qing casual remarks that argue for modest liberation of economic policies, some recognition of the contributions of merchants, and the impracticality of banishing self-interest altogether. Mild and scattered, these entries are not in the same class with the revolutionary thought held by their

Western contemporaries. All boiled down, capitalism was championed in the West with a degree of sweeping thoroughness akin to what the ancient Chinese writers put down as reaching a state of sincerity from a rectification of the mind, through which one's self can be cultivated and one's household unified, and ultimately what is under the heaven put in good order. Never was capitalism promoted incidentally, half-heartedly, and capriciously to simulate flowers of special specimens that bloom suddenly one morning and then vanish overnight.

At this point the reader may visualize the kind of trouble we had brought upon ourselves in the mid-1970s. Without a clear vision of our own standpoint, we had walked into that black hole called "capital-ism." We encountered Marx's complaints about a proprietor of a bak-ery in London who, dissatisfied with the sixteen-hour work day, demanded that his employees attend the ovens twenty hours a day. We also read Sombart's essays, which seemed to keep pace with Hogarth's paintings and Thackeray's novels. We knew that capitalism was a monster that had been there for centuries and had caused turbulent changes that involved many nations. We could even claim that we had seen its silhouette. But we remained ignorant as to whether it was a walking animal or a flying bird. The fundamental difficulty was that the subject matter required an interdisciplinary treatment. As such, it was not so easy to set up a procedure for a synthesis that included all the connecting factors.

In retrospect, the delay we had to put up with did not constitute a total loss of time. During the interval, especially in 1976, Mao Zedong and Zhou Enlai died, the "gang of four" was arrested, and China set out to reexamine the "Great Proletarian Cultural Revolution." The events provided an excellent opportunity for historians to reevaluate the entire situation; they might feel like those tourists who, on their way to reach a river's estuary, looked back upstream and gained a new perspective that enabled them to see the mountains and ravines in the middle section with a better understanding. This is not basically different from Schumpeter's statement, cited earlier, that current writers have to inter-pret the past in such a way as to rationalize their present positions. Our view of the formation of capitalism in Europe is developed from the standpoint of China. If we have a better understanding of our own footsteps, the knowledge should add to the depth of our vision when Europe is under observation. Another way to put it is that since we are entangled with one of the major problems in world history, the more we are able to clarify our own immediate surroundings, the more will our confidence be boosted in making overall judgments.

In this connection, I have to say that my book *1587* is not a specialized work dealing with the Ming Dynasty as some commentators claim it to be. Rather, it is a profile of traditional China prior to its full-scale conflict with Europe. It explains that the imperial court of China and Chinese society, with their own sense of justice and thought system, had arrived at a different organizational order. Their operations and functions also necessitated unique styles and manners. Implicitly, this is to explain how the two sides differed. From "what did not occur" to "what actually took place" on the side of China, I was still addressing the same problem.

For the following several years, the problem of capitalism in Europe came to mind often. If, I reasoned, the formation of capitalism cannot be separated from law, and law must have state organizations in its backing, then we should treat the subject matter within each country's national boundary. The fifteenth year of Wanli in China may differ considerably from the year 1587 in Europe. Similarly, what happened in France and Belgium could not be on the same footing with what took place in Britain. I had by then recognized capitalism as an organization and a movement, and that its development embodies a linear progression and, once reaching a point, it becomes irreversible. Those conditions serve to stress that time is an important factor. Between Dr. Needham and myself, an agreement had been reached that the formation of capitalism had much to do with the Renaissance and Reformation, the relation being verified by the timetable of the emergence of modern banks. With those presuppositions on hand, why should we not divide the history of the development of capitalism in Europe into three segments, as in Italy, Northern Europe, and England? In that case, the passage that I composed in 1975 could serve as a checklist. If we flesh out the three geographical regions with deeds and events that initiated commercial practices as general organizational principles applicable to the nation as a whole, the record arranged in chronological order should give us some clear ideas of how capitalism took shape.

In 1978, when I arrived in England for a fourth time, a pile of drafted papers and more than thirty books filled my suitcases. Dr. Needham had retired from his position as Master of Gonville and Caius. His new office on Brooklands Avenue, called the East Asian

History of Science Library, was not too far from Cambridge's railroad station. In that office I drafted such an outline. Parts of it were read aloud during our weekly conference for Dr. Needham's criticism and revision. The case of Venice was selected to present the city states on the Italian peninsula. The Dutch Republic stood as an example of Northern Europe. This on the whole served our purpose. Only the part concerning England, for obvious reasons, was dealt with in considerable detail. At a public lecture in Shanghai on September 23, 1981, Dr. Needham disclosed that we had a new understanding of capitalism in the West. It was mentioned by the *Xinmin Evening News.*

In November 1983 at his hotel in New York I saw Dr. Needham one more time. On that occasion he indicated that the material would be included in volume VII of *Science and Civilisation in China,* with some details still to be worked out. When I met him for the first time, I had suggested to Dr. Needham that although my draft could be used as a bottomline repository of source information, I would like to see the text come from his own hand, because as a work of erudite distinction, *SCC* manages to retain the personal style of the author, whose English, coming out fluently with the longer sentences stretching four or five lines in places, is not something that anybody else can imitate. At the time this article is being prepared, I have a feeling that Dr. Needham is still too busy to work on volume VII. Originally, when he planned *SCC* at the midpoint of the century, each "volume" was supposed to be a physical volume. But as the work progresses, one volume has expanded into four huge printed books; another, six. The author himself refers to the situation in terms that "the work is enlarging according to some form of geometrical progression." Moreover, section 33 is in print prior to section 32. This he feels to be in line with "Taoist natural irregularity and surprises." All I can say at this point is that volume V and VI may continue to engage him for some time.

But I also have an agreement with Dr. Needham. I can feel free to use my drafted portion for publication and lecture, provided that acknowledgment is made that the ultimate authority is *SCC.* It is a fact that thirteen years have elapsed since we started our weekly walks on Saturday afternoons along the banks of the Cam River. It is most difficult to say which portion of this article comes from his original thought and which is my suffix. When the editor of *The Chinese Intellectual* urged me to write a "critical review on the rise of capitalism in the West," I felt that it might not be a bad idea to include in the article the story of our own struggle. The best way to enable the reader to visualize the complexities of the problem is to lead him through the steps that we ourselves have gone through before arriving at the current state of understanding. It has also become necessary for me to disclose our standpoint, since we are introducing a new perspective on the subject.

But our preliminary draft remains preliminary. Although this article freely borrows from the 1978 version, it has also incorporated an amount of new material. So I alone am responsible for it. In this way I seem to take a free ride on the prestige and influence of *Science and Civilisation in China* yet remain unaccountable to its author. But a knowledgeable reader, appreciative of Dr. Needham's magnanimity, should realize that the role of an original thinker who has initiated the whole project differs from that of his associate who endeavors to solve technical problems. What makes the present case really complicated is that having assumed the role of such a technician, I still have to present a critical review to fill a timely need, and for that I have to maintain an independent position.

Although opinions vary, writers on the formation of capitalism hold one thing in common. From Marx to Sombart, from Henri Pirenne to Fernand Braudel, they unanimously trace its origin to the Italian peninsula somewhere near the fourteenth century. Many causes can be credited for that, such as that Roman law, accommodating to early commerce, was not restrained by the feudal influence of the Middle Ages. Another factor, even more important, is the rivalry between the papacy and the Holy Roman Empire, which left many city states on the Italian peninsula autonomous, the foremost among them Venice.

That city resides at the end of the Adriatic Sea, remaining a pivot point between Western Europe and the Eastern Empire. In a lagoon and separated from the continent by a body of water of two and a half miles, it remained unaffected by the affairs on the mainland. Its population since the fourteenth century for a great part of the modern era had remained on the whole stable. Rarely did it run away from the one hundred thousand level. Black Death had at one time cut down that figure. But replacements were found with planned immigration. On the other hand, living conditions in modern times did not cause the population to climb steadily, as often happened in other places.[5]

There were aristocrats of Venice who could trace their noble origins to landed baronage on the continent. From the fourteenth century onward, however, they appeared in the main as the ruling class of the plutocracy. Intermarriage with commoners was widely practiced. The status of the children followed the male line. In 1381, after Genoa was defeated, Venice conferred noble ranks on thirty citizens who had established merit during the war, including some artisans and small merchants. The city moreover established a pension fund to subsidize unemployed nobles.[6] At times the Venetian nobles were divided into factions; disputes and clashes of interest occurred. Yet the nobility as a whole, for most of the time remaining within the range of one hundred to two hundred families, managed to stay together as a rather stable and coherent group.

Venice had no agricultural foundation. Its food came from the southern tip of the peninsula, Sicily, and even Asia Minor and the Black Sea region. The city state seemed to have elected to be a grain broker rather than producer. The territorial possessions on the mainland had no decisive effect on the city state's politics. As a rule, its military operations on the continent were entrusted to the condottieri. The cities under its rule were encouraged to form self-governing bodies of the communal type. In contrast, colonies overseas that affected international trade were developed and exploited by Venice with full vigor. No local autonomy of any kind was allowed. The island of Crete, being a part of the reward for Venice's participation in the Crusade, was arbitrarily managed by it for several centuries and frequently experienced native resistance.

When Europe moved from the Middle Ages to the modern era, the broad interpretation of "usury" by the Church remained a serious inhibiting factor to the development of commerce. After the twelfth century, the prohibition applied to laymen. But Venice, with its commercial practices antedating the new restriction, was able to ignore it. Nominally, the city stayed within Catholicism and was under the papacy. But the clergy in the city state remained docile; the priests were even elected by the citizenry. Excommunication by the pope, ordered more than once, troubled Venice a great deal but never succeeded in breaking the independent spirit of this business community.

The major industries of Venice were shipbuilding, salt production, and glass manufacture. Its weaving industry had at one time in the thirteenth century become prominent. The lack of unsalted water in the city limited its growth. In the fifteenth century the cloth exported by Venice came from Milan; it was no longer locally produced.[7]

Industrial guilds were organized by the handicraft workers, but not seamen. The latter and the ship construction workers were under stricter governmental control. The navy personnel were drafted from the entire population. Citizens were organized into units of twelve men each, so that they could rotate to answer the draft call. In its heyday, Venice maintained a formidable navy. The galleys in the fleet engaged 150 to 200 oarsmen each. Similar galleys appear in Chinese sources as "centipede ships," for the large number of oars made them look like those many-legged insects. The manpower gave the vessels a high degree of mobility. In combat, the oarsmen also turned fighters. In novels and movies, those oarsmen are often presented as slaves pressed into service. In reality, that happened in the mid-sixteenth century and beyond, but by then Venice was already in decline. When the city was in the prime of its life, all hands on board were free citizens. Those details enable us to see the close connection between the free city's population and its sea power. It should also be noted that major items of trade were under governmental monopoly. The ships moved in convoys.

When we study capitalism by using the source material of continental Europe, it is easy for us to see the movement from a monolithic social order toward a plural society, sometimes dramatized by the demand for liberalization by an urban population from the feudal authorities. But if we start with the Mediterranean source material (which is the proper chronological order), especially from the history of Venice, we instead see a commercial organization, under a most unusual situation, feed itself to grow on its own logic and its own power. It may even be described as a society of single-mindedness. Without a revolution, it simply banished all the things incompatible with its own organizational structure, and remained uncompromisable at accommodating everything and anything that went along with commerce.

Historians of Venice often bring forth two outstanding features of the city state, which, at a glance, seem to contradict each other. One is that some form of democracy was apparently at work. For instance, the single executive, the doge, was elected. Forty noblemen who exercised that privilege formed an electoral college; the election was conducted by casting a secret ballot. The legislative branch of the government consisted of a senate and a general assembly. But behind-the-scenes maneuvering remained important in Venetian politics, suggesting the use of steering committees and caucuses. The other side is that it might appear as a police state. Its secret service was active. Legal provisions against treason were severe. The two points can be explained by the constitution that was rooted in trade alone. Venice's kind of democracy had not been installed to effect democracy for its own sake. It only happened that by maintaining its monolithic order, everything was mathematically manageable. Political stability would be secure if all persons involved in the city's commerce were invited to participate in its governance, with the distribution of power in parallel with the distribution of wealth. But it is difficult to say that its decisions on the expansion of trade, control of sea lanes, and matters of war and mobilization always met with the approval of the entire population. The fear and suspicion of the general public by the government could not be avoided, the more so because of subversive influence of hostile nations. What the government counted as firmly in its control was the largest industry—ship construction—which was publicly owned and operated. Other industries, such as soap manufacture and metal works, could be watched through their guilds. Social mobility softened class barriers considerably. The feeling of discontent was also mollified by opportunities for business participation. A kind of partnership called the *colleganza* permitted the workers and widows to invest their modest savings in overseas trade. Seamen were authorized to carry private cargo. For all these, it seems unrealistic to exaggerate the situation to the point of making Venice a police state, just as it is out of proportion to overglorify its democratic institutions.

A modern scholar has referred to Venice as a "city without territory" and a "merchant republic." It is said that "the government was that of a joint-stock trading company, the Doge its president, the Senate its board of directors, the populace its shareholders."[8] The semblance might have been overstated; the incisive statement nevertheless seizes the true character behind the organization and delivers it directly to the reader.

Not all the city states in Italy could imitate the style of Venice. Take Florence for example: Its economic maturity had come before that of Venice. Prior to 1300 it had established itself as a woolen manufacture and banking center. At one time seventy-two money exchanges surrounded the city's new market. The Florentine bankers functioned as financial agents of the nobility and bishops of many European countries, a part of their work being the remittance of church income to Rome. But Florence was landlocked. From its landlords it became entangled in the politics of an agrarian society. The conflict of interest between manufacturers and the land nobility occurred. Nor could Florence remain aloof from the contest of power between the Empire and the papacy. Thereafter Florence was tossed into a political test tube, undergoing "the rule of nobility, the tyrannies, the struggle of the middle class with the proletariat, limited and unlimited democracy, pseudo-democracy, the primacy of a single house, the theocracy of Savonarola, and mixed forms of government that prepared the way for the Medician despotism."[9]

Under those circumstances, it is difficult to say what stage of development Florence found itself in during the Renaissance. Its polity had the ingredients of capitalism; it also had those of "communism" and "national socialism."[10] It can be observed here that merchants and merchant capital alone do not constitute capitalism. Even when production relations progressed early, such as in Florence, which saw the antagonism between capitalists and the urban proletariat in the fourteenth and fifteenth centuries, there was no guarantee that the development would precipitate capitalism. In this connection, we are more convinced by Braudel, who has said, "Capitalism only triumphs when it becomes identified with the state, when it is the state."[11] Only the "whole hog" prevails.

To go back to the story of Venice: It enables us to see that the formation of capitalism in its early state benefits from the constitutional simplicity of the state, not from its complexities. The advantage of such a state of simplicity is that everything is mathematically manageable.

An important factor emerged when Europe moved from the medieval period to the modern era: The dynastic states transformed into national states. The financial operation of a dynastic state did not hold the hereditary monarchy responsible to the entire population. The kings took care of public finance as if it were a private matter. For that they often borrowed from the merchants, sometimes placing crown jewelry as collateral. Beyond that, loans were forced; debt obligations were unilaterally canceled. All this would not secure the legal rights of property holding and therefore remained an obstacle to the development of capitalism. New nations of the modern era, on the other hand, accept national debt as a public liability, instead of letting the kings be responsible.

In 1160, the government of Venice borrowed 150,000 silver marks from the merchants. With this borrowing it established the earliest precedent of national debt. Twelve years later, a Bank of Venice was established. It was authorized to issue negotiable notes on the strength that it was the lender of this loan, antedating by five hundred years a similar arrangement that gave birth to the Bank of England.[12] These two cases fulfill Professor Braudel's criterion that capitalism triumphs when it becomes identified with the state and when it is the state. In history, such a development creates an irreversible situation. Since the government operates like a corporation, commercial law can be utilized as the basis of the civil code. When those conditions prevail, the entire society is moving ahead with capitalism.

But Venice, starting from a community that relied on fishery and salt production as the mainstay of its economic life, had to wait until the advancement of ship construction and the expansion of large-scale business under the influence of the Crusades to demonstrate its mature capitalist character. Its law code was enacted in the early thirteenth century, when Giacomo Tiepolo served as doge. When the Venetian Republic entered its golden age after about 1300, most public institutions supporting capitalist adventures were in place. With the exception of the permanent corporations capitalized with common stocks that had yet to appear, precedents had been established for business adventures that involved several or more partners and that might be concluded in several months or over a longer period. Modern commercial practices involving maritime insurance, letters of credit, double-entry bookkeeping, bills of lading, and residential business agents overseas had been set in order. After 1400, markets for import-export business of the modern type existed in Venice, enabling foreigners to enter into contracts with native merchants. The *curia di petizion* was the arbitrating agency for legal disputes. As a rule, the lawyers were appointed by the court; but the contesting parties could also bring in their own attorneys. The books and correspondence could be subpoenaed for examination.[13]

Why, in discussing the formation of capitalism, do we have to touch upon so many technical details? To answer the question we may refer to what was said earlier, that any law, to be enforceable, must have thought and belief and social compulsion behind it. The legal practices of the city of Venice, while supported by its Senate, were contrary to the customs of medieval Europe and at odds with its moral standards. The city state nevertheless went on, substantiating its conviction with deeds and accomplishments. Only in this way did capitalism under its patronage appear as an "ism"; it started with a new concept about man's nature and ended with a new world order in view. The ideology was fulfilled by action.

The weakness of the Venetian Republic rested in the fact that it had no base of production. Its organizational principles could not be readily applied to agriculture and industry. In 1453, the Turks took Constantinople; in 1488, the Portuguese circumnavigated the Cape. Traditionally historians have held the two events to be milestones that marked the decline of Venice. Yet, the fall did not start immediately. In terms of art and letters, the sixteenth century had yet to be recognized as the advent of a new era—the Renaissance—during which time the brilliance of both Venice and Florence had yet to shine. The decline of the Venetian Republic thenceforth happened, sliding down to the final point when it was handed over to Austria by Napoleon without causing a fuss. It happened not because its system was outdated, but because a free city, relying solely on the commercial strength of its island base, could not withstand over a prolonged period the onslaught of the land powers of an enormously greater numerical superiority.

When we read European history, it seems puzzling why the advanced commercial organization put to work by the Italians had not been copied by the greater powers of Western Europe such as England and France sooner than it was. After some length of study, especially a close count of the background factors, it becomes evident that what we call economic matters are in fact interwoven with a variety of social issues. A major overhaul can never be executed without reconditioning all the related components. The extent of work may be comparable to the metamorphosis that turns a walking beast into a flying bird. Unless there are internal and external pressures, will such a transformation even be taken up? Often the leading figures of the movement, deeply involved in the struggle over decades, are not consciously aware of the true meaning of the roles that they themselves are playing. There are cases in which it takes several hundred years for historians to discover the cause-and-effect relationship among the events, and it can only be done by taking a comprehensive view and comparing them diligently with similar affairs in history.

Take England, for example: After 1300, its foreign trade was under the influence of the Italians. Traders from Venice, Florence, and other

Italian cities who resided in London were known as Lombards. The banking district of the city was accordingly designated as Lombard Street. For one thing, the foreign bankers were more substantially capitalized. For another, before the Reformation those Italians had ready access to remittances to Rome. Either from the endowments to the clergy known as chantries or from ordinary properties from which tithe went to the church, rural England handed a significant portion of its annual income to the ecclesiastics, which of course included the pope. In reality, tax farmers handled the lower-end collection. Nor were the funds directly dispatched to the papacy. Instead, the Italian bankers issued drafts that satisfied that requirement. The cash, through the monasteries, was offered as advance payments to purchase wool, which was shipped to Flanders to feed its weaving industry. Since the business made connections with many quarters, Italians were entitled to extraterritoriality. If a lawsuit involved both a Lombard plaintiff and a Lombard defendant, an Italian consul would preside over the case. Only when one of the contestants was English would the litigation be taken to a mixed court.[14] Differences in social customs between the two sides, often with a touch of religion, had made the arrangement necessary. But if modern commercial laws had been widely observed in England, the host country would not have allowed the Lombards or Italians to manipulate its international trade by dipping a finger into its agrarian economy.

What actually took place in history proved that from the late sixteenth to the early seventeenth century, the nation that adapted to the new organizational order had to be larger than the autonomous cities of Italy, yet significantly smaller than England or France. The United Netherlands, generally known as Holland (in reality Holland was one of the seven provinces), did not enjoy the extent of de facto independence of the cities in the Italian peninsula; yet never was it placed under the effective control of a strong monarchy as in the cases of England and France. The fact that capitalism in its second stage of development finds a foothold in such a country may serve to affirm that history, while working toward an evolutionary process of a longer term, always manages to maintain a logical sequence.

The Netherlands, or the Low Countries, comprising today's Holland, Belgium, and Luxembourg and located on the coast of the North Sea, remained a region of relative inconspicuousness during the age when feudalism took hold of Europe. Toward the end of the Middle Ages, the autonomy of the local towns became prominent. Many feudal lords conceded to the privileges of those towns and cities. After the twelfth century, the construction of city walls became a fashion. The territorial lords, upon receiving financial aid from them in the name of voluntary contributions, in general allowed those towns and cities to maintain their judiciary independence. The unwritten laws in those days recognized the burger status of a villein who had taken residence in one of the municipalities over a year or a hundred days. But in the Low Countries, forty days would be sufficient.[15] With a wider circulation of money, there was a steep increase of prices. The commuted services, not adjustable to the new circumstances, worked more in favor of the inhabitants of the boroughs at the expense of the manorial lords. The written and unwritten laws, based on local custom, at the same time showed a great deal of variety over a wide geographical region.

In the fifteenth century, all the Low Countries fell into the house of Burgundy, whose territory also included parts of today's Germany and France. It seems, on the map at least, that the Burgundians would have an opportunity to wedge in with a third kingdom between the two. In fact, that was what they had in mind. The centralized administration started with a new court system; judges were appointed to the districts. Taxation was anticipated to take the entire territory into count. But soon after those measures were contemplated or about to take effect, the designated king, Charles the Bold, was killed in action. That happened in 1477. The heiress, Mary, was only twenty years old. The municipalities of the Low Countries called a meeting at Ghent and presented to the duchess a document called the "Groot Privilegie," similar to the Magna Carta in spirit and coverage. It declared that the supreme court of Burgundy should not take up cases that fell within the competence of the law courts of the districts. Without the consent of the municipalities the duchess could not declare war or collect new taxes. She could not appoint anyone except natives to office. Even Mary's own marriage had to be approved by the assembly of towns and cities.[16] Acceptance of these terms by the duchess confirmed the autonomy of the self-governing units.

Economic expansion in the Low Countries in the sixteenth century enhanced their importance, with the weaving industry in Friesland and the appearance of Amsterdam as a major port in particular tipping the balance. At this point Emperor Charles V, aspiring to be overlord of Europe and counting the Netherlands as a household asset, proceeded to tighten control over the provinces. The banner of the Counter-Reformation was utilized as an instrument, so that the tightening of political control worked hand in hand with the persecution of heresy. In this way the political, economic, and legal problems of the Low Countries became entangled with a new element of religious belief.

The edict issued by Charles in 1550 is a terrifying document, capable of causing the reader to shudder to this day. It decreed that anyone who printed, copied, kept, or circulated the heretic literature by Luther, Calvin, Zwingli, and several others, along with anyone who read, preached, or discussed the scriptures in private or in public without authorization, was to be put to death. For those who repented, the execution was to be carried out with the sword for men and burial alive for women. Those who refused to recant were burned at the stake. It is said that Charles, busy with many other matters, did not enforce this edict to its fullest. But in 1546, five years before the proclamation of the edict, a contemporary witness reported that in the two provinces of Holland and Friesland alone, more than thirty thousand persons lost their lives on the charge of heresy.[17]

After the abdication of Charles, his son Philip II reactivated the decree. Upon the establishment of new bishoprics in the Low Countries, the Spanish Inquisition proceeded in full force, the details of which are covered in most textbooks. When Alva (or Alba) served as governor general, he assumed supreme military and civil authority in the Netherlands. Eighteen thousand persons are said to have perished under his reign of terror. To provide for the Spanish forces, a 10 percent sales tax was imposed. When an article changed hands ten times, it was taxed ten times. The unpopular move provoked a full-scale resistance of the native population. Declaration of independence took place in 1581. The sympathetic support of England provided Philip the needed justification to dispatch the armada. The fighting on land dragged on, until an armistice was reached in 1609, by which Spain virtually accepted Dutch independence. But the full-scale recognition came only at the conclusion of the Thirty Years' War, sixty-eight years after the declaration of independence by the Dutch Republic, and eighty-one years after the people in the Low Countries took up armed resistance.

For students who are concerned with the development of capitalism, this chapter of history offers several points of interest: Ever since its independence, the Dutch Republic has shown its capitalist character as a nation. But the war of independence had little or nothing to do with class struggle. The Low Countries had never been a region for feudal influence to take a firm hold. When the armed clash with the Spaniards broke out, the nobility rallied with the commoners in a nationalist struggle. Most of the houses of noble titles, as an eyewitness reported, were ruined by the war. Striving to live up to their previous standards, thereafter they became employees of the urban bourgeoisie.[18] The war also provided an opportunity for the new republic to go on with an industrial and commercial expansion. When Antwerp sustained the destruction meted out by Philip's army, Amsterdam as a major seaport received a lift. The weaving industry and metal works in Holland greatly benefited from the war disturbance, which had motivated skilled labor to migrate northward. When these new factors were cast against the Dutch background of urban autonomy, the basic structure of a capitalist society was already in place. The country's agriculture, with more emphasis on cattle farming than crop planting, was again in need of water transportation and commerce to exist.

It is difficult, however, to pin down quickly the relation between religious belief and the forming of capitalism. The common notion that the Calvinist doctrine of predestination will immediately fill in as the gospel for the capitalists is not verifiable with the deeds of Dutch independence. Catholics participated in the war against Philip II. The Spanish Inquisition was not aimed at protecting the creed alone. But Philip, by establishing new bishoprics and subjecting the entire populace to religious discipline, was strengthening his own hand for political centralism, which clashed with the doctrine of a priesthood of believers held by the new sects. William the Silent, who led the Dutch in the war of resistance, was converted from Catholicism to Lutheranism before settling down as a Calvinist. As soon as independence was secured, the Calvinists quarreled among themselves with varied interpretations of predestination. The Reformed Church continued to turn back usurers from communion; universities denied them degrees. Politicians took advantage of the doctrinal schism to promote their own interests. Only when Holland and Friesland declared that the church had no power to interfere with matters of banking and Maurice of Nassau, the new stadtholder, took a firm stand on the matter, allegedly saying, "I don't know whether predestination is blue or green,"[19] did the dispute gradually quiet down.

This multifaceted development does not present a picture of a capitalist system that owes its origin to the inspiration of a religious concept. Rather, the settlement of a large number of factors had cast the Dutch Republic into a prototype suitable for bourgeois leadership, and only then was the doctrine of predestination interpreted in such a way as to stress that a man's materialistic well-being is predetermined, so that a pious believer must work diligently to manifest his worldly success as a sign of God's blessing. In this connection, a specialist of Dutch history may be quoted to compensate for our lack of decisive voice in such a subtle matter. He said: "In questions relating to the world above, many may be seduced from their convictions by interest, or forced into apostasy by violence. Human nature is often malleable or fusible, where religious interests are concerned; but in affairs material and financial, opposition to tyranny is apt to be unanimous."[20] He did not point out that often the materialistic interest works inside the individual, without his full awareness of it, to determine his outlook, including religious convictions.

The Hollanders had no prior experience in organizing a national state. Continental expansion was neither their ambition nor a task that suited the best of their ability. Only navigation and trade appeared as strong points. The iron ore they needed came from Sweden, spices from the Far East. The Hanseatic League could not be relied upon for maritime safety, as it had no effective political organization in back of it. The Dutch Republic filled the void. Immediately it became the pioneer of maritime insurance, which absorbed a large quantity of capital. The Bank of Amsterdam, accepting deposits in a variety of currencies and bullion but crediting the depositors with a uniform bank money (*florin de banque*), could be said to have kept an international currency in circulation. It was highly praised by Adam Smith. Those practices, unprecedented, contributed to what we call a capitalistic system. The cardinal point is that the Dutch Republic, founded on an organizational structure of commerce, had no better logic to maintain its raison d'être but to enrich its populace. The constitution necessitated the upholding of the inviolability of property rights and the guarantee of the disproportionately more influential role in public life played by private capital. At this point the reader may take these conditions along with what was mentioned earlier, i.e., wide extension of credit, impersonal management, and pooling of service facilities, as our definition of capitalism.

Because of those conditions, the United Netherlands could not abandon its urban autonomy, with which it demonstrated another characteristic of capitalism. It might appear to be aggressive and innovative without; yet it must remain customary and conservative within. For its integration, the Dutch Republic applied the principle of federation. The national government handled only those matters beyond the competence of the provinces. In principle, the administration of civil laws followed local precedents. One good thing was that the province of Holland alone had two-thirds of the population of the federal republic, and after independence it contributed three-fourths of the federal funds.[21] Thus even with the unevenness among provinces, the administration of federal affairs never deviated from majority rule.

After the Dutch Republic, England was the next nation to complete its capitalistic reconstruction. For England, the seventeenth century was an age of sorrows. At first the king clashed with Parliament, taxation and finance being the focal point of controversy. Religious issues added a dimension to the conflict, to be further complicated by policies dealing with Scotland and Ireland on one side, and with Spain, France, and Holland on the other. The nation experienced civil war, regicide, republicanism, commonwealth, protectorate, restoration, and the second (Glorious) revolution, not to count plots and assassinations, pamphletering, banishment of religious nonconformists, bribery and secret pacts, and acceptance of foreign subsidies by the king. The population of the country might have grown from four to six million over the period, on the whole less than 1 percent of China's in the twentieth century. Yet the ungovernable situation of England in the seventeenth century is comparable to that of China in our own days.

An enormous body of literature has been produced on England in the seventeenth century. For the general reader the first hurdle may appear to be, as a specialist has pointed out, that in the array of studies the "fertility of hypothesis was running far ahead of factual research."[22] Another specialist, while exposing the inaccuracies of other authors, had to turn the review into a rancorous attack. Still another confesses his own past prejudice in treating the subject matter; he goes so far as to list an earlier work of his own in the bibliography of a new volume and call it representative of an opposite view. Such controversies are many; the ground is never secure or level. An outsider is not expected to walk in, make comments, and leave unscathed.

But rancor does not contribute to good historical reading. Nor will fear of criticism in any way strengthen the credentials of the outsider. We feel that, with the knowledge of modern Chinese history on our side, what happened in England in the seventeenth century is not difficult to summarize. The different perspective can in fact be utilized to our advantage.

Every nation must have a superstructure and an infrastructure. The links in terms of religious beliefs, social customs, and economic interests have to be represented by law. Mutual compatibility is essential to the proper functioning of the system. When discord occurs, repairs can be done in a variety of ways depending upon the cause of the malfunction. The top may be reorganized; the bottom may be restructured; or the middle echelon may need readjustment. Sometimes a new tax law or a revised legal code will suffice. The situations of England in the seventeenth century and China in the twentieth century are alike in that both the superstructure and infrastructure are in need of reconstruction, and the middle-echelon components affecting religious, social, economic, and legal factors simultaneously require renewal. Therefore, we see England in the seventeenth century facing an all-embracing problem, not a bundle of small problems.

Let us leave the abstract theorizing here. To review how it happened, we propose to establish a sequence by starting from the infrastructure. The central core of the problem was land tenure. In the seventeenth century it had lost its accountability.

Land tenure in England, following feudal usage, should in theory be difficult to alter. But even in the Middle Ages, there were already legal loopholes. If a man wished to combine his property with that of his wife, he could enfeoff the tenements to a third person and ask the latter to return to him the properties intact in the form of subinfeudation, this time jointly with his wife. A landholder could also sell the estate that he theoretically held but did not own to another man. He might, upon receiving payment, enfeoff the purchaser in exchange for the nominal service of "a rose in midsummer." In the seventeenth century, the common law courts faced numerous such cases. A legal historian charges them for "piling fiction upon fiction to escape the heavy burden of history."[23]

Our general impression is that a freeholder is the owner of the land. But until the mid-seventeenth century, he might still have a landlord behind him, to whom he paid rent. His freedom rested only in the fact that his rights could be freely transferred or inherited. Yet the most controversial were the properties of the copyholders. Their ancestors being villeins, they held the properties in question according to the copies of the manorial records. Historically, villeins indeed could own property. But they were also assessed with duties and services to the manors in a bewildering range. Part of the records were destroyed during the Black Death, some three hundred years before. There were manorial lords who had received payments from the copyholders and converted their tenure to freehold. Other manors, however, treated them as if they were renters. A manor as a territorial unit might have been dissolved; its rights holder could still demand service obligations from the heirs of the villeins, usually commuted to payments. The monetary payment was not referred to as rent, but as an "entry fine," to sustain the legal fiction that the occupant had taken possession of the property with a false title. The general trend in the seventeenth century was an increase of the fine, and forcible conversion of copyhold into leasehold. The background was that after the flow of silver bullion from the Western Hemisphere, there was a currency inflation. The improvement of transportation and the expansion of commerce atop it had caused a general increase in prices. From 1500 to 1600, farm produce in England had gone up about four times, with no end in sight. When the property was recognized as rental, the lease set up a time limit, running from seven, fourteen, twenty-one, or more years. The rental relationship could be terminated when the contract expired; the payment would be adjustable. To the end of the sixteenth century, copyhold still counted as the most popular form of tenure. In Yorkshire, for instance, copyholders amounted to perhaps two-thirds of the tenants. The constant inquiry of manor customs, survey of the estates, and check of the tenant's title affected a large segment of the population, as it was generally known that "a yeoman who failed to protect his title was lost."[24]

Enclosure has in the past been recognized as a chief cause of displacement of small peasants and social disturbances. Recent research, however, points out that it was not always the case. Enclosure could be amicable or antagonistic, depending on the region and circumstances. Moreover, the movement started before the sixteenth century, carried through during the entire seventeenth century, and was completed only in the early years of the present century. In the main it stood as a necessary measure toward the rationalization of land utilization in the face of population growth. The problem of the seventeenth century had largely arisen from the sale of manor rights and the handing down of landed properties to the heirs by the users. Both could involve parcelization and legal ambiguities. The common law courts, capable of sustaining the right to possess (seizin) but inadequate in clarifying ownership in a modern sense, appeared to be no help. This must have generated an atmosphere of uncertainty among the farming population. While the displacement of agrarian workers occurred, there were also landlords who were unable to locate their possessions in the field or to contact their chief tenants. Those who relied on fixed incomes could have been ruined. On the other hand, a new group of landlords prospered; they had amassed their capital elsewhere, such as in business and in office holding, and subsequently had speculated in landholding and risen to be the new gentry class. In sum, the dislocation reflected an entire range of legal provisions concerning land tenure that was no longer in accord with the rural scene.

When the agrarian economy could not be coordinated with the rising commerce, the deadlock also became a cause of the social predicament. According to common law, farm produce must be sold at "fair prices" in the designated markets. Private marketing was unpopular and regarded with suspicion. The principle against waste could be interpreted to disallow duplication and the slightest change of procedure. But in the seventeenth century, urban population growth had revised the supply-and-demand situation in large areas. Wayfaring merchants made a substantial contribution in closing the gap and bringing the regions together. Their life was hazardous and their business insecure. A major cause remained the common law, which had never prepared itself to be an instrument for modern business transactions. For one thing, it never accepted that chattels, being perishable, should ever come up with entail. Under its rule, there was no equity of redemption; mortgagors in general gave up possession to the mortgagees. Of course, no adequate provisions had yet been made for insurance and bankruptcy. Even in a lawsuit involving a breach of contract, the damage was limited to what the plaintiff actually sustained, not the claim for missed opportunities. And there was a long waiting period, usually seven years.[25]

The superstructure of England was represented by an uneasy state of balance between Parliament and the king. Following feudal usage, the king in peacetime had to live on his own; his income from land paid the court expenses. Only under an emergency situation could he call Parliament into session and ask for a subsidy. No tax was to be collected without consent. When the conflict flared up in the seventeenth century, both sides claimed to have acted on precedents. In reality, the current development had already overstepped the bounds of past experience, to which neither side could retreat. Another cause leading to the collision of power had to do with Henry VIII's Reformation. When he called himself the head of the Church of England, he virtually conferred on himself and his successors the position of another pope. In the early seventeenth century, a large segment of the population preferred a congregational form of worship. About the same time, the exercise of judicial power also brought the two sides to cross purposes. Since the common law could not adequately handle a number of situations that arose in the new era, a remedy was found in the prerogative courts, more under royal control. Those courts were enumerated by the authorities in different ways. With broader coverage, they included the Court of Chancery, which handled petitions to the king's council; the Court of Exchequer, which dealt with litigations in which the Crown property was an issue; the Court of Requests, which traveled with the king; the High Commission, which functioned as an ecclesiastical court to continue the papal authority left from the Tudor Reformation; the Star Chamber, which dealt with sedition and libel; and the Court of Admiralty, which handled cases arising from maritime trade. Those courts were not bound by the common law, but were committed to dispose of the cases with equity. In other words, the decisions were aimed to be equitable, not necessarily legal in the sense that they were always supported by precedents. The jurisprudential innovation, in effect since the sixteenth century, speeded up the litigation and broke the rigid tradition that what had not been done before could not be done later. But in the seventeenth century the king had already been at odds with the parliamentarians on taxation and on religion. The parliamentarians were more concerned that in the name of equity Charles I could use judicial power to advance his absolutism. On the eve of the civil war, the most offending of the courts, the High Commission and the Star Chamber, were abolished by a parliamentary resolution.

The political events between 1642 and 1689 will not be covered in this article. As mentioned, there is a large collection of books dealing with the period, including some excellent textbooks. In tracing the formation of capitalism, we can in fact jump to the latter date. It is connected to what was mentioned earlier, that having progressed to a point, the social environment promoting the wide extension of credit, impersonal management, and pooling of service facilities may push all these to an irreversible position, making the nation's capitalist feature unmistakably clear thenceforth. For England, the success of the Glorious Revolution in 1689 marks such a point.

William III, the son-in-law, came with the "protestant wind" to overthrow his father-in-law. But as a Dutchman he had no intrinsic interest in the domestic politics of Britain. Answering the invitation of his supporters, he became an elected king. Five years later the Bank of England was established. When national debt became a public institution, the king or queen was no longer personally responsible for the deficit. Constitutionally, this forever removed a major cause of controversy reminiscent of the seizure of bullion at the Royal Mint by Charles I, the stopping of payments at the exchequer by Charles II, and even the forced loan on the East India Company by Cromwell. Indirectly, the termination of such infamy was the best assurance of the inviolability of property rights, without which the feeling of trust would not prevail. A year earlier, that is, in 1693, the Mines Royal Act was proclaimed. Until then the Crown had a claim to the previous metals found in private mining. In reality, the provision held back the population at large from costly mining adventures, while occasionally exemptions were granted the privileged few, with no significant results one way or another. The renouncement of the royal claim immediately set off private investment. Mines Adventure of England, with capital of 125,000 pounds fully subscribed in a short period, appeared as an industry of mammoth size for those days. The investment launched in such a vital area should stimulate the business of allied interests.[26] The round of development convinces us that the formation of capitalism is more feasible under a democracy or a constitutional monarchy. Absolutism generally obstructs the growth of private capital.

The bloodless revolution of 1688–89 is called "glorious" because it actually restructured the top strata of England. Thereafter the king became a ritualistic ruler, parliamentary supremacy growing into a reality. Toward the end of the seventeenth century, the prototypes of political parties and the cabinet form of government were in place. Although not yet fully mature, they followed a linear progression of growth and development. The political stability made it easier to leave religious controversy behind.

Why was such a splendid achievement possible in the closing decade of the seventeenth century but not in the middle of the century, when England had the vigorous leadership of Cromwell? Based on what we have learned from Chinese history, we can assert that when the superstructure experiences such a breakthrough to reach maturity, the infrastructure must have also been significantly tidied up, otherwise the legislation would not be able to make connections. We imagine that toward the end of the century, land tenure in England must have differed from what it was several decades before. Statistical data are still lacking. How exactly it happened is far from clear; it may never be. But one item may give us something to think about. The uniform land tax of 1692, applied to the entire nation and without the service of tax farmers, turned over to the exchequer more than two million pounds, more than the annual income of the Crown of previous years.[27] This could not have been accomplished some fifty years before, when land tenure was in great chaos and England remained mathematically unmanageable.

The following items we do know: Before the civil war, many enterprising landowners were already working to rationalize their holdings. The profitable tracts were preserved and consolidated; the unprofitable portions were sold or discarded. During the years of the civil war, tenant farmers and yeomen followed their landlords and local squires. The tendency toward land consolidation and rationalization should continue to gain ground, not to lose momentum. By the mid-seventeenth century, the freeholders ceased to pay rent; they turned toward proprietorship. The substitution of leasehold for copyhold continued unchecked.[28] We can, therefore, believe what Tawney said, that the civil war provided a "melting pot." And his statement that foreclosure was cheaper by war than by litigation may not have been flippantly tossed out; it may well be a sober observation unnoticed by the participants themselves.[29] In sum, there was a new class of landowners who, persistently working toward the regularity of landholding, dispelled others who failed to keep up. Great pressure was felt by the copyholders as a class. Some of the lucky ones among the descendants of villeins managed to elevate themselves to freeholders. Others were either turned into leasers or squeezed out from agriculture altogether to provide cheaper labor for the rising industry. But this was a movement with a prolonged historical standing, connected to the events before and after the war. Thus even in the eighteenth century, copyholds still existed.[30]

Accordingly, when we say that by 1689 the infrastructure of England must have been remarkably regularized, there is no absolute measurement to back it. The observation provides an explanation for the formation of capitalism in England, not as a conclusion derived from the study of the civil war, nor from the study of land tenure itself. Authorities working on those topics take different views of the melting pot, and their divergent views are not likely to converge.

With this explanation, we can clarify the role of law. Even though the parliamentarians championed the supremacy of the common law courts, the position became untenable as that body of legal practices was too far behind the times. The application of equity, especially by the Court of Chancery, went on in strides, even more so after the Restoration of 1660. The cases involved equity of mortgage redemption, protection of women's property, bankruptcy, contracts, shipping partnerships, and the principle of undue influence applicable to fraud and deceit.[31] Equity had started with the idea that no legal precedent was necessary. Yet its application after some length of time had also accumulated a body of precedents of its own. The situation was ripe for the merger of equity with law. In 1689, Sir John Holt became chief justice of the King's Bench. He decided that thereafter, in cases where merchants were involved, commercial practices would be applicable.[32] Had there not been parallel social changes in the background, the directive, if opposed by the public, would have been unenforceable.

Before and after the Glorious Revolution, legal reform rarely had anything to do with the executive or legislative branch of the government. In the main it was accomplished by judicial review. On that Sir George Clark has said: "The courts and law offices went on working without interruption except for a few months, so that the development of the rules of law by judicial decisions went on. There was much agitation for law reform, but not even in the most revolutionary phases of the crisis was there any important legislation in the land law or commercial law or law of contracts."[33] Clearly enough, an executive order or a bill passed by Parliament still carried the effect of an ordinance by which the will of the top was binding on the bottom layer. But capitalism affects the property rights of private individuals. The technicalities had to be clarified in each particular situation; only the court could handle them with patience and with leisure. Starting with the spirit of experiment, the accumulation of precedents builds up a system in a more practical manner. Clark's interpretation enables us to visualize what was at issue: It is the interlink between the superstructure and the infrastructure.

When we reexamine the founding of the Bank of England, we can appreciate what Professor Braudel has said, that capitalism triumphs when it becomes identified with the state. The list of stock subscribers of the bank in 1694 starts with the king and queen, followed by 1,267 names. They were, "without exception," rich through generations of trading or associated with the city government of London; many were members of Parliament. In terms of creed, they were "protestant to the last man." The capital was not paid in cash, but with receipts of silversmiths and tallies issued by the exchequer for the military supplies that the stock subscribers had provided the government. Those assets, 1.2 million pounds in all, were loaned to the government at an annual interest of 8 percent. The income from customs duties and excise on liquors was pledged as a guarantee for the loan. But as long as the annual interest was paid, the indebtedness could carry on in perpetuity, at the same time as the bank was authorized to issue sealed bills in the same amount, which it also loaned to its business contacts at interest. By receiving the double interest, the bank was on its way to the career of credit inflation.[34]

In September 1694, not long after the bank opened for business, the government asked it to remit 200,000 pounds to the Duke of Marlborough, who was fighting the French in Flanders. This was by no means writing a check and asking John Churchill to cash it in Belgium. No overseas branch of the bank had been established, nor had international credit advanced to such a stage. It required the directors on the board to arrive at Churchill's headquarters. Agents were dispatched to Spain, Portugal, the Netherlands, Switzerland, and Italy, especially Venice and Amsterdam. European merchants, upon hearing that the merchants of London were standing behind the British forces, made the assets under their control available to Churchill, who organized the war effort. With the financial support of Northern and Southern Europe, England defeated France. The proceedings advanced the organization of international credit, with Britain taking the leadership role.

Credit inflation continued in the meantime. The annual expenditure of England increased from five million pounds in 1702 to eight million in 1714. National debt during the same period advanced from thirteen million to thirty-six million pounds. The capitalization of the Bank of England also expanded.[35]

From these conditions, we can deduce that land tenure in England had been relatively stabilized, that farm management was generally in firmer hands, and, with the merger of equity with the common law, that commercial laws were now applicable to the agrarian society. An era was entered in which agricultural capital could interflow with industrial and commercial capital, the inland sector and the coastal region were tied together, and the distance between production and distribution was shortened. Epitomizing the situation was the appearance of land banks in the closing years of the seventeenth century. They stood for the flamboyant hope that while the real estate on hand remained secure and intact, cash could be obtained elsewhere on the strength of this ownership. On the whole they failed because of inadequate organization and impatient operation. Only after the midpoint of the eighteenth century and beyond did the mushrooming of local banks and country banks in England and Scotland establish a permanent trend. A number of small private banks also appeared in London. Not only did money and credit continue to expand, but they also now had a national organization.

The checklist worked out by Dr. Needham and myself has yet to deal with management and services in business under a modern capitalist system. It covers prevention of fraud and deceit, punishment for embezzlement, formation of insurance companies, organization of joint-stock companies of limited liability, establishment of a postal service, construction of turnpikes, and the appearance of newspapers and periodicals. All those steps were completed after the eighteenth century, but they all owed their origins to before or immediately after the Glorious Revolution. So, when we consider that capitalism stands for an organization and a movement, 1689 should be taken as a crucial point as far as England is concerned. If there is no such timing in history, capitalism can only be reviewed either as abstract concepts or as disconnected components. But our notion of capitalism is that it is something integrated, substantial, and identifiable.

The fact that England enters into the capitalist stage of development is a vital event in history. From today's point of view, a nation of six million persons on sixty thousand square miles is rather small. But England in seventeenth-century Europe was a substantial power. Such a country, with a considerable agricultural base and a firm and solid legal tradition, turned itself into being mathematically manageable, until everything inside became integrated so that the entire nation appeared almost like a city state—this had never been done before. In the past, the military strength of England was below that of Spain and Portugal. Nor could its commercial organization rival that of the Italian cities or the Dutch Republic. At this point, by adapting to a firmer and tighter organization, it exceeded all the aforementioned nations in efficiency. The accomplishment enabled it to remain as the top nation over several centuries.

Even though Marx did not use the word "capitalism," he sketched in his works a polity corresponding to the conditions that result from it. Obviously, his description is closer to the historical development of capitalism in England than to anything else. The class struggle theme in the *Communist Manifesto* also has some relevance in English history, except his narrative of two or three sentences can never cover the intriguing complexities over several hundred years. This serves to indicate that a revolutionary pamphleteer who writes inflammatory literature takes a different role from that of a general historian.

Dr. Needham's curiosity and mine had at least been partially satisfied when I said good-bye to England in 1978. As I said, we became involved in the above question because we wanted to know why modern science and technology originated in the West, not in China. After several years of groping, we had become convinced that there is no simple answer to the question. To understand the situation fully, we have to take social organizations of the two sides and their movements into account. With what we have learned, we see in the capitalist society a modern society as compared with the medieval society of Europe or the society of traditional China, noted for its bureaucratism.[36] Insofar as capitalism is capable of rendering the entire society mathematically manageable, members of the society are made to appear as interchangeable parts, with which a further ramified division of labor is feasible. When the rights of private property of the individual are held inviolable before the law, the authority to perform and the obligations that come along with it can also be added, subtracted, multiplied, and divided to correspond to the more refined division of labor. Those conditions provide an incomparable advantage in developing science and technology over a society not yet so restructured.

But his preliminary conclusion is made for medieval Europe and traditional China only, with a time limit of the fourteenth to the seventeenth century, or roughly corresponding to the duration of the Ming

Dynasty in China. Of course this does not represent our view on current politics. Dr. Needham, ruggedly independent, has expressed his views on current affairs in writing and in lectures, with clarity and forcefulness. It would be ludicrous for me to try to be his spokesman.

This article was written at the request of *The Chinese Intellectual*, whose editor indicated that a number of young historians, intrigued by my previous essay in volume 1, number 4, hoped that I would provide a more detailed account on the subject. With such a background, it is only fitting that I conclude this follow-up piece with a summary that speaks for myself alone.

When the topic of capitalism is mentioned in the late twentieth century, several points require our attention. Seen from a technical rather than an ideological angle, capitalism is only an organizational device of the state. It penetrates many social and economic factors and, as Adam Smith puts it, applies the "system of commerce" to enrich the people. Without explicitly saying so, naturally the premise requires the enlightened self-interest of the individual, without which no adequate infrastructure can be made to reside within such an organization or device. Once this structure is set up, legal protection of property rights and the allowance for private property to play a significant role in public life come as necessary corollaries.

This type of organization rose from the Mediterranean region, spread to Northern Europe, and carried into England. It started from nations surrounded by water and went to nations with long coastlines, and from nations that have agricultural bases to nations in which living style is very much determined by tight agrarian organizations, thus establishing a world trend. Nations that hang on to an agricultural order as their organizational principle tend to cling to the current state of balance. Nations that have adapted to commerce as their organizational principle are more interested in the dynamics of exchange. As time moves on, the latter become even more apt to take advantage of science and technology. The former, left behind with their crude and simple organizations, further expose their weaknesses. Their citizens are more disillusioned by the outmoded management.

From Venice to the Dutch Republic to England, we can see that it is by no means easy for a nation to abandon its medieval background to fabricate a capitalist system. Within the characteristics of its own geography and history, each nation has to grope in darkness for some time before it unexpectedly succeeds. In this connection, the word "constitution" in the English language serves an illustrative purpose. By constitution we may refer to the fundamental law of a nation. Yet the same word, when applied to any organic being, means its function, organization, and bodily structure. To draft a fundamental law is a relatively simple matter. To change a nation's function, organization, and bodily structure is by no means so simple, as no one can command a walking beast to turn into a flying bird. The more the case will be if the nation to be so converted is agrarian, since farming affects the livelihood of the entire population, and any rushed innovation can easily lead to a general famine. Such a simple truth easily escapes our attention because we are usually under certain illusory influences in reading American history and Japanese history.

Way back during the colonial period, land tenure of the future United States involved few feudal factors. In general, land changed hands freely. The merger of equity with the common law had as a whole been completed in England. Very few territories of colonial America saw the coexistence of the two kinds of law courts. We can say that since the inception of the United States, its agriculture has remained consonant with industry and commerce. Moreover, timed with the development of technology, the nation was pushed from coast to coast over virtually empty space. Even then, the United States experienced Shays's Rebellion, the Whiskey Rebellion, Nullification, and a civil war that lasted four years. To organize banks, institute a national currency, regulate labor unions, proceed to antitrust activities, and coordinate interstate commerce, the nation had to go through a long list of struggles. But the United States had benefited by a rather long period of growth and gradual development, the history of which does not reflect the difficulties when the problems crowd time and space, with nowhere to turn around, yet with the influence of an old society that cannot be shaken off.

Japan, an oceanic nation, in the late Tokugawa period saw the *daimyo* (territorial lords) designating their *kuramoto* (business agents) in the major cities, where *kabu-nakama* (business associations) and *tonya* (wholesale dealers) arose, and *kaisen* (scheduled shipping services carrying on an insurance business on the side) came into being. In the background, political centralism has never been a part of Japanese governmental tradition; commercial organizations and commercial capital nevertheless achieved steady growth. On the surface, the Meiji Restoration made long strides ahead of its time. In reality, it merely capped an infrastructure, its archetype already in place, with a super-structure. When we put aside the unusually favorable situation in this case, it will be easy for us to believe that if the Japanese could do this, so should everybody else.

Yet, whether they are unique or routine, difficult or easy, these cases have established an irreversible trend in world history. The development does not mean that capitalism is always appealing or desirable. Its unsatisfactory features did not even need to wait for Marx to unmask. They had been exposed by Adam Smith. In *Wealth of Nations,* the author took the side of the colonies, denouncing the unfair and shortsighted practices of British merchants and the British government. In recent times, John Maynard Keynes and Joan Robinson have made severe criticisms of modern capitalism. For all these, I believe that we can fall back on Dr. Sun Yat-sen's writing: he has distinguished capitalism as that seen by a physiologist and that by a pathologist. Besides, for the shortcomings, modern socialism provides remedies; it also gives self-defense to those nations that have only lately taken steps to modernize.

But at rendering the entire nation mathematically manageable by adapting to the organizational principle of commerce, socialism is not different from capitalism. It too has to recognize the individual's right to private property; it too has to promote the circulation of capital and the best employment of talent and the sharing of service facilities. The differences are only in degree. After World War II Britain has sometimes shown strong socialist tendencies; yet at other times it shows strong capitalist characteristics. No fundamental constitutionalist restructuring is necessary for the switch. The United States is one country in which capitalism is developed to the utmost; its public policies sometimes still show socialist inclinations. A crucial point here is that when capitalism was organized some three hundred years ago, it appeared to contradict the beliefs and customs of contemporary Europe on every turn. It had to go all the way to provide itself with a theoretical justification that is perfect and flawless. Today there is no longer such a need, not to mention that such an absolute position would be most difficult to maintain. Is man's nature good or evil? What is the true meaning of predestination? Those are religious problems. Locke's labor theory of value was worked out in the seventeenth century when the production methods were simple. It was still believable to say that a man, by mixing his labor with an amount of natural resources, could claim ownership of that amount. Today, commercial advertisement is carried by electromagnetic waves for dissemination, and that alone could throw the claim out of focus and make a strict adherence to the labor theory of value most difficult.

Therefore, I feel that concerning China's reform today, any effort to ascertain whether it is ultimately capitalist or socialist in nature may have some propaganda value, but it is academically meaningless. The only thing to watch is the absurdity that a developing nation, having not yet completed the most basic modern reorganization, talks extravagantly on fulfillment in communism, to the extent of negating the individual's self-interest. That has to come out as a distortion of history. We have seen enough of the literature that attempts to rationalize such a movement. Routinely it starts from the terminological inexactness and works toward a wrong sequence of world history. In the end, the writing separates itself from time and returns to the traditional Chinese practice of constructing a pyramid upside down.

Notes

Source: Chinese Intellectual II:4 (summer 1986); *Chinese Studies in History* XX:1 (fall 1986).

1. The term "food and money" in the *Twenty-four Dynastic Histories* carries a large connotation of national economy and people's livelihood, often presented as a variable in the course of time. For instance, the "Food and Money Monograph" of *Ming shi* mentions that during the Ming dynasty, taxpayers were assessed with service obligations called *lijia, junyao,* and *zafan.* The one sentence covers the evolution of a tax system over several centuries. The lack of logical consistency in the text can easily lead the reader astray.

2. About the impact of the Black Death on land tenure in England, see Theodore Plucknett, *A Concise History of the Common Law,* 5th ed. (London, 1956), pp. 32–33, 311. For the incident at St. Neots see Joan Thirsk, ed., *The Agrarian History of England and Wales,* vol. 4, *1500–1640* (Cambridge, 1967), pp. 502–3.

3. Braudel, *Civilization and Capitalism, 15th-18th Century,* vol. 2, *The Wheels of Commerce,* trans. Sian Reynolds (New York, 1982), pp. 237–38; Clark, *The Sixteenth Century,* 2d ed. (New York, 1947), p. 11.

4. Weber, *The Protestant Ethic and the Spirit of Capitalism,* trans. Talcott Parsons (New York, 1930), pp. 22, 36, 48, 50. See also R.H. Tawney's foreword.

5. Frederic C. Lane, *Venice: A Maritime Republic* (Baltimore, 1973), pp. 20–21.

6. Ibid., pp. 252–53; John Julius Norwich, *A History of Venice* (New York, 1982), pp. 257–58; Jacob Burckhardt, *The Civilization of Renaissance Italy,* trans. S.G.C. Middlemare (New York, 1958), vol. 1, p. 86.

7. M.M. Postan and E.E. Rich, eds., *The Cambridge Economic History of Europe* (Cambridge, 1952), vol. 2, pp. 352, 393.

8. Edward P. Cheyney, *The Dawn of a Modern Era* (New York, 1936), p. 11.

9. Ibid., p. 42; Burckhardt, *The Civilization of Renaissance Italy*, pp. 99, 102; Oliver C. Cox, *The Foundation of Capitalism* (London, 1959), pp. 143–44; Leonardo Olschki, *The Genius of Italy* (Oxford, 1949), p. 169.

10. See Lauro Maritines, *Power and Imagination: City States in Renaissance Italy* (New York, 1979), pp. 251–54. His explanation is based on the relationship between Florence's multifaceted political thought and the Renaissance.

11. Braudel, *Afterthoughts on Material Civilization and Capitalism*, trans. Patricia M. Ranum (Baltimore, 1977), p. 69.

12. Cox, *The Foundation of Capitalism*, p. 81; Charles A. Conant, *A History of Modern Banks*, 4th ed. (New York, 1909), p. 10; Norwich, *History of Venice*, p. 108.

13. Norwich, *History of Venice*, pp. 155–56; Lane, *Venice*, pp. 51–52, 141–47; Braudel, *Afterthoughts*, p. 22; Lane, *Andrea Barbarigo, Merchant of Venice, 1418–1449* (Baltimore, 1949), pp. 18, 98, 112.

14. M.M. Postan, E.E. Rich, and Edward Miller, eds., *The Cambridge Economic History of Europe* (Cambridge, 1963), vol. 3, pp. 102, 117; Cheyney, *Dawn of a Modern Era*, pp. 16, 29. But extraterritoriality seems to have been reciprocal; English consuls also tried cases in Italy. See E. Lipson, *Economic History of England*, 11th ed. (London, 1956), vol. 1, p. 590.

15. J.A. Houtte, *An Economic History of the Low Countries, 800–1800* (London, 1977), p. 29. See weak feudal influence in the Low Countries, pp. 74–75; M.M. Postan, ed., *The Cambridge Economic History of Europe* (Cambridge, 1971), vol. 1, p. 337.

16. John Lothrop Motley, *The Rise of the Dutch Republic* (London, n.d.), vol. 1, p. 51.

17. Ibid., pp. 114–14, 254–57. A similar decree was issued earlier in 1529, but Charles was not yet emperor. See Emile G. Leonard, *A History of Protestantism*, trans. Joyce M.H. Reid (London, 1965–1967), vol. 2, pp. 77–78.

18. Herbert H. Rowen, ed., *The Low Countries in Early Modern Times* (New York, 1972), pp. 221–22.

19. R.H. Tawney, *Religion and the Rise of Capitalism* (New York, 1926), p. 238; Rowen, *The Low Countries*, p. 116.

20. Motley, *Rise of the Dutch Republic*, vol. 2, p. 277. The quoted statement is made in connection with the sales tax imposed by Spain.

21. Rowen, *The Low Countries*, pp. 215–16; Harold J. Grimm, *The Reformation Era* (New York, 1954), p. 443.

22. Lawrence Stone, *The Causes of the English Revolution, 1529–1642* (London, 1972), p. 29.

23. Plucknett, *Concise History*, pp. 159, 539.

24. Thirsk, *Agrarian History*, vol. IV, p. 304; see also Plucknett, *Concise History*, p. 538.

25. Plucknett, *Concise History*, pp. 665, 677; Edward Jenks, *The Book of English Law*, 6th revised ed. (Athens, Ohio, 1967), pp. 258, 285.

26. For royal obstruction to investment in mining in sixteenth- and seventeenth-century England, see B.E. Supple, *Commercial Crisis and Change in England, 1600–1642: A Study of a Mercantile Economy* (Cambridge, 1964), p. 227; William

Rees, *Industry Before Industrialization* (Cardiff, 1968), p. 386. For the organization of Mines Adventures, see ibid., pp. 526–30.

27. J.S. Bromley, ed., *Cambridge Modern History* (Cambridge, 1970), vol. 4, pp. 285–86; Maurice Ashley, *England in the Seventeenth Century* (Cambridge, 1977), p. 175.

28. Thirsk, *Agrarian History,* vol. IV, pp. 684–68; Stone, *Causes of the English Revolution,* p. 73.

29. Tawney, "The Rise of the Gentry, 1558–1640," *Economic History Review* 11 (1941), pp. 1–38.

Anyone who has browsed the history of land tenure in England in the seventeenth century realizes the complexities of the problem. From the civil war to Restoration, there were also proceedings of confiscation, leasing of the confiscated properties, redemption, and recoveries by the former owners. Even experts cannot provide comprehensive coverage. Yet, while the details cannot be ascertained, a general picture is not too difficult to sketch. Moreover, historians seem to have reached some kind of consensus, as summarized by a recent work on the subject.

In the 1640s, numerous disputes arose over land titles. They continued in the 1650s. Even in the 1660s, they had not completely died down. But as a whole, after the Restoration the number of cases was diminishing. Solutions to the problem were limited to the turning of copyholds into freeholds and conversion of them into leaseholds. The focal point of the debate among specialists is which social group benefited most during the turnover, which, in one way or another, does not affect our observation that having gone through the turmoil, England became "mathematically manageable."

See John Thirsk, ed., *The Agrarian History of England and Wales,* vol. 5; pt. 2, *1640–1750: Agrarian Change* (Cambridge, 1985), pp. 198–208. The author of this chapter is Christopher Clay. His summarized view is that wherever the landlords worked on the spot with fresh capital, they reaped most of the benefits; otherwise they had to make concessions to the tenants.

30. G.W. Southgate, *English Economic History* (London, 1970), p. 108. Also see G.E. Mingan, *The Gentry: The Rise and Fall of a Ruling Class* (London, 1976), p. 173.

31. Plucknett, *Concise History,* pp. 690–91.

32. Ibid., p. 246.

33. Clark, *The Wealth of England from 1496 to 1760* (London, 1946), p. 114.

34. The best reference on the subject is John Giuseppi, *The Bank of England: A History of Its Foundation in 1694,* reprint (Chicago, 1966).

35. Ibid., p. 35; P.G.M. Dickson, *The Financial Revolution of England: A Study of the Development of Public Credit, 1688–1756* (London, 1967), pp. 42–46; Bromley, *Cambridge Modern History,* vol. 6, p. 285.

36. An article written by me offers a preliminary explanation for the traditional Chinese bureaucratism. It appears in *Explorations in the History of Science and Technology in China* (Shanghai, 1982), pp. 115–30. The English translation appears in *Ming Studies* 16 (Spring 1983).

—— 4 ——

The Merger of Chinese History with Western Civilization

In our general conception, the Central Intelligence Agency of the United States is a secret service apparatus whose good and bad deeds, given a legendary touch, readily become themes of fictional thrillers, sometimes put on movie screens. Yet a specific function of the Agency is not always appreciated by the general observer. It also collects data of academic value in a nonconfidential manner. For instance, a meteorological report on China is produced annually by the CIA, with illustrations, and copies are made available to educational institutions on request. At this point on my desk is a copy of a twelve-page report entitled "China's Economic Performance in 1985." The text comes from the CIA's report to the Joint Economic Committee of the Senate and the House of Representatives on March 17, 1986. After the session, copies of this report were offered to the public for the asking. My copy came by return mail after a request was sent on a postcard.

Focusing on the results of 1985, this report starts with the negative aspects of recent Chinese performance. For instance, grain production is 7 percent less than the level of 1984. Industrial production, due to the relaxation of control by the center, resulted in a flurry of hasty actions that overburdened the transportation system, causing congestion and dislocations at various places. Inflation was three times the previous year's level. The imbalance of payments in international trade led to a serious depletion of foreign exchange reserves.

Yet, the main purpose of this report is not to sound the alarm of a catastrophe. There is no prediction that a collapse is imminent. Most of the negative factors have been admitted by the Chinese government and given notice in print before. The CIA analysis further points out that behind them are inner causes indicative of positive influences, on the whole inevitable due to the current reform. The decline of grain production was in part caused by natural disasters. But food surpluses over the years more than made up for the shortfall. Even though China purchased 5.4 million tons of grain from abroad in 1985, it also exported 9 million tons during the same period. Against the 1984 level, Chinese industrial output showed an 18 percent increase. That of rural industry was a hefty 35 percent. One of the reasons that less grain was harvested was more peasant participation in industrial works. Despite inflation, the standard of living of the population still marked a significant improvement. Imports of consumer goods in part accounted for the depletion of foreign exchange reserves. But a major portion of spending overseas was for production tools and raw materials, steel products included.

In conclusion, the report observes that in view of the negative factors the Chinese government decided to slow down economic development. Zhao Ziyang's report of September 1985 promised a period of readjustment over two years to improve control of the macroeconomy. The CIA suggests that China can do well by pursuing indirect controls, such as taxation and monetary policies that influence interest rates. Actually, China is moving in that direction. For instance, the 1985 budget makes substantial cuts in government expenditures. It calls for the sale of material and goods by public enterprises and the tightening of credit and an increase of interest rates by the central bank.

As a historian, I am impressed by this report, for it confirms my thought that the hundred-year Chinese revolution has been completed in the 1980s. A major achievement that comes from it is that China is now mathematically manageable. Because of this breakthrough, not only does modern Chinese history require a vigorous review, but the general history of China also needs to be rewritten. Moreover, a review of China may open the door for reconsideration of European history, American history, Japanese history, and so forth. It seems that a unitary movement is taking hold of the history of mankind. Historical works of the past, having been composed from a narrower vista, can, in the light of the new development, either be reinforced in order to appear to be more substantial or be modified with new additions and abridgements so that they can be brought up to date. This is an opportunity that does not appear more than once every five hundred years.

At a glance, my proposal may appear grossly unrealistic.

Isn't That Absurd?

Not only is the per capita income of the Chinese people currently way below that of the advanced nations, but also, for several decades to come there is no prospect that the difference can be bridged. At this moment, China is encountering great difficulties in its population control. With the increase of agricultural and industrial production, new problems have arisen with soil conservation and pollution on land, in water, and in air. An article by Qian Jiaju in *The Chinese Intellectual*, volume 2, number 2, has exposed the many anomalies of the current Chinese pricing system. Coal purchased from the free market costs somewhere between six and seven times that of the same material supplied by the government. Steel products, when meeting the prescribed standard, are mandatorily surrendered to the government at low prices. The rejects are in the meanwhile sold on the market to fetch at least a fourfold profit. Some government functionaries, still entrenched behind their "leftist" line, deliberately obstruct foreign trade. Illiteracy and partial illiteracy to this day afflict 23 percent of the population nationwide, including a segment of the membership of the Chinese Communist Party. According to the interview given by Wang Daohan, former mayor of Shanghai, to Lu Keng, correspondent of the *Sino-Daily Express* of New York, the mayor still functions like an economic czar. He makes decisions on the government budget and salaries and pays factory workers, and he even has a say in the television sets sold on installment to employees by the manufacturer. Isn't it absurd that at this time I venture to say that China is mathematically manageable? A more outspoken critic might charge me with being self-deceiving.

I must at the outset emphasize: The observation is that China is mathematically manageable. It maintains some distance from the position that the country is mathematically managed, and it is still farther away from the position that it is being managed mathematically in a rational order. My viewpoint, derived from macro history, focuses its attention on the function of the social structure, giving less consideration to the immediate capability of the state apparatus. The latter derives its strength from the former. If the foundation of the former is secure, the latter will sooner or later work its way to suit the circumstances. The aforementioned case has already proven a point: When the macroeconomy is moving out of control, a remedy can be found by ordering a two-year period of reevaluation and readjustment.

My rush to produce an outline of macro history at this point can be explained as follows: Traditional Chinese society has an immense reach. Since the control by the government is limited, the organizational principle precludes incessant changes. Chinese history, following this pattern, always marks time to register a movement of any kind. It is no match for the nimbleness and dynamism of the modern societies of the West and Japan. When we seize a single element of culture or one person or event to compare with a similar item on the other side, the study serves no useful purpose. Qian Jiaju's article, mentioned above, contains a point of interest. It points out that the population of Tokyo matches very closely that of Beijing. Yet there are more than 170,000 restaurants of various sizes in the Japanese capital compared with some 5,000 such establishments in the Chinese capital. Indeed, as the author of the article claims, ideology has a bearing on the few restaurants in Beijing. But fundamentally, the sharp difference in numbers of public eating places reveals not only two types of economic structure, but also different social backgrounds. Tracing it further back, we can even make an issue of its origin in history. The prosperity of Tokyo goes a long way back, to the life of *chonin* during the Edo period, made evident by the literature of the *ukiyo-zoshi* and contemporary woodcuts. Japan's basic social organization, having survived World War II, has enabled Tokyo to make a fast recovery and come back to exceed its prewar level. The 170,000 restaurants stood for no more than a link in the chain of commerce.

If, when a casual question is raised on the reason why there are fewer restaurants in Beijing, an explanation has to be built up from the brushwork of Ando Hiroshige and Kitagawa Utamaro, will that not make historical study disjointed and cumbersome? My own teaching experience in the United States has told me that the cause-and-effect relationship coming out from the circular route usually makes the presentation ineffective. There is the necessity to reconstruct history in larger frames.

Of course, there must be various ways of doing it. Our own method starts from a systematic review of European, American, and Japanese history with special attention on their differences with Chinese history. Along with this, the entire length of Chinese history from the Spring and Autumn period and the Warring States era is examined. An outline is constructed from the "Food and Money Monographs" of the *Twenty-four Dynastic Histories*. From it the study is extended to other monographs and biographies in the series. Then, the general summaries and specific explorations by present-day authors are scrutinized for new insights and particular connections. For source information from both sides, the continuity of the outstanding features is noted in such a way that the historical proceedings of hundreds of years can be seen as if they were events occurring in a single day. The many years of reading and reflection have now crystallized into the conclusion that the hardships and discomfiture that China has endured over the past hundred years are the necessary steps within a full-scale reconstruction in preparation for the merger of Chinese history with Western civilization. When China becomes mathematically manageable, this reconstruction can be considered to have been completed. The details fill up the following sections and paragraphs.

Another advantage of such a survey in macro history is that it enables us to visualize a number of factors unseen by contemporaries of the period under study. When history is recast in panoramic views of longer time segments, the dynamics of the social structure and the role of mass movement become major themes, to outweigh the importance of the words and deeds of the great personalities on stage. In this way, it is closer to the true nature of modern history. World War I started with a clash of pan-Germanism and pan-Slavism in the Balkans, which affected the collective security of the major powers in Western Europe. But when the war concluded, going down the drain were not only the central powers but tsarist Russia as well. The outcome could be summarized as that the old-fashioned autocracy, with an outdated structure sprawling over a large geographical region, had been liquidated under the strain of war, to make the flurry of events in 1914, including the sending out of ultimatums and orders for mobilization, irrelevant. World War II started in Europe with Hitler's drive for the doctrine of racial superiority and his design for a *Lebensraum* for the German people in Eastern Europe. When this movement failed, not only was Nazi racism defeated, but the equality of the entire human race became a worldwide principle. The liquidation of colonies has since been extended into regions not even directly engulfed in the war, so that self-determination can be held as a global doctrine. Unforeseen by Hitler, the consequence was apparently also not anticipated by Chamberlain and Churchill.

Chinese history of the past hundred years also involves mass movements of different kinds, although not exactly on a par with the international war fought on a global scale. But it follows the pattern that after the great upheavals, social changes tend to equalize the elements that previously have been unbalanced, with the infrastructure rather than the superstructure being the determinant. The cause-and-effect relationship can only be clarified from the vision of macro history; it cannot be assessed from the biography of Zhang Xun and the collected lectures of Yan Xishan. It also bears little connection to Cao Kun's election by purchase and Duan Qirui's declaration of war at Machang.

But to many readers, I may appear to be demagogic and provocative in asserting that the merger of Chinese history with Western civilization marks a rare occasion that does not happen more often than once in five hundred years, and that China is now mathematically manageable. Historians of the traditional Chinese school refrain from disturbing settled themes, to which they attach a kind of moral relevance. Even with the freedom of speech in the West, when a scholar invades the territories of other specialists to offer revisions, he is not likely to be cordially received. The difficult situation compels me to disclose fully my own background in relation to this article, portions of which have appeared in previous issues of *The Chinese Intellectual:*

- I am a naturalized American citizen. Both this article and my writings on the macro history of China are derived from a larger historical perspective of mankind, not restricted by the mental barrier of nationality. If not, the content cannot qualify to be macro history.
- I graduated from the Central Military Academy at Chengdu during World War II, and thereafter served as a junior officer with the Chinese Nationalist Army for more than ten years. In that capacity I have conducted personal observations of China's countryside and rural towns. It can also be said that I have interviewed numerous persons of major and minor importance.
- During my youthful years I became acquainted with a number of leftists who were or later became members of the Chinese Com-

munist Party, including Tian Han, writer of the national anthem of the People's Republic; Fan Changjiang, who served as president of *People's Daily* and the Xinhua News Agency; Liao Mosha, one of the three writers first under attack during the Cultural Revolution; Tian Hainan (Tian Han's son), who fought in Korea; Lu Yi, who, the last time I heard, was on the Municipal Committee of Shanghai; and Deng Jianzhong, a member of the Nanjing Municipal Committee. My analysis of official and unofficial publications has benefited from my conversations with them. Thus my understanding of the Chinese Communist movement is derived from views within and without.

- While with the Chinese Nationalist Army, I went to India and Burma. After V-J Day I visited Manchuria and Taiwan. Also, I have resided in Japan for three years and in England for one year. Short visits have been made to continental Europe and Korea. Viewing the relationship between each nation's history and its social customs is part of my travel experience.

- My book *Taxation and Governmental Finance in Sixteenth Century Ming China* (Cambridge, 1974) took seven years to prepare. Forty Ming local gazetteers were consulted. The *Veritable Records of the Ming Dynasty,* 133 volumes in the present reprint, was read from cover to cover. My idea that until today China has not been mathematically manageable emerged from that round of research.

- Aside from my academic degrees earned from the University of Michigan, I am also a graduate of the U.S. Army Command and General Staff College at Fort Leavenworth, Kansas. I consider the military science taught there, especially the segments concerning mobilization and army logistics, as most beneficial to a historian's training. It compels us to gauge the possible support of manpower, material, and civic organization behind a mass movement or public enterprise. The sense of calculation enables us to see whether a project is feasible or not as determined by objective factors; beyond that, excessive adulation or unreasonable upbraiding of historical personalities unsupported by those factors adds little to the role of the historian.

- I have conducted historical research at Cambridge, England, and several universities of the Ivy League, including collective research and research on the history of thought. My teaching career, however, is restricted to institutions of less influence. This combination of circumstances gives me unique experience to understand the difficulty in delivering the results of advanced research to the general reader. The task can be eased much if we abandon the current procedural formalities and start anew.

The Chinese practice ceremonial humility. Self-promotion has to be done in a subtle manner. American society encourages frankness. Self-introduction can incorporate an element of advertisement. Yet, behind the scenes people still feel scornful toward those who bring out their own works as commodities for quick profit. When I lay my background on the table, I realize that I may risk negative reaction on both sides. My purpose, however, is to explain to the reader that with an immense subject matter, the author does not suggest covering it with a bird's-eye view. Instead, he wants to assure the reader that he has done his ground work in many areas at a snail's pace. With this understanding, cumbersome footnotes are omitted from this article. I shall try to keep its length within the space allocated by the editor.

"The First Thing Is Poverty, the Second Is Emptiness"

Mao Zedong once commented on China with the statement that the first thing is poverty, the second emptiness. At first I did not think of the connection between the two. As for poverty, it has been my personal experience since childhood. From my family friends to relatives, to my schoolmates whom I met in primary school, middle school, college, and the military academy, extending to wider circles including my colleagues in the army, my superior ranking officers, and my friends who later became members of the Chinese Communist Party, we could all be classified as poor. With a few extremely exceptional cases, none of these people maintained a standard of living comparable to that of a middle-class family of an industrial nation. In novels, biographies, and *belles lettres,* poverty usually is a common theme. During the war with Japan, on the main axis of Chongqing-Kunming-Guiyang-Liuzhou, everywhere it was dilapidated, and material shortages were universal. Even those who were accused of being war profiteers might not have exalted themselves too far above the poverty line. When the civil war came on the heels of V-J Day, I was a student officer at the Staff College at Fort Leavenworth. In March 1947, the Nationalist Army captured Yan'an. At that time television was not so popular; movie theaters usually showed newsreels before the main features. The cave dormitories of Yan'an appeared on one of the news-reels not long after the city changed hands. We encountered questions from our American classmates: they wanted to know what we were fighting for, in a nation so poverty-stricken. We, the handful of Chi-nese students, feeling embarrassed, did not know how to provide an adequate answer. Unexpectedly, some forty years later, rich nations still remain peaceful and secure. It is again the nations suffering from poverty that are troubled by internal strife.

Poverty is linked with so-called emptiness. I can bring up another personal experience for illustration. In 1941, I served as a platoon leader of the 14th Nationalist Division on duty in Yunnan province. We were stationed in Maguan county, immediately behind the bound-ary with Vietnam, which was then occupied by the Japanese. Our troop movement was done entirely on foot. There were times when we marched from the eastern end of the county to the western end without seeing a highway, a bicycle, a telephone, a basketball court, a copy of a newspaper, or a dispensary. In brief, all the cultural elements implying a modern society were not there. The background was that the peasant population of the Ailao Mountains, working from hand to mouth, could not support such a thing called modern commerce. If they even traded, they rarely went beyond the exchange of their corncobs for salt and cloth in the village markets. The Nationalist Government in Chongqing, hard pressed itself, certainly could not offer aid of any kind. The undevelopment of the service sector of the economy, includ-ing transportation, communication, health, and recreation facilities, is a common feature of all developing nations. It runs in parallel with the extremely few restaurants in Beijing. Poverty and emptiness moreover come hand in hand. When one is poor he possesses nothing; when he is empty-handed he remains poor. A nation that is hard pressed by the people's livelihood is not likely to possess a great deal of organiza-tional capacity.

This problem is given attention by American scholars. Albert Feuerwerker, for one, in his account of Shen Xuanhuai points out that China's failure in providing forced savings for industrialization in the nineteenth century allowed the Japanese to move ahead. Actually, on the eve of the French Revolution Adam Smith already visualized the fundamental cause of China's poverty. He said: "China has long been one of the richest, that is, one of the most fertile, best cultivated, most industrious, and most populous countries in the world. It seems, however, to have been long stationary. Marco Polo, who visited it more than five hundred years ago, describes its cultivation, industry, and populousness, almost in the same terms in which they are described by travelers in the present times. It had perhaps, even long before his time, acquired that full complement of riches which the nature of its laws and institutions permits it to acquire. The accounts of all travelers, inconsistent in many other respects, agree in the low wages of labour, and in the difficulty which a labourer finds in bringing up a family in China." (*The Wealth of Nations,* Book I, The Wages of Labour.) (Note that by labor Smith included farm labor. Also, he was in the age when the general consensus held that a large population was always a good thing to have.)

Smith's criticism made a point. From archaeological discoveries and contemporary paintings we can reconstruct the living conditions of the previous dynasties including the life of the working class. During the Han dynasty China went ahead, to reach a standard of living that did not seem to be inferior to that elsewhere in the world. Progress was made during the Tang and Song, but not most perceptibly. Stagnancy could indeed be the word to describe the conditions of the Ming and Qing, which was no comparison with Western Europe in the modern age, where improvement was made so steadily that the features of one century might be visually recognized as different from another in the first glance at the illustrations. The reason for China's inability to keep up its early lead is not that the fertility of the soil was exhausted, nor that the people turned indolent. But, with the suggestion of Smith, we should look into Chinese laws and institutions to locate their limitations.

The most outstanding feature that separates the Chinese polity from those of Western Europe, the United States, and Japan is China's perpetual political centralism. But before I bring in the primary sources to elaborate on the point, let me first introduce an American author.

Karl A. Wittfogel is German by origin. While in Europe, he was a Communist Party member. Migrating to the United States on the eve of World War II, he subsequently severed his partisan connections and turned out to be fervently anti-Communist. He set himself to exposing Communist suspects and leftists among American writers as if on a mission. One book of his, *Oriental Despotism: A Comparative Study of Total Power* (Yale, 1957), launched him to prominence. This is a work thickly entwined with ideology. John K. Fairbank has this to say: "His thinking made theory the ultimate truth. Abstractions were the basic facts." In this book Wittfogel calls the Soviet Union "Russia's Asiatic Restoration" and Mao Zedong "a genuine Asiatic Restoration" (pp. 438–43), although he gives each of them a question mark. The West must remain combat ready, to check against the totalitarian systems in order to safeguard the democracy of Western tradition. The publication of *Oriental Despotism* came not long after the ceasefire in the Korean War. At the time, most learning institutions in the United States were scratching their resources to promote Chinese studies, and the author's ideas and suggestions had a tremendous impact on American Sinologists. Whether agreeing or disagreeing with the author, Frederick W. Mote, Jerome Ch'en, and Ping-ti Ho in their publications have cited Wittfogel and his thesis.

Wittfogel believes that in the Oriental countries, those in Asia in particular, agriculture requires irrigation systems, which in turn call for huge hydraulic projects. The total mobilization of manpower has set up centers of control, which provide the origin of Oriental despotism. To him the term also becomes interchangeable with "hydraulic society" and "Asiatic society." Yet by "Asiatic" Wittfogel brings in Egypt and Peru but excludes Japan. The reason is that while the Japanese also cultivate rice, their civilization did not start on the banks of a major river. With irrigation done on a smaller scale, Japan manages to keep the political power within the territorial region, therefore avoiding Oriental despotism. Consequently, Japanese society is not "hydraulic" but only "hydroagricultural"; it is "fragmented" rather than "coordinated" (p. 197).

It is Marx's original idea that a different "mode of production" creates a different society. But, having coined the term "Asiatic method of production" and casually related it to the artificial irrigation system, Marx does not elaborate further. Wittfogel's thesis could be said to be his personal understanding of Marx's theory; it could also be said to be his own revisions. Its greatest shortcoming is the lumping together of elements of history that cannot be adequately combined. What he calls a "comparative study" is actually hostile and selective picking, and in doing so he mixes an academic work with his own political opinions. For instance, he goes so far as to assert that the art work in all hydraulic societies, including architecture, always consumes a maximum of material but comes out with a minimum of ideas. Only after the Islamic style began to blend with Hellenistic influence did the region show signs of being loosened from its massive building structures. He cites the pyramids of Egypt ("little more than a huge pile of symmetrically arranged stone"), mausoleums in Mesopotamia, and the city gates in China as evidence (p. 44). The terracotta soldiers recently unearthed near Lishan, China, show realism in great variety, down to such details as each individual's facial expressions, hair and beard, and shoes and armor, which are all close to life models. They bear no resemblance to the mystic figures of Egypt, whose human bodies carry the heads of birds, or the idols of India, who come out with three heads and six arms. Nor are they similar to the soldier figures decorating the audience hall of Darius of Persia, which seem to have been cast from a stereotype. In sum, China's political centralism, despotic as it is, from its early stage has been supported by an integrated bureaucracy. It has never lacked its own ideological, technical, and artistic accomplishments. The details will be introduced as we move on. Here it suffices to say that it does not fall into Karl Wittfogel's categorization.

Yet, this is by no means to say that Wittfogel's book has no factual backing. After irrigation, Wittfogel also laterally mentions flood control, the importance of which is confirmed by classical Chinese records. The incident in 651 B.C. in which Duke Huan of Qi convened his league of principalities at Kuiqiu (*Zuochuan,* Xingong 9), is an indication of the close relationship between China's political centralism and flood control. In the Spring and Autumn period (722–481 B.C.), the small principalities, when constructing flood dikes, were only concerned with their own requirements and paid little attention to the consequences to the adjacent states. Duke Huan represented the hegemon who called the convention, during which an oath was taken by the participants and later recorded in various sources as "not to execute improper dikes," "not to hinder the water flow," and "not to clog the ravines." In the *Book of Mencius,* water control is mentioned no less than eleven times. As if to echo these passages, the book also carries a short dialogue: "How can stability under the Heaven be reached?" "It can be reached through unification." In his conversations with Bai Gui, Mencius said: "Yu took the Four Seas as a receptacle [of overflowing water]. Now you instead take adjacent states as receptacles. When water reverses its direction of flow, it would be turned into flood, that is one of the things which humane administrators dread. Sir, you are wrong!" All these serve to indicate the endless controversies associated with the flood control problem when it was handled by the small principalities. After imperial unification, the First Emperor of the Qin erected stone tablets to commemorate his achievements. One of the inscriptions cited the "neutralization of the barriers that obstructed water flows." The Yellow River was redesignated by him as *Deshui,* or the "Virtuous River," and the State of Qin was called "the era that begins with water's virtue" (*Shiji,* chapter 6, Biography of the First Emperor of the Qin). Apparently, he had never forgotten his own leadership in coordinating the effort at water control as essential to his imperial quality. *Oriental Despotism* gives a one-sentence reference to the First Emperor's hydraulic works but leaves all the above evidence untouched.

Wittfogel suggests that although the power of hydraulic despotism is unchecked, it is far from being efficient enough to exercise control over everything. In areas unreached by the state apparatus, such as the villages, a kind of "beggars' democracy" exists (pp. 108–26). Even though here his diction is vicious, the argument we do not challenge. In fact, it comes close to the main point that we ourselves wish to bring up.

One more useful observation made by *Oriental Despotism* is that the hydraulic state continues to impose fiscal demands on the mass of all commoners (p. 70). That is to say, most state revenue comes from direct taxation, collected from the entire population. It stays away from the management of a feudal system, where the feudal lords deliver tribute to the king's coffers. Nor does it follow the procedure of a modern state, which derives large portions of income from indirect taxes, corporate taxes, and the proceeds from progressive taxation. This is undoubtedly true in the case of China, where taxation is normally a matter between the emperor and all the imperial subjects, and it remains one of the key issues that exercise a decisive effect on the making of Chinese history.

When the fiscal foundation of the state is built on such a taxation system, the bureaucrats are compelled to encourage reclamation. Whenever possible, they assist the peasants to obtain tools and draft animals. The agriculture-first policy must have contributed substantially to China's early stages of growth and development. But all things considered, the same arrangement also constitutes one of the major hindrances to the country's further progress in the recent several hundred years. To maintain a large tax base, the government had to foster numerous small self-cultivators, and to prevent the takeover of them by stronger hands. Such a takeover, called *jianbin* (annexation), has since become a target at which the bureaucracy is determined to rush. Technically, this is not a commendable policy. On the one side it is difficult to carry out. Once *jianbin* becomes widespread, the state revenue diminishes. Political instability comes as a result, and it may even lead to the fall of the dynasty. On the other side, even if the policy is carried out to the fullest, the numerous self-cultivators, either from hand to mouth or even worse, do not provide an economic foundation to improve production techniques, increase farm wages, and provide "forced savings" from the agricultural sector to invest in industry and commerce to diversify the national economy.

This financial organization did not start with the Qin. The following paragraph appears in the "Food and Money Monograph" of *Hanshu;* it deals with Li Kui, a statesman of the Wei during the Warring States period (403–221 B.C.):

> The conditions went on until the Warring States period. . . . It was Li Kui who offered a plan to Duke Wen of the Wei, which would derive the maximum benefit from the soil. His calculation comes as follows:
> A territory of one hundred *li* square consists of nine million *mu* of land. Take away a third for mountains, waters, towns, and residential areas, and there will be six million *mu* of land for cultivation. When the field is worked to its maximum benefit, each *mu* will yield three quarts ore. If not, there will be a shortfall by that amount.
> Therefore, for the one hundred *li* square, the production could go up or down by 1,800,000 hundredweight . . . .
> A farmer in a household of five works on one hundred *mu* of land [about 11.4 acres by the measurement of those days]. Each *mu* produces 1.5 hundredweight of grain. Total harvest, 150 hundredweight.
> Food, 1.5 hundredweight per person per month. For the household of five, 90 hundredweight for the year. Remainder, 45 hundredweight. At 30 copper cash per hundredweight, worth 1,350 cash.
> Deducting 300 cash for community sacrificial and festival services, available for household expenses, 1,050 cash.
> Clothing, 300 cash per person, 1,500 cash needed. There is a shortage of 450 cash.
> Incidental expenses for sickness and funeral service, as well as tax surcharges for military campaigns, not included.

We can vary the numbers in these paragraphs to represent the different conditions of the different dynasties. But the basic formula remains unchanged over a two-thousand-year period. Historians of idealist inclination usually follow the lead of earlier writers to speak against *jianbin*. Some routinely condemn the statesmen of the past who have increased taxes or advocated tax increases. What is unsaid is that the argument precludes the possibility for providing the service sector of the economy altogether, as without *jianbin* no private capital is provided to organize it, and without tax increases, no public funds are available to launch the various projects either. The tragedy arising from the kind of unthinking egalitarianism is the wholesale poverty systematically manufactured over a prolonged period in history.

"Without Guangzhong, I Would Have Buttoned My Coat on the Left Side"

Water works for flood prevention furnish only one of the geographical conditions for China's political centralism. Along with it is the effect of the seasonal winds on agriculture. In China's agricultural area, 80 percent of the rainfall comes in three summer months. The summer monsoon comes from the direction of the Philippine Sea. The moisture in the air current depends upon cyclones moving from west to east and northeast as the cooling agent, so that it can be condensed to give rain. When the two kinds of air currents constantly converge over a given area, the place will suffer from floods. Conversely, if they repeatedly miss each other over some area, drought sets in. There are times when China suffers from both drought and floods over its wide geographical span. The meteorological maps prepared by the Central Intelligence Agency indicate that there is often rainfall on spots in amounts doubling the annual normal amount or coming to less than half of it. The situation can be verified by the classical sources. In the "Biographies of Prominent Merchants" in the *Shiji,* there is the statement: "Six years of good harvests will be balanced by six years of drought. In every twelve years there is a general famine." Following it, the "Food and Money Monograph" of *Hanshu* says: "It is the will of heaven that the world has good harvests and famine." Many wars in the Spring and Autumn period can be attributed to natural disasters and crop failures, as cited in *Zuochuan*. We can imagine that if the people had not actually been pressed by hunger, the military campaigns during the War-ring States period would not have grown to the intensity as recorded. As things stood, only larger states that controlled sufficient territory and resources could adequately solve the relief problem. An illustra-tion is provided by King Hui of Liang, who told Mencius: "When the west of the Yellow River is stricken by famine, I relocate some people there to the east and ship food to the west. When disaster befalls the east, I will act likewise." The imperial unification by the First Emperor of the Qin took place in 221 B.C. Prior to that, several particularly bad years occurred during the period when he eliminated the other six states. In 235 B.C. the drought is said to have "hit what is under the heaven." "Great famines" are recorded for 230 and 228 B.C. (*Shiji*, Biography of the First Emperor). When the First Emperor claimed that he had "saved the common people, and provided stability to the four corners," the political platform was not unsupported by the logic of history. Since then, the central government of unified China has al-ways taken famine relief as one of its major responsibilities, calling it "famine administration" as does the *Rituals of the Zhou*.

Rainfall not only causes uncertainty for China's farm production because of its overabundance or scarcity, but also sets up a limit on the country's north and west, beyond which farming is impracticable. China's Great Wall in general follows the "fifteen-inch isohyet line." That is to say that to the north and west of this line, the annual rainfall is usually less than fifteen inches, inadequate for planting crops. The steppeland becomes a staging area of nomads. Either when they them-selves are pressed by bad weather or when China is divided and pro-vides no effective frontier defense, it is the time for an invasion. Confucius, who was active in the sixth century B.C., at one time said: "Guanzhong became the premier of Duke Huan, assisting him to be-come the presiding prince of the territorial lords and to create a general standard for what is under the heaven. If it had not been for Guanzhong, I would have combed my hair down and buttoned my coat on the left side!" What he meant was that without a central authority, the Chinese would have been subject to the rule of the barbarians, and would have had to change their hairdo and costumes and their alle-giance. Lacking hard evidence, to this day we are unsure of the making of the barbarians that he referred to. But we know that toward the end of the fourth century B.C., the nomads began to take up cavalry tactics. Their mobility had been greatly improved.[1] In the third century B.C., soon after the Qin unification, the emperor ordered Meng Tian, commander of three hundred thousand troops, to wage war against the Xiongnu tribes. In a sequence, the south of the Yellow River bend was recovered and the construction of the Great Wall began. The action, however, only furnished a prelude to usher in a protracted campaign which had yet to commit the Han Chinese majority on one side and the Tungusics, Mongols, Turks, Uighurs, Tibetans, and so forth on the other. The clashes in the steppes and in desert land never ceased during any dynasty or any century; and rarely did peace reign over a decade or at most a score of years. The events had a profound historical consequence. For one thing, merely to provide an adequate defense political centralism cannot be abandoned. In the meantime, the two-thousand-mile frontier makes it impractical to maintain a smaller force of top quality. For China, from mobilization to military operations, from army personnel to logistics, numbers always count more. When national defense sets the pace, civil administration follows suit. Homogeneity and uniformity have to be given the first consideration on every turn.

Writing in the late twentieth century, it would be out of place to take a position on Han chauvinism. When we read the accounts of the Xiongnu wars waged by Wudi of the Han, we can say that his policy was nothing short of an effort at genocide. Even the defense measures taken by the Ming people, setting the grasslands in the buffer zone afire, causes us to think of the reaction of the nomads, whose livelihood was in jeopardy. But to praise or condemn is not the purpose of writing macro history. Under consideration here is the long-term historical consequence. It points out that under the peculiar geographical conditions, the majority is compelled to abandon its initiative to readjust to the minority groups, owing to the fact that North China can be occupied but the desert and grasslands cannot. The short histories of the Uighurs, Tibetans, and Turks in the *Jiu Tangshu* and *Xin Tangshu* contain many episodes little known to the general reader, such as on the minority groups who entered and looted Changan (now Xian) at will and took thousands of Chinese as prisoners to their territories, and the sorrows of the Tang princesses who were married to the chieftains as part of the pacifying measures. Even under Empress Wu, when Tang prestige was still at its height, Chinese troops in today's Hebei failed to stop Khitan incursions. Only after the invaders withdrew did they seize the innocent people for questioning and execute some. The woman ruler was such a heroic figure that, unafraid of truth and un-compromisable by flattery, she managed to cut through the bureau-cratic red tape to bring the case to justice (*Jiu Tangshu,* chapter 89; *Xin Tangshu,* chapter 115, Biography of Di Renjie). The story bears wit-ness that political centralism in China wraps up many problems never adequately solved. The bureaucrats, lacking technical means to deal with them, tend to rationalize their handling by dehumanizing a num-ber of pertinent factors. In this way truth always comes from the top hierarchy, binding on the lower echelon. So long as the "responsibil-ity" for a problem is located, the logic of bureaucratic management is protected and the case can be closed. The minority groups may be innocent as they themselves are the victims of geography; neverthe-less, as the tools of history they impose a difficult problem for China because of their numbers, and at no time have adequate technical means been found to deal with it.

North China in the middle centuries was a melting pot for numerous ethnic groups. That the Han Chinese managed to assimilate them all is a gross overstatement. The details are far from being clear; a great deal of research is still required. But a few items may be mentioned here: While the "Food and Money Monograph" of the *Liaoshi* indicates that under the Liao, sheep and horses were not permitted to be shipped to the Song, we see in the painting by Zhang Zeduan, *Qingming shanghetu* ("River Bank on a Festival Day"), that the carts are teamed with water buffalo, depicting how it was in twelfth-century Kaifeng. The *Liaoshi* also mentions that one of the major reasons the Liao lost to the Jin was that its combat horses could not be replaced. This im-presses upon us more the influence of geographical factors on history. For civil administration, the Liao separated the Han Chinese from the non-Chinese. Yet the Han Chinese were conscripted as "country sol-diers" and "transferred troopers" and formed separate contingents within the Khitan battle formations, each with a quota assigned (*Liaoshi,* Military Monograph). Under the Jin, the Jürcheds intermin-gled with the Han Chinese. Of the mixed population, about forty to fifty households formed a *mouke;* generally eight *mouke* were grouped into a *mengan.* The *mouke* and *mengan* households had to be Jürcheds. They supervised the conscription and taxation of households under their control, similar to *li* and *jia* chiefs of the Chinese system (*Jinshi,* Food and Money Monograph). Thus the Mongols did not act without historical basis in calling the natives already under the domination of the pastoral peoples the Han, while those who were not were classified as *nanren* or southerners (appearing in Marco Polo's journal as *manzi*). After the Ming dynasty was founded, Zhu Yuanzhang composed a pamphlet called *Dagao* (Grand Premonitions), in which there is a section entitled "Hu Yuan zhizhu" (The Barbarian Yuan Weighing Down Their Masters). It incites the nationalist sentiments of the Han Chinese to justify his reign of terror. All told, the political centralism in Chinese history is inseparable from the frontier defense of the north and west.

Zhu Yuanzhang decreed that the ethnic minorities must marry outside of their own racial stocks (*Da Ming huidian*). China, moreover, was twice under minority domination, during the Yuan and Qing. Therefore, today a dominant majority of ethnic Chinese, including this writer and a great many readers of this article, must be of mixed strains, similar to the situation in which most English people are of mixed strains of the early settlers (Celts), Italians (Romans), Norwegians and Danish (Angles), Germans (Saxons), and French (Normans), and most Japanese are of mixed ancestries of Chinese (Qin), Koreans, Hokkaido Ainus, prehistorical stocks of horse-riding peoples from the continent, and maybe oceanic strains from the far south. Under these circumstances, it would be of doubtful value to distinguish who is "pure Han Chinese," if possible at all. Yet, the historian must point out that for China, the mixing of the majority with the minorities did not occur as a short-term military migration. It comes out as the result of the heavy burden of history, of which both the intensity and duration are exceptional. For this reason, the traditional Chinese government always proclaims the platform of being "gently with people coming from afar and welcome to technicians of every sort," a Confucian doctrine, yet at the same time imposing over the population the Legalist principle of military organization, grouping households into fives and tens, latently supporting political centralism. If those conditions help to create an "Oriental despotism" in China, then more than being "hydraulic" by itself, Chinese society has been constantly under the tremendous pressure of a steppeland culture for a long time.

The above sketch, summing up the opinions on the left and right, findings in classical literature and ideological discoveries, events of the B.C. period and those close to recent times, lessons in textbooks along with my personal experience, comes to the conclusion that traditional political centralism in China is both man-made and dictated by nature. It leaves a long-term influence on history in that, before the development of technical means, the Chinese government was already compelled to handle enormous problems that involved large numbers and as such had no alternative but to take them in whole. Consequently, it has been obligated to produce ideological explanations to rationalize its handling as far as possible; on the other hand, it resorts to administrative and technical shortcuts to avoid the confrontation with reality. This article, being a summary, cannot do more than cite a handful of exemplary cases here and there for illustration. But the reader may realize that once the contours are mapped, it should be easier to fill in with notes and details. The following sections, while attempting to develop the central theme more fully, will also bring in more deeds and events that serve to elucidate the argument.

A Pyramid Built Upside Down

The *Zhou Li,* or the *Rituals of the Zhou,* is an interesting and curious book. When Liu Xin brought it out near the Christian era, it was immediately branded a forgery. Since then, it has been controversial over the millennia.[2] Its alleged author is the Duke of Zhou. Had that been the case, the work should date back into the B.C. era more than a thousand years, or have preceded the first appearance of bronze coins in China by several centuries. Yet the *Rituals of the Zhou* not only mentions these coins, but also describes the organization of a royal mint that produces them. It even deals with consumer protection, discussing at length why the prices of the merchandise in the market must stay fair, and how the quality can be examined to meet an official standard. Along with those there are sections that genuinely refer to the systems of the Zhou dynasty, which seem actually to have existed.

My personal observation of the work is very simple: It can be best described as the blueprint for constructing a pyramid upside down. Starting from a mathematical formula, it has the ideal perfection of Natural Law. Regardless, it is superimposed on a nation whose boundary is zigzag and whose population, many millions of them, has as much variety as any other nation on earth. Of course, the book does not openly acknowledge that whenever its provision becomes infeasible, compromises have to be accepted. Thus the meticulous elaboration on the top could end with numerous untied odds and ends on the bottom. In other words, the adherence to the fidelity of the design diminishes as the program is carried downward, or the pressure and demands are weakened when the distance to the source of power is lengthened. For the present-day reader, there is no urgent need to verify the authorship of this work. The demonstrative function of the *Rituals of the Zhou* serves its best historical purpose. A short verse repeatedly appears in this work, of which Biot's French translation reads: "Seul, le souverain constitute les royaumes; il détermine les quatre côtés et fixe les positions principals. Il trave le plan de la capitale et des campagnes. Il crée les ministères et sépara leurs fonctions, de manière à former le centre administratif du peuple." These few sentences encompass the spirit of the basic design of the Chinese polity for more than two thousand years. Max Weber has much to say about the *Rituals of the Zhou:* "A very schematic state organization under the rational leadership of officials."[3] It is an incisive appraisal.

Broadly speaking, schematic design is inseparable from the traditional Chinese state apparatus. When it had barely gone through the Bronze Age, when letters and official documents were written on wood and bamboo strips, it had already been compelled to take up political centralism over a wide region, to solve problems of a dimension already anticipating the present. It had no alternative but to compensate, through structuring a huge literary bureaucracy, realism with idealism and vice versa. This confusing situation is further compounded by the structure of the Chinese writing system, which from the very beginning was determined by the style of the oracle bones. It delivers only the essential elements of the message, leaving many parts of speech out and waiting for the reader to fill them in. As a result, the *Rituals of the Zhou* and several other classical works, such as *Zuochuan, Yugong,* and the Book of *Mencius,* when bringing up institutions of ancient times, always carry a tone of mystery.

The feudal system of the Zhou, the *Rituals of the Zhou* describes, started from a king's domain one thousand *li* from the capital and extended four directions with strips of territory that also connected together to form concentrated squares. They all had an additional width of five hundred *li*. Each belt of the square frame was called a *fu*. These nine *fu*, depending on their distance from the capital, determined the functions and duties of the feudal lords whose territories were found within them. In general, the services they provided the king diminished as they got further away from the capital. In reality, the Zhou capital was not the geographical center of China at the time. Nor could the latter's domain embrace a reach of five thousand *li* in each direction.

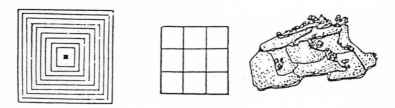

Technically, it was beyond the capabilities of the contemporaries to produce such a gridded map, not to mention clarifying the straight boundaries on the terrain. Yet, the general concept that there was a king's domain and the functions of his vassals were differentiated into nine *fu* is unmistakably clear from this short description.

A land allocation plan of the Zhou, according to the several sources cited above, was incorporated into the so-called well-field system. Eight households formed a "well," each of them allocated a square plot of one hundred *mu*. An additional plot in the center, of the same acreage, was designated as the common for the surrounding eight households, and its harvest paid the taxes for them.

Whether such a neat yet fanciful system was actually put into effect or not has been debated by Chinese and foreign scholars. I have compared the description with the general plan of *juntian* (equalization of land allotment) under the Sui and Tang, the fiscal management of the Song, and the taxation system of the Ming and Qing. My conclusion is that the aforementioned allocation is not entirely infeasible. If there was level land to be divided, the Chinese bureaucrats would not hesitate to follow the plan literally. But usually, even in an ideal situation the actual allocation probably never exceeded the approximated extent as shown in the picture above, that is, to project the geometrical symmetry and balance to the terrain as far as the contours and slopes would permit. So far as the design and purpose were not deliberately violated, the variations would not be considered irreconcilable obstacles. In a less optimum situation, a "well" could also consist of six or seven households. Still, isolated households not included in the well formations would be registered as the "rat's tail"; for them special arrangements would allow them to pay taxes. This is close to what the Japanese call *ryo-to-ja-bi* (a dragon's head teamed with a snake's tail), or my metaphor of a pyramid built upside down. The solidity and heaviness on top are not matched by the actual conditions on the bottom.

The type of "system" has a decisive effect on the development of Chinese history. The infrastructure of Chinese society is artificially created by the superstructure. It exists to serve an administrative or managerial purpose. Protection of the logic behind this organization becomes an obsession to the bureaucrats, for which not only the interests at the lower level can be obliterated, but also, if necessary, the lives of those bureaucrats and their families can be laid down as sacrifices, as Etienne Balazs once said. This type of design, setting back democratic potential and obstructing the growth and development of regional and local institutions, also presses the technical impracticalities downward to the bottom. It is one of the major reasons why in the modern era China is found to be not mathematically manageable.

Three Empires

My vision of macro history develops from positivism. Although exposing the unsatisfactory features in history, the study does not intend to negate China's historical accomplishments. To put it personally, since political centralism has been necessary for the survival of many millions, the author of this article has to urge the reader to follow in the steps of Confucius, who, loathing Guanzhong as an individual, cites his historical accomplishment to the extent that "to this day people benefit from his bestowal." That is, had it not been for political centralism, our ancestors might not have survived. There is no need to speculate on what would have happened to their descendants.

The enormous structures of the Chinese polity and Chinese society stand for some form of maturity ahead of their times. Before their weaknesses were exposed, they had been greatly admired. For a great length of time, China exceeded Europe in science, technology, literature, philosophy, and the fine arts. Not only did the fragmentation of Europe in the Middle Ages make it no match for China, but also, until Adam Smith commented on China's stagnancy, continental Europe had been in the age of Enlightened Despotism, and even then, Chinese institutions were still admired by Smith's contemporaries, such as Franklin and Voltaire. All these things have been pointed out by many other writers. Their themes do not contradict this article.

Nevertheless, the main purpose of this article is to investigate the reasons why, until very recently, China has remained mathematically unmanageable. For that we have to count the negative influences. In the following analysis, China's imperial period is divided into three segments. Since these three "empires" have all vanished, our review has to place more emphasis on the decline and fall. Once more I have to stress that the negative influences underlined in this essay should be divorced from the "praise and condemnation" method of traditional Chinese historians. They are provided as instruments for a broad analysis.

The First Empire: Qin and Han

Imperial unification under the First Emperor took place in 221 B.C. But the Qin collapsed during the short reign of the Second Emperor. It was replaced by the Han, which, with the interruption of Wang Mang's usurpation, held the reigns of the Liu family for about four hundred years, somewhat evenly divided between the B.C. and A.D. eras. In history, the Qin and Han can be taken as a larger unit. It is not so easy to summarize this entire segment of history in some four thousand Chinese characters.

I propose to start with the fiscal administration of the empire, and to avoid being confused by the figures in the records. The qualities of statistics of various kinds in Chinese history are determined by the qualities of the regimes that have supplied them. For instance, under the Former Han, the land tax took one-fifteenth of the yield, less than 7 percent. The poll tax set the standard of 120 copper cash per capita annually; the exact rates differed for age groups, between males and females, and between commoners and slaves. It is most questionable that such a complicated system could have been carried out to the full over a population estimated to be close to sixty million. The reader is reminded that only a score of years ago the vital statistics of the People's Republic still contained inaccuracies and falsifications on an enormous scale. How could the above tax formula be applied to a nation with such a huge population, before paper was even invented (the invention, traditionally credited to Cai Lun, came about in the first century A.D.) and when official documents were still written on wood and bamboo? Yet, if we take an extremely skeptical view and say that the so-called tax laws are merely fabrications existing in the writers' imagination, how could the formidable empire have been maintained? And on what basis can we discuss its history? When hard evidence fails us, logic has to be allowed to prevail. The large frame of macro history permits us to assume that the tax law was also part of the schematic design, to be enforced as far as the circumstances would allow but to remain inoperative beyond that feasible limit.

A "scientific" inquiry into the statistics of the Qin and Han is impossible due to the remoteness of the data and their incompleteness. But when the related factors are examined, the following trends become evident: (1) The efficiency of the fiscal system depends on the pressure exerted by the emperor. Its prime mover is political power, not economic factors. (2) It reaches a high level of performance in the midst of successful military operations. Nevertheless, too much pressure could also cause rebellion and mutiny. (3) The easing of the pressure, on the other hand, may encourage local autonomy; the decentralizing tendency could lead to disintegration. (4) The entire system depends on a huge body of small self-cultivators to form a tax base. With such an infrastructure, there is no possibility to break away from the pattern to reach a significant qualitative improvement.

After emerging during the Qin and Han, the above features of traditional fiscal management reappeared in later periods. There were cases when the national wealth increased, but the dynasty was unable to keep pace. The collapse of the political system ushered in disorder, which ruined the economic accomplishments, and the rebuilding had to start from scratch. Traditional historians, without the benefit of our historical perspective, often seize the less vital factors as the causes of the downfall, and indiscriminately charge *fuhua* (corruption). This type of historiography can no longer serve as a model.

The Qin, after the prolonged warfare and total mobilization of the seven states, accomplished imperial unification through military conquest. The First Emperor, moreover, standardized China's writing system and the axles of Chinese carts and carriages. He himself claimed that his administration was noted for "devotion to duty by everyone low and high, and a general aversion to sloth and negligence." Lu Sheng and Hou Sheng, who he had commissioned to search for medicine that could prolong life, commented on him as "having used a scale to weigh the documents and set up levels to be reached for each night and each day, and resisted to rest until the level was reached." In the background the official documents were written on wooden and bamboo strips. The energetic emperor therefore stretched his working hours to meet the quantity that he set for himself to read and to act upon, counted by so many pounds (*Shiji,* Biography of the First Emperor). We can surmise that his financial system worked to its possible maximum efficiency. On the terracotta soldiers buried with him, even the bronze buckles on the leather belts and the iron studs of the soles of the boots simulated the real objects down to the smallest detail. In his lifetime he organized construction projects of all kinds and ordered the relocation of personnel in large numbers. His own claim, that he had "timed the progress of [his many kinds of] works, to make things productive and multiplying," boastful as it might sound, must have had a factual basis.

Learning from the lesson of the Qin's quick downfall, the Han allowed itself a mixed constitution, which made the territories of the appointed prefects adjacent to the domains of the princes and marquises and tightened the proclaimed Confucian humanism with the Legalist stringency. It survived the coup of the family of the first empress and experienced the gentle rule of the third and fourth emperors. Only under the reign of Wudi, or that of Liu Che, was the policy of centralism reaffirmed; by then the dynasty had been in place for more than sixty years. Wudi reigned for fifty-four years (141–87 B.C.), during which time he waged Xiongnu wars eight times and sent expeditions to today's Korea, Koko Nor, and Vietnam. Historian Sima Qian claimed that his military supplies effected "in general, more than ten *zhong* to deliver one hundredweight" (*Shiji,* Essay on Equity and Standards). Each *zhong* being 6.4 hundredweight, the statement asserted that less than 2 percent of material collected on the home front was eventually to be delivered to the field. The literary style offers no assurance of precision. But there is little doubt that the mobilization was both intensive and extensive, a fact that was further substantiated by the number of grand councillors and imperial secretaries who were either imprisoned by the emperor or committed suicide.

The military exploits of Emperor Liu Che were tied to his policy of affirming centralism. Under the Han, ever since the rebellion of 154 B.C., which involved seven principalities, the remaining fiefdoms were either converted to prefectures under civil administration or reduced in size. The dynastic founder had established 143 marquisates. Of these, 68 had been escheated before Liu Che's accession; there were only 75 when he inherited the throne. Before his reign was over, another 70 were abolished, with only 5 remaining. All except one were escheated by Liu Che (*Shiji,* chapters 18 and 19). The most frequently cited causes for the forfeiture had to do with the material supplies delivered to the emperor, either less than the demand quota or inadequate on other counts. The tightening of financial control supported the military operation and vice versa.

We cannot accept the notion that Liu Che ever allowed "mercantile participation" in his government. When Dongguo Xianyang, Kong Jin, and Sang Hongyang served as his financial advisers, they did not utilize mercantile organization and commercial capital to widen systematically the government function, nor did they employ governmental influence to work for commercial expansion that might eventually lead to an enlarged source of revenue. The public monopoly on salt and iron was assaulted by the literati, as recorded in the *Discourse on Salt and Iron*. Other measures taken during the period, such as leather currency (forced loan), counting the *min* (capital tax), and price leveling through storage and long-distance hauling (government engagement in business) were all short-term methods of raising funds; no effort was made to accumulate capital. For this reason, it could not escape the criticism of the contemporaries, who considered that the officials should never compete with the populace for profit.

But when the indirect governance of the feudal system was banished, a commercial organization was not created. This left the many millions of small self-cultivators directly under the emperor, without any economic interest in the middle to function as a link. The ruler or regent or his executive had to perform his part by invoking the mandate of heaven and justifying his position in the name of morals. The infrastructure, made up of the peasant masses, had no way to speak for themselves except, when pressed by cold and hunger, to resort to open rebellion. The tens of thousands of bureaucrats maintained an organizational logic unsupported by economy and unguarded by legal precedents. The drawback of substituting morality for law was that there was no precise yardstick to go by. An element of subjectivity prevailed, as government authority was exercised, by its own claim, to release the power of ideal perfection at punishing the most wicked evils. A consequence of translating the technical problems into moral problems was that the losers of major political debates had to be given the death penalty, which only intensified the political instability.

The efficiency of the Former Han government had been brought to the high point by Wudi. When Huo Guang became regent, the operation could not be continued. The entire situation became untenable in the days of Wang Mang. From Wang's policies and pronouncements it is difficult to say that his intention to give the Han government a new lease on life to benefit the populace was not genuine. After his take-over, he exposed the evil of the bureaucratic practice of the time as "Those who have received official appointments in the court go to the private residences of their patrons to express their gratitude. The government, after granting the ranks and honors, sees its own function unattended." These remarks confirm the fact that when the lives, limbs, and property rights were insecure, government employees all took the "back-door approach" to ingratiate themselves with those who wielded power. When they put duties and services behind their self-interest, the peasant rebels, such as the Red Eyebrows and Green Forests, ran rampant. Yet the situation could not be cured with additional secret service. Wang Mang, not resolute enough to cut himself off from the existing bureaucratic circles, fancied a revolutionary reconstruction on the scale of the *Rituals of the Zhou.* He had not fully seen through his own historical background.

The founder of the Later Han, Guangwu Di or Liu Xiu, had been a student at the Imperial University. Once a merchant, he earned his living as a grain dealer and acted as the attorney of wealthy landowners to collect overdue rents (*Hou Hanshu,* Biography of Guangwu). By nature he was calculating. Claiming that he was to govern the nation with "softness," he set the land tax at one-thirtieth of the crop yield and discontinued all the government monopolies of the Former Han. Some historians believe that laissez faire was indeed his policy. Yet his annals show that in 40 A.D. he executed more than ten prefects, including one in the metropolitan district, for having submitted inaccurate land data. It serves to testify that soft as he assumed himself to be, Liu Xiu was far from incapable of harshness. His son Ming Di, or Liu Zhuang, prided himself as a scholar. But his biography in the *Hou Hanshu* describes him as "skillful at the trial of criminal cases and meticulous in applying the penal code. He presided over the cases day and night, determined to uncover the wrongs and hidden angles." The biography concludes with a skeptical question: "Is it that he has not excelled in developing his magnanimity?" The father and son took charge of the restoration of an empire over half a century. Having rebuilt a political system through military conquest, they attended to financial matters with practical diligence. They could not be lightly treated as lenient or easy-going. The unnoticed traces in the records lead us to believe that they, like the Yongle Emperor (Zhu Di), belong to the class of monarchs who know how to promote their publicity by employing a literati retinue.

During the Later Han, in 57 A.D., the population under state control was reported to be twenty-one million. In 105 A.D. it suddenly jumped to fifty-three million. Liu Zhuang's biography claims that during his reign, "all the functionaries fulfilled their assignments, the populace was content with its pursuits, the near and afar were obedient and disciplined, so that the population increased rapidly." But it is extremely doubtful that in a span of forty-eight years within the first century, the population could actually increase by two and a half times. If those figures as fiscal data had any validity at all, they suggest that a great deal of pressure had been applied downward over some length of time to achieve results.

The Later Han's promotion of classical studies exceeded that of the Former Han. In the earlier period, only a handful of learned men of distinction, such as Jia Yi, Zhao Cuo, and Dong Zhongshu, became imperial advisers on their merit. During the later period it became a custom that scholarly excellence was inevitably linked to official appointment. The Imperial University, according to official records, had 240 buildings comprising no less than 1,850 rooms. During the reign of Huan Di (Liu Zhi, r. 147–167 A.D.), persons claiming university student status counted thirty thousand. Still, the *Hou Hanshu* named many private tutors who gathered around themselves several hundred disciples each, and in several cases over a thousand. A bad consequence came from this pattern. Without any other outlet, book learning served only the purpose of entering the government, which to some was also a leverage for acquiring wealth. Eminent households were formed upon several generations of successes. The inability of the government to mete out justice objectively compounded the problem. The passing of moral judgment by the literati-bureaucrats confused justice with their own hidden motives. Even when they were sincere, they regarded their own standard as inviolable as Natural Law, for which they are criticized as being "narrow" by Qian Mu, a modern scholar who retains a classical way of thinking (*Guoshi dagang,* chapter 10).

The partisan crisis of the Later Han rose under such a background. The immediate cause was supplied by *jianbin.* Many wealthy households in the countryside, making connections with men of power in the capital, employed large numbers of auxiliaries. They loaned money to the small self-cultivators and systematically took over their home-steads. Acting on the popular ideology, the local officials were obli-gated to intervene. Often they found that behind the powerful households were influential figures of the imperial court, sometimes eunuchs. The top eunuchs even maintained close ties with the imperial family. (Eunuchs had foster sons. After 135 A.D. their noble titles and civil service ranks were inheritable.) For instance, Chief Chamberlain Zhang Rong's daughter-in-law was a sister of Empress Dowager Dong. The classical sources cite that "visitors wishing to call on him arrived with carriages that counted by the scores and over a hundred" (*Hou Hanshu,* Collected Biographies of the Du and Ho Families, Col-lected Biographies of Partisan Leaders, and Collected Biographies of the Eunuchs). The cases in dispute reflected that in the age of eco-nomic expansion, the court system remained inadequate in legitimating the accumulation of wealth at the middle level. Nor had the social system any provision for taking care of the small self-cultivators if they were displaced. Championed by the majority of university stu-dents, officials of righteous reputation took the law into their own hands to fulfill the role of popular heroes. Colonel of Censure Li Ying earned his intrepid name by arresting Zhang Rong's brother and put-ting him to death. Ling Zhi, a prefect's assistant, went even further. He ordered the execution of more than a hundred persons whom he con-sidered to be evil, including a principal offender who had received the pardon from the emperor. Almost two millennia later, it would be most difficult for us to judge who was right and who was wrong. What is clear is that the social progress had gone ahead of the statute. As the capital accumulated from agricultural production found no appropriate way to be reinvested, the central government was in a dilemma itself, not to say providing a guideline for the operations in the regions and districts. Public opinion, while condemning back-door approaches, constantly confused legitimacy with morality. When the bureaucrats were unable to handle the controversy, the source of power was in-volved. Plots and conspiracies thus implicated the palace eunuchs and the families of the empresses.

One more contributing factor had to do with the "election" system of the Han. The entire procedure, having gone through some lengthy fluctuations, was rather complicated. But it can be said to have devel-oped along the lines that periodically each district with a population of 200,000 should recommend a "filial pious and incorruptible" person who could assume the leadership role. Bureaucrats of higher ranks were also required to nominate candidates to offices and remain responsible for their conduct. Sons and younger brothers of important courtiers were commissioned as "young gentlemen" on palace duty to gain experience for future appointment. Networks of connections were thus built up to tie the patrons and protégés together, which could be carried on for generations.

The fall of the Later Han is sometimes traced by historians to the peasant rebellion of the Yellow Turbans, or the lawlessness of the eunuchs, or the call of frontier troops under Dong Zhuo to the capital. In reality, the large-scale civil war commenced only after the Yellow Turbans had been suppressed, the eunuchs had been chastized, and Dong Zhuo had paid with his life for his undisciplined role. What happened was that during the period of a moribund imperial court, the landholding interests in the regions had organized themselves into armed camps under civil leaders of celebrity. Now they could not find an adequate logic to support a mutually acceptable central government. The Battle of Guandu in 200 A.D. ushered in the most prolonged period of disunity, which was to last for more than three and a half centuries. The side representing the rising landholding interests was Yuan Shao. His seventh-generation ancestor Yuan Liang had started the family fortune as a specialist on the *Book of Changes* and one time served as literati attendant to the crown prince. He handed his specialty to his grandson Yuan An, who, having been nominated as a "filial pious" person, rose to become prefect and minister and eventually was elevated to grand councillor. Since then not a generation of Yuans had gone by without occupying key positions in the Han court. Yuan Shao was a fourth-generation descendant of Yuan An (*Hou Hanshu*, Collected Biographies of the Yuan, Zhang, Han, and Zhou). He had served as an officer of the capital garrison and colonel of censure. The Yuans, having provided three grand councillors in four generations, claimed disciples and former office subordinates over the entire nation. When Yuan Shao set up his standard, his one hundred thousand soldiers were contributed by his associates. The supplies came from North China on ten thousand carts (Wang Zhongluo, *Wei-Jin-Nanbeichao-Sui-Chu-Tang shi,* 1962, p. 24). To check him was Cao Cao, who at this point was still trying to strengthen the central government. His foster grandfather was Cao Teng, a eunuch. As a palace attendant he became the crown prince's reader-in-waiting. In the later stage of his career he received the title of

Marquis of Feiting. Cao Cao's natural father Cao Song was Cao Teng's foster son. He himself was nominated as "filial pious and incorruptible" (*Hou Hanshu,* Collected Biographies of the Eunuchs; *Sanguozhi,* Weishu, Biography of Wudi). His army was mainly made up of the surrendered Yellow Turbans; the food came from military farming. In other words, for the two sides, both manpower and supplies were derived from elsewhere than the present imperial system, to underline the fact that the Han dynasty collapsed under the weight of the abundance it had itself fostered.

For literati-lords turned warlords, the sequence of events established a world record that has yet to be broken. It also reveals that the private interests of the individual must be given adequate outlets for fulfillment. If constantly suppressed as if water were unchecked by earth against its natural direction of flow, a breakaway could do more serious damage. Classical education and a status called "filial pious and incorruptible" could all be turned into instruments of self-gain and equipment to enter the battlefield. Visualizing the pitfalls, centuries later the Sui abandoned the nomination and recommendation system of the Han but institutionalized the open examination system for recruiting its functionaries.

The Second Empire: Sui, Tang, and Song

In 220 A.D., the last Han emperor performed the ritualistic surrender of his throne to the Wei, and with this episode China entered the Wei-Jin and the North and South Court period, the prolonged disunity lasting more than three and a half centuries. During the long period, even though the Jin reunited the country in 280 A.D., ten years later the campaign to challenge Empress Jia's authority opened the door of the "Riot of the Eight Princes." Civil war went on. By 317, both Changan and Loyang had fallen to the invading Xiongnu. The Eastern Jin established an exile government south of the Yangtze. Reunification did not come until 589, when the Sui finally annexed the Chen, the last succession state in the south.

Unprecedented and never to be repeated, this long period of disunity presents some problems for the historian. The chronicles of the short-lived dynasties routinely give courage to the so-called imperial courts, which most of the time were cornered and without substance. The shattered superstructure provides few clues for us to assess the situation as a whole. In the eyes of traditional historians, Empress Jia, the source of all troubles, was not only cruel and wicked but also ugly in appearance. Her husband, Sima Zhong, when told that people had no rice to eat, was supposed to have replied, why not let them eat minced meat, which came too close to Marie Antoinette's cake to be credible. In reality, the disunity was no longer a problem with the superstructure. The works of such modern scholars as Lien-sheng Yang, Tang Zhangzu, and Wang Zhongluo, however, direct our attention to the infrastructure. The views developed from the bottom and from the sides often prove to be more useful.

In short, toward the end of the Later Han, the residents of North China under the leadership of the powerful clans constructed defense works around the villages. Those fortified units had little offensive strength. But scattered and self-sufficient, they were most difficult to raze. Even the invading nomads, classified by Chinese historians as made of five different ethnic groups, found them impregnable. Around 350 A.D., north of Taiyuan in today's Shanxi, more than three hundred such fortified villages clustered together one hundred thousand households, Chinese and non-Chinese. About 400 A.D., Shaanxi Province had three thousand of those villages surrounded by forts of pounded earth. They formed alliances and elected regional leaders (Tang Zhangzu, *Wei-Jin-Nanbei-zhao shi luncong,* 1962, pp. 178–81, based on *Jinshi,* chapters 110, 114, and 115). Even the migrant population who followed the Jin exile government to the south maintained the same autonomous stance. For instance, Xie Lingyun, the famous *fu* composer who was executed in 433 on the charge of sedition, was described as having "inherited enormous fortunes from his father and grandfather, becoming prosperous and enterprising. His bondservants were numerous. His disciples and retainers counted by the hundreds. He executed engineering projects of tunneling mountains and dredging lakes. He worked on them without end" (*Songshu,* Biography of Xie Lingyun). The narrative provides a glimpse of the semi-autonomous clans in the south.

With these conditions in view, the reunification had to start from forces completely outside the present order of things. It required the sinification of the nomads so that their military power, which centered around the cavalry, could be used for the task. A new bureaucracy had to be structured, unhampered by either the tribal nobility or the powerful Chinese clans, so that, once again, the members could pick up classical literature to build up a uniform ideology around traditional political philosophy. Yet, more important, an infrastructure had to be set up, again with independent self-cultivators forming the backbone. Those difficult conditions necessitated the prolonged preparation. In the end, the work was pioneered by the sinicized state of the Northern Wei and completed by the Sui dynasty, whose ruling house of Yang could be considered marginally Chinese.

The founders of the Northern Wei, the Tabas, were a Xianbei people. Being nomads and with a population seemingly less than one million, they occupied the northern portion of today's Shanxi Province in the early fourth century when Jin power was on the wane. Repeatedly and systematically, they netted other nomadic groups in their entirety and forcibly converted them into agricultural laborers. The leadership families of the captured, including women and children, were put to death. The rest of the tribesmen were assigned to plots of land and distributed farm tools. In the fifth century the Taba records indicated that the ethnic lines separating the agricultural population had blurred. If they had one time been state serfs, by then they all appeared to be small self-cultivators. As Taba power continued to be extended, they also resettled large numbers of Koreans and Murongs (also of Xianbei stock) in today's Hebei Province. Their first priority was to build up a homogeneous agricultural base. Until their position was sufficiently consolidated, they refrained from venturing into central China. (See Tang Zhangzu's introduction; his primary source is the *Weishi*.)

The resettlement of the Northern Wei capital in Loyang in 494 A.D. is an event of significance in Chinese history. A half century earlier, the Northern Wei emperor, Taba Tao, had delivered a severe blow to the powerful Chinese clans within his reach, in particular the Cuis, Lus, Lius, and Guos (Wang Zhongluo, p. 402). The sinification of the Tabas nevertheless continued. The imperial family had so customarily taken Chinese consorts that by the fifth century the Xianbei blood must have been running thin within the line of succession. Taba Hong's decree to adopt Chinese surnames, language, and costumes at this point only confirmed a trend already in progress. Even more important than the relocation of the capital, in 485 the Taba state had proclaimed the "land equalization system," by which all agricultural land was in principle nationalized. The entire population was allocated per capita acreage. In 486 the "three chiefs system" came into being. Every five households formed a neighborhood; every five neighborhoods formed a village community; and every five village communities formed a precinct. All the chiefs of those units were appointed by the officials. These provisions could not have been carried out down to the smallest detail, but they considerably tightened up the slack conditions of the past, described as follows: "The registration was remiss; evasions were many," "purveyors and tax farmers crowded the country" (*Weishu,* Food and Money Monograph), and "thirty or fifty households were registered as one household" (*Weishu,* Biography of Li Chong). All told, after the fall of the Han, the Northern Wei finally succeeded in returning to the traditional schematic design to put the mass of farm laborers directly under state control. The Tabas themselves took sinification voluntarily; they also furnished China with a new infrastructure. Good or bad, this provided a matrix from which the conscription and taxation systems of the Sui and Tang could emerge.

With the relocation of the capital, the Northern Wei fitted Loyang into a state of gildedness, as the *Loyang jialanji* testified. This dissatisfied the Xianbei nobility, who still look nostalgically to their own cultural tradition. Nor would the cavalry base in the North feel content to be left in oblivion without a struggle. Internal strife flared up, playing into the hands of the generals of mixed blood. The coups and conspiracies split the Xianbei state into two parts. The eastern portion gave birth to Northern Qi; the western portion to Northern Zhou. It would take some doing to cover the details. But from the viewpoint of macro history, it can be said that for China's Second Empire, the prototype of a social organization was already in place. Its superstructure, however, had to go through some struggle to suit the leadership role. The opportunity befell Yang Jian, a man of mixed blood and the father-in-law of the Northern Zhou imperial house. He at first annexed Northern Qi in the name of Northern Zhou. Then he took over the latter as well. He mobilized all the forces to capture Nanjing, site of the headquarters of the remaining southern state.

The unification movement took a north-to-south and west-to-east direction and embodied an organizational structure of simplicity and uniformity to eliminate rivals of greater complexity. The Northern Zhou, the nucleus of this last stage of the unification movement, was located in today's Shaanxi Province, less influenced by either the Xianbei nobility or the Chinese clans of long social standing. Its longtime adviser and finance minister, Su Zhuo, was under Buddhist influence. He "read all the books, and was especially good at math."

Organizing the Northern Zhou institutions, he took the *Rituals of the Zhou* as his guide. Further military operations required of the unification movement nevertheless assigned the main part to the marine force, an area in which the Xianbei commanders could not become proficient. Yang Jian, or Wendi of the Sui, picked up all the favorable conditions to accomplish his career as the second greatest unifier in Chinese history, a role that a modern scholar has cited to compare with that of Charlemagne.[4] Yet, he had to slaughter the Northern Zhou noblemen by the dozens to safeguard his position. His campaign to take the southern capital over large spans of water had indeed been swiftly and rapidly carried out. But the next year, 590, saw a wide rebellion that affected all the influential clans in the South. Luckily, it was promptly put down by the new dynasty before those family groups managed to work out a system of resistance (*Suishu,* Biography of Gaozu; also see *Zizhi tongjian*). The above proceedings clearly reaffirmed the proposition that a unified China relied on a large body of small self-cultivators as its source of manpower and tax revenue, not interfered with by any middle-level privileged groups. The Han lost the First Empire because this condition was compromised; the Sui helped to create the Second Empire by restoring it.

The dynastic founder's son, Yang Guang, initiated construction on a grand scale and fought a winless war in Korea. He exhausted the nation and made the Sui merely a pacesetter for the Tang, similar to the way in which the Qin had paved the road for the Han. Yet, after taking into consideration the events before and after, including the unifier Yang Jian's cruelty, and the equally cruel performance of the enlightened ruler of the Tang, Li Shimin, who extended the butchery to his own brothers and nephews, we may have to acknowledge that to construct a huge empire at a time when technology was not ready to give support and public education was at a minimum, there was probably no better way than to throw the peasant masses into a gigantic movement and keep the momentum going and resist interference of any kind, ruthlessly, by all means. This is a situation that can be better explained by Machiavelli.

The Tang dynasty lasted for close to three hundred years (618–906), which appeared to be a brilliant era in Chinese history. It enjoyed a benefit unknown to other dynasties. After the long period of struggle, the obstacles to integration had one after another been eliminated by the minor dynasties preceding it. Once and for all, the Tang could actually institutionalize the type of management reminiscent of the *Rituals of the Zhou.* As its territory was extended, more population was brought under the control of its schematic design.

What is the system of *zu-yong-tiao* about? Briefly, this is a system of applying a horizontal tax rate to the entire agricultural population. The level of taxation is low, the amount payable in manpower, farm commodities, and village produce is within everyone's reach, and its calculation is direct and simple. As it was put into effect by the Tang, it was supported by the land allotment plan, which theoretically at least had assigned an acreage of land in proportion to each household's manpower and therefore equitable in terms of its tax liability. When there were practical difficulties, the imperial government was willing to compromise with *guafu* (clemency and further reduced rates offered to the households that had evaded tax registration, so as to induce them to turn themselves in voluntarily). Those provisions enabled the Tang to increase its tax-paying population from three million households in the early seventh century to a reported 9.6 million households toward the middle of the eighth century.

The pressure applied by the dynasty was not greater than that of other dynasties, with the exception of the Song. But such a plan remained effective only when the agrarian economy was crude and simple. Once its level began to advance, the complexities began to set in. For one thing, previously the bureaucracy had been organized to model after the agrarian population. Its personnel and logistics structured to administer the system had also paralleled its simplicity and uniformity. Now, with the more advanced sectors of the national economy coming into the picture, the bureaucracy was also under pressure. In between the old and new, the simple and complicated, it started to split.[5]

Western scholars often take 755 A.D. as a dividing line in the Tang to separate a period of growth and contentment from a period of decline and morbidity. More than a military campaign, the An Lushan Rebellion arising in that year marked major changes within the state, revealed by its finances and by its constitution. The *zu-yong-tiao,* as mentioned, relied on the land allotment plan for effectiveness. Having been in place for close to one and a half centuries, the institution had used up its feasibility. Now another factor tossed the state affairs into an unmanageable situation: It appeared that North China and South China could no longer be effectively administered under the same center. When An Lushan began as an armed uprising at Fanyang (in today's Hebei Province), "the warehouses in the two capitals [Loyang and Changan] were stocked with articles at unprecedented levels" (*Jiu Tangshu,* Food and Money Monograph). "Premier in Charge of Finance Yang Guozhong felt that the items in storage were not appropriate to be distributed to the soldiers. He dispatched censor Cui Zhong to Taiyuan to raise funds by selling licenses for Buddhist monks and Taoist priests [which entitled the purchaser to tax exemption]. In ten days, this method netted one million *min* only" (*Xin Tangshu,* Food and Money Monograph, differing slightly from the entry in *Jiu Tangshu*). The episode revealed that for two economic systems that had no channel of communication between them in peacetime, it would be most difficult to mobilize one to support the other in time of emergency. Many centuries later, China under the Ming had to scrape up silver in the South and deliver it to Manchuria to meet a crisis situation; the effort was laborious and the result not rewarding. The lack of delivery vehicles in those cases can be explained with the parable that it would not help the situation if the United States closed the Boston Symphony and the Metropolitan Opera of New York in order to win the Vietnam War.

Yang Yan's "two-tax system," proclaimed in 780, never openly nullified the *zu-yong-tiao.* But the latter, along with the land allotment plan, was in fact shelved. Nor did Yang's innovation constitute a system. Its net effect was a tacit authorization for the provincial officials to collect taxes as they saw fit, so that portions of the proceeds could be delivered to the capital. But "the amount delivered counted no more than two or three out of ten" (*Jiu Tangshu,* Food and Money Monograph). Political centralism of course had no place under those conditions. When the trend carried, the regional military posts became inheritable. It went on until the Five Dynasties period, when it was the norm that everywhere army officers took charge. Taxation fell entirely into the hands of provincial strongmen.

The Five Dynasties, altogether occupying a span of only fifty-four years (906–960), is not to be compared with Wei-Jin and the North and South Court period. Without an effective central government dictating what could be done and what could not, regional economy, following its own impulse, made robust advances.[6] Throughout China's imperial period, tax legislation had never before been decided on the regional level yet formally institutionalized. (Curiously, tax legislation during the Five Dynasties period remained in local gazetteers of some districts. They apparently served as guidelines for those districts during later dynasties. See, for example, the 1566 edition of *Huizhou fuzhi*.) After its founding in 960, the Song took advantage of the situation by consolidating the revenues and armament of the autonomous regions from the top.[7] There was no need to rework the bottom layer. Thus, even though the Tang and Song were separated by about half a century, the infrastructure continued its long-term evolution. There was no drastic break.

A development that occurred during the interim period in the area of frontier defense had a more enduring effect. When China was again divided, the Khitans, a semi-nomadic people, took the sixteen border prefectures inside the Great Wall, including today's Beijing. The effort by the Han Chinese to dislodge the squatters repeatedly failed. Beijing had yet to become a capital of alien rule, to witness the rise and fall of the Liao, Jin, and the Yuan of the Mongols. More than four hundred years had yet to pass before it was recovered by the Ming, the last indigenous Chinese dynasty.

The Song differs from all other Chinese dynasties because of its governmental finance. From the beginning it chose to support its state institutions with the more advanced sectors of the national economy, paying attention to ship construction, minting money, opening mines, collecting commercial taxes, and installing governmental monopolies on wine, vinegar, salt, and alum. It made no effort to disturb landholdings. It remained as the only major dynasty in Chinese history to try to fill its army ranks exclusively through recruitment, staying away from conscription. The dynastic founder, Zhao Kuangyin, intended "to accumulate two million bolts of silk fabrics to purchase the heads of the enemy" (*Songshi,* Food and Money Monograph). This meant that he had in mind to solve the problem with the northern minority groups, whose economy was lagging behind, with the advanced sectors of the economy in the South. If this scheme had succeeded, the entire length of Chinese history would have been rewritten. And the history of the world would never had come down as it was in the nineteenth century. Since this basic direction set up by the dynastic founder was never abandoned by the Northern Song, we may take Wang Anshi's "New Policies" to explain the paradox of how the approach had to fail.

With Shenzong or Emperor Zhao Xu's trust, Wang Anshi worked to reinforce the national economy of the Northern Song to drive away the Khitans and Tibetans, who also took China's northwest region. As it happened, not only did the Khitans remain unshakable, but the Tibetan state Xixia also turned back the Song army, with huge casualties. The New Policies became the crucial point of debate after military setbacks. The technical problems turned into moral issues. The direction of the government fluctuated; laws were proclaimed and drastically reversed. The partisan controversy continued until the fall of the capital in 1126, which terminated the Northern Song.

With today's perspective, it can be readily seen that the New Policies aimed at no more than speeding up the money economy and commercializing government finance, the success of which would have hinged on the maturity of the civil components in supporting the program. Yet the organization of the latter would not have gone very far until rights to private property were secured by law, and the interchangeability of services and goods was generally recognized and widely practiced, to the extent that all accounts could be summoned to check against one another. Even for Western Europe, a great length of struggle had to occur to make the necessary preparation in areas of thought, religion, and jurisprudence before such a state of economic structure would emerge. The Chinese bureaucratic management made truth descend from top to bottom, undebatable wherever authority was involved. In administering the affairs of the huge number of peasants, officialdom was more interested in discouraging lawsuits than attending to justice. Nor could the court expenses arising from the legal proceedings be bearable for a government deriving major revenue from small self-cultivators. When the New Policies were proclaimed, the Song government started to do business with the populace. Yet the traditional method of financial management continued, including application of pressure from the top downward. With it the program's impracticalities reached to the bottom, where the efficiency of the operation mattered most.

As records show, Wang's *fang tian fa,* which was supposed to provide a graded land tax according to soil productivity, was not in effect twenty years after its proclamation, as the land survey, even in the vicinity of Kaifeng, ran into technical difficulties. The *mian yi fa,* intending to commute labor service into monetary payment, was held onto by Wang's critics to enforce the circulation of money in rural areas. The *shi yi fa,* which authorized the government to engage in trade, was not utilized to stimulate the wholesale business, but to turn government functionaries into retailers, some of them peddling fruit and ice blocks in the streets. And the *qing miao fa,* effecting a government loan to peasants during the planting season, could not be carried out in an orderly manner due to the lack of institutional supervision. There were no banks to handle the funds and no court proceedings to oversee the rights and liabilities of borrowers. The prevailing method was for parcels of money to be handed out to groups of peasants, regardless of whether they had applied for a loan, and then to hold them mutually responsible. One man's delinquency thus encumbered all others in the group. Once the law was put into effect, every county was assessed a quota of interest. There were districts that did not provide the funds as principal. With no money loaned out, the alleged "interest" was collected from the population as a surtax. (See *Songshi,* Food and Money Monograph.)

In its more than three hundred years (960–1279), the Song, intermittently involved in war and peace with the minority groups in the North, compiled a military history that was inseparable from its financial history. The Wang Anshi story was only an obvious example. Actually, the technical impasse of taking the more advanced sectors of the national economy as its financial basis on one side and retaining small self-cultivators as its social infrastructure on the other troubled the entire period. Jia Sidao's compulsory purchase of agricultural land from private landowners in the Yangtze Delta region toward the end of the Southern Song attempted to break this impasse without noticeable success. Throughout the dynasty, the fiscal figures, running into serious inflation, could not be audited. The twelve chapters of the military monograph in the *Songshi* provide many entries on the desertion of soldiers, on soldiers begging for food in public, and on unfulfilled recruitment quotas. At this point the urban standard of living of the Chinese people compared favorably with that elsewhere in the world, yet China was struggling against the northern states, unable to gain an upper hand, in the face of all indications that the adversaries had smaller populations, lower cultural levels, and an economy that was crude and less developed. The outcome appeared to be most unusual in world history. The main reason was the background simplicity and uniformity of the steppeland, which made mobilization technically easier. The nomads continued to enjoy the advantage of controlling the Han Chinese in North China, so long as they retained their organizational simplicity and uniformity. But after occupying the territory over a period of time, they too became involved in the complexity of the national economy. Liao established offices in charge of salt and iron monopoly, transportation, accounting, and minting, "until the closing years, when expenses were mounting, the state obligations were not met, even though the operation of the mint never ceased." The situation went on until "scarcity was to the end felt by the high and low, and supply dumps and warehouses were empty" (*Liaoshi,* Food and Money Monograph). The dilemma was passed to the Jürchen state of Jin, under whose rule the outcome was an even greater surprise. The Jin occupied Kaifeng in 1126. Therefore it set itself up for a career of printing notes, until, progressively, inflation reached sixty million fold, a world record (Peng Xinwei, *Zhongguo huobishi,* 1954, pp. 364–65).

The Third Empire: Ming and Qing

In Chinese financial history, the less than one-hundred-year rule of the Yuan dynasty merely provided a transition between the second and third empires. This is to say that the Mongols had never provided an adequate solution to the problem arising from the divergence of North and South, and the lack of integration between a commodity economy and a rising money economy. The dynasty printed paper currency, employed Uighurs as tax farmers, and authorized fiefs for the Mongol princes and princesses, with the provision that the enfeoffed could send their stewards to the local districts (*Yuanshi,* Food and Money Monograph). It also declared large-scale tax reductions south of the Yangtze. To promote agriculture, it compiled the *Nongsang jiyao,* the first printing of which ran to ten thousand copies. For taxation, it acknowledged that two separate systems governed North and South China. The Food and Money Monograph of the *Yuanshi* indicates that "Revenue derived from interior prefectures was divided into a land tax and a poll tax, which imitated the Tang *zu-yong-tiao.*" This means that taxation followed horizontal rates, applicable to all households and every individual. The monograph continues: "Revenue derived from south of the Yangtze was divided into a summer tax and an autumn tax, which imitated the Tang *liangshui.*" This means that in principle taxation was based on the acreage of agricultural land and productivity, and actually quotas were farmed out to the local districts.

The Ming dynasty was founded in 1368. Against the expansion background of the Tang and Song, the third empire marked a long step backward. It was introverted and lacking competitive character. Its leaning on the pool of small self-cultivators was obvious. The Qing historian Zhao Yi made a point when he let it be known that the founder of the Ming was an imitator of the founder of the Han.

Against the trend of the modern world, our criticism of Zhu Yuanzhang could never be too harsh. Yet, in reviewing the failure of the second empire, we cannot say that he formulated his policies without any vision at all. His return to an agricultural emphasis, printing of paper currency merely for awards and famine relief, adoption of the backward elements of the economy as a national standard, and ceaseless work for homogeneity and uniformity at the low level reflected a total retreat from the direction that had already proven to be disastrous. Moreover, he achieved a unifying drive that turned toward the North from the South, historically unprecedented. Facing these factors, we must say that in the perspective of macro history, praise or condemnation would be out of place. What we can assert is that within Chinese history, the influence of geopolitics is profound. Unless we lift the horizon of our vision, we cannot explain the puzzling factors of the recurring political centralism, the need to anticipate wartime organization in time of peace, and the undue value placed on quantity rather than quality. Once those elements are understood, we can say that the development of Chinese history from the B.C. era to the present time has been persistent. Its linear progression overrules the dynastic cycles, which are no more than internal fluctuations.

Although Zhu Yuanzhang did not overturn the entire landholding pattern, he imposed punitive taxes in the name of "confiscation" on the estates in the Suzhou-Songjiang region. He enlarged several seditious cases to deliver fatal blows to the affluent families and powerful clans, until "many of those households of middle-class background were ruined" (*Mingshi,* Monograph on the Penal Code). A report of 1397 by the Ministry of Revenue indicated that across the nation, only 14,341 households still possessed more than 700 *mu* of land (about 120 acres) or more. The list of owners was presented to the emperor (*Ming shilu*). Under imperial rule, merchants were not allowed to wear silk. The entire population was forbidden to take to the sea. Large numbers of office workers, attendants, and runners were requisitioned from village communities and remained unpaid; also requisitioned were bows and arrows, office furniture, and stationery. The *weisuo,* a chain of military colonies, was nevertheless an imitation of a similar system under the Yuan.

The state, relying on the small self-cultivators as its foundation, was not only intolerant of anything that intended to insert itself between the superstructure and infrastructure, but it also restrained its own government from operating in the middle, such as providing more effective logistical functions. Under the Tang and Song, public income and expenditure began to converge at the middle level, as indicated by financial commissioners and transportation agencies in charge of large geographical regions and the accounts established at such a level. From the Hongwu years of the Ming, China's financial resources were again split into numerous small segments and parcels and delivered laterally by the lower level agencies or even by the population who paid the taxes. The Revenue Ministry thus became a huge accounting office with no operating capacity, a telephone switchboard that paired the revenue collectors and dispensers while itself was not a party in the conversation. With this, a curious combination was achieved: the high-level political centralism was teamed with a thoroughly diffused fiscal apparatus. The effect of the constraint was apparent, since all the governmental offices were watching one another, none of them able to enlarge its function because none could increase its operating budget. No doubt the commercial organizations were likewise restrained. As the experience of the advanced nations shows, the beginning of modern commerce always comes with government contract. The Hongwu mode of governance required no such service rendered by mercantile circles; nor would the government feel compelled to solve the problems of the merchants. All the measures taken by Zhu Yuanzhang, outlined above, could be considered to have emerged from his reaction to the Wang Anshi experiment. His discussion of the Song reformer confirms this.

The "Single-Whip Reform" in the sixteenth century is generally recognized as having made a significant improvement. Yet, to restore the integration of financial responsibility and function was beyond its scope. Liang Fangzhong, an authority on the topic, referred to the reform as "merely minimizing the crisis of the old system on the brink of a total collapse." After the reform, he pointed out, the "Hongwu mode" of production relations changed little (*Linan huebao,* vol. 12, no. 2). What he labels as production relations is what we recognize as the "Hongwu mode of financial management." It deliberately divided the nation's financial resources into small segments to facilitate lateral transactions. This mode was not altered in the late sixteenth century, when silver was in wide circulation (see Shen Bang, *Wanshu zaji*).

Even with modifications under the Qing, the basic scheme of management survived in the twentieth century (see Chen Gonglu, *Zhongguo jindaishi,* 1965, pp. 665, 687). It is therefore not an exaggeration to say that the reform in China today is targeted at the socioeconomic system left by the Ming dynasty.

Undeniably, historical incidents were instrumental in sending the Manchus to be masters of China. When Li Zichen's Da Shun had the mandate of heaven in his grasp, the last Ming emperor, Chongzhen, chose to die rather than perform the traditional handover. Although North China surrendered to the Qing in a state of shock, and the South was unable to turn the tide even if it had had the resolve, and regardless of the unpredictable timing, the recognition of history's rationality induces us to see that the Qing dynasty did compensate for China's deficiency on many counts. When the Ming *weisuo* was replaced by the Manchu banners, the expenses of recruiting an army were reduced. When government expenses, including military expenditures, incurred a large amount of silver in circulation, it was passed around in the South so as not to contradict the operation of the civil economy. The low level of culture of the Manchus fit well with the Ming approach to government, which actually favored uncouth simplicity. Functionally no break occurred, as the conquerors were bound by the institutions of the conquered; they imposed on the latter only their particular ritualistic trappings.

The Manchu takeover thus featured disciplinary and technical touches only; institutional and organizational renewal was not the emphasis. Under the Qing, the positions of ministers and vice-ministers were doubled to accommodate Chinese and Manchu officeholders in equal number. At the direction of Kangxi, the quota of the *ding,* or able-bodied males, was permanently frozen as of the record of 1711, which made it possible later to merge the poll tax with the land tax. The Yongzheng Emperor ordered that the collection of melting charges on payments made in silver be institutionalized. He also organized the Grand Council, by which a handful of top bureaucrats could meet the sovereign regularly to improve governmental efficiency. These several items exhausted the major innovations of the Qing.

The institutionalizing of melting charges has recently been studied by an American scholar.[8] She points out that with it the Yongzheng Emperor wished to strengthen the contact between the governors general and the throne. Aside from eliminating the abuse of public funds, he also hoped that with a widened revenue, the government could provide more services to the populace, to break away from the pattern of merely holding them at bay. But its effect was manifested for a very short period only. The fundamental obstacle to a more enduring reform rested in the fact that when taxes were collected from the small self-cultivators, the revenue could not be significantly expanded. The resolution of the emperor and his top advisers was unable to bring about a turnaround. The population increase in the early Qing made the situation worse. After 1800, the meaningfulness of this reform had already vanished. The unsatisfactory conditions of the late Ming began to reappear, regardless of the desire at the top. That is to say again: Poverty and emptiness came together.

Bureaucratism: An Organizational Reality

Traditional China's political, economic, and social system appeared as an interlinked whole. supported by its own literature and philosophy. It cannot be easily lumped together with any of the great systems of world history. Numerous modern Chinese writers call it *fengjian,* by which label they try to approximate it to the feudal system in Europe. The result is awkward.

The word "feudalism" was coined only after the French Revolution, by scholars who used it to denote certain political, social, and economic features of medieval Europe without giving it a precise definition. Only in the present century did a number of scholars examine those features at close range, enabling us to have a clear perception of what the European feudal system was like. Only in the 1950s did a number of American scholars gather to reach a consensus as to how the term could be applied to various civilizations in the world, the Chinese included. The conference observed that feudalism embraced the following three prominent characteristics: (1) Fragmentation of authority. Within the feudal society, monarchy existed. Yet the most effective government that held the reins of taxation, administration of justice, and providing military service existed at the local level. Decentralization was the key. (2) Public affairs becoming private domains. The enfeoffment involved the custody of a territory that, through inheritance, became inalienable. Under its provisions, from the king's domain down to the manors, all the holdings remained private estates. The chain of superior-inferior relationship applied to the entire population. Feudal Europe forbade the sale of landholdings, because once the estates were freely transferred, social mobility would ensue, and the system would no longer be tenable. (3) Warrior tradition. The above conditions cast the social status of the entire population into a pyramidal order; it already embodied the spirit of a military organization. Naturally, the warriors represented the landholding class as well as the political power. The knight, being a professional soldier, was also part of the nobility. Based on these three conditions, a participating Sinologist concluded that the feudal system occurred in Chinese history only during the Shang and early Zhou. In the Wei-Jin-Nanbeichao period, certain feudal elements emerged, but they did not reappear as a system.[9]

Even within traditional Chinese historiography, the word *fengjian* is also contrasted with *junxian,* a centralized system. To equate the great empires of the Han, Tang, Song, Ming, and Qing, which feature political centralism, power in the hands of the literary bureaucracy, land changing hands freely, and social mobility no more in check than anywhere else in the world, with *fengjian* rather than *junxian,* and further to put them on the same footing with the feudal system in medieval Europe is nothing short of adopting a false premise. The observations coming out of this type of scholarship do not deserve the serious attention of the learned, to say the least.

Nor could the Marxist "Asiatic mode of production" be the right garment for China. To begin with, Marx himself did not develop the term fully enough to allow us to make a judgment. The ambiguity only gives those who are ideologically motivated an excellent opportunity to advance their own ideas under the armor of authority. China's reliance on the small self-cultivators—more than a mode of production, also a fiscal requirement of the huge empire—is unique in world history. For one thing, it bears no resemblance to the jajmani system in India, another Asian country, which makes not only agricultural production but also the trades of carpentry, laundry, pottery making, and so forth collectively hereditary within the villages and ties the exchange of services and goods likewise in a collective and hereditary manner.

I believe that from the three empires described above, an inductive method can sum up the main features of China's "bureaucratism," a political system. It was achieved under an imperial order, which, while taxing the entire population, disallowed economic entities from operating at its middle level. Those features were: (1) the assumption that the Natural Law was within its grasp. For example, it proposed to write history in order to praise and condemn. Instead of introducing to historiography an element of objectivity that was based on technical reasoning and was readjustable over the course of time, the position took for granted that the judgment passed by its own moral standard had a permanent validity. The supposition differed from the attitude of the Greek thinkers, who believed that Natural Law must be continually discovered. (2) Its permanent tie with the Chinese monarchy. Without going through the stage of "separation of church and state," the Chinese monarchy always retained its religious tone. The emperor's directives were referred to as "saintly decrees." His presence injected a "heavenly countenance" and his pronouncements were delivered by a "jade voice." All these mobilized the ideal perfection within Natural Law as the source of power behind the superhuman authority. The success of this system required the integration of the bureaucracy and its demigod presiding officer, a most difficult task. In Chinese history, strong rulers manipulated their bureaucrats; weak emperors turned themselves into the instruments of the latter. Li Shimin or Taizong of the Tang seemed to have avoided the imbalance and come close to the desired state of harmony with his top bureaucrats. But then, he had to eliminate his brothers to maintain such a state of integration. (3) Make-believe as part of its operation. A child emperor in China could be honored by the bureaucrats as "our fatherly emperor." During the Ming dynasty, no prince regent was ever appointed to take charge. There were many cases wherein mediocre rulers were dressed up as brilliant and sagely, and ruthless ones were made to appear kind and generous. The Yongle Emperor of the Ming, or Zhu Di, being a cruel tyrant as many sources later suggested, was given the following title after his death: "Our Cultured Emperor Who Has Embodied Heaven and Magnified the Way, Heightened Enlightenment and Widened Our Destiny, Combined Saintly Valor with Divine Accomplishment, and Served with Pure Kindness as Well as Absolute Filial Piety."

The principle was to stage the ideal perfection as far as possible and to substitute it with pretense whenever the effort failed. Make-believe could stand for reality. In all events, the form was important, sometimes taking precedence over substance. Ritual was not merely an ostentation; through it business was considered actually to have been transacted. (4) The acceptance of a performance standard fixed by the upper echelon rather than decided by the actual feasibility at the lower level. To carry out this rule, pressure had to be applied to the lower units. The setup drove the irrationality of the system to the operational level. Traditional historians never ceased to call the crisis situation a result of *fuhua,* or corruption, thus ignoring the fundamental cause of constitutional inadequacy, but turning the symptoms of the ailment into its causes. (5) The claim of exclusiveness. Proclaiming that "heaven does not allow two suns," Chinese bureaucratism took an exclusive position. It would not tolerate, ideologically, the manifestation and patronage of the ideal perfection by another body or agency. Technically it could not compete with an efficiency-oriented organization. These conditions compelled it to maintain an introverted outlook. To prevent the populace from external contact became its obsession. Wendi of the Sui, or Yang Jian, prohibited the construction of ships over thirty feet long. The Yongle Emperor of the Ming, or Zhu Di, dispatched Zheng He on maritime expeditions. Yet in 1404 he decreed that all seafaring ships in private possession be converted to flat bows, so as to eliminate their ability to make distant voyages. The claim for exclusiveness dictated those measures.

Leaning toward religion, bureaucratism of the Chinese type took an idealist approach to practical problems. When obstacles arose from its own impracticality, often it avoided the real issue. Instead, it claimed that *yong* (function, or modus operandi) was supposed to differ from *ti* (body, or prototype). In this way it connived in the noncompliance with the law.

From the standpoint of macro history, the exploitation of the population by the ruling class was not the center of the problem. When the mass of small self-cultivators was set up as its fiscal foundation, the bureaucracy excluded a potential warrior group or a nobility from becoming its middle-echelon apparatus, nor would it permit mercantile interests to act as its agents. In this way, no machinery for systematic exploitation was put in place. The civil service examinations, in the effort to recruit talent, created sufficient social mobility to prevent permanent exploitation. Looking from the angle of developing a national economy, the problem existed on the other side. It was that the accumulated wealth was unable to take hold.

Furthermore, China's poverty amidst emptiness should not be handled as a moral problem; it must be treated as a technical problem. To sum up the organizational structure of China's bureaucratism, its greatest weakness lay in the fact that it was not mathematically manageable. It developed this way because at a time when technological support was not yet available, the country was already committed to solving political and military problems larger than itself.

Capitalism: A Term That Is Already Outdated

If we say that China has been mathematically unmanageable, we must recognize that until about 1600, none of the nations of the world could have been mathematically managed as some of them are today. Merely four hundred years ago, some of the modern states such as the United States and the Soviet Union had not yet come into existence. Those that were there, such as Britain, France, and Japan, differed enormously from what they are at present. The most crucial factor that separates the past from the present is the so-called rise of capitalism, which makes some of the nations mathematically manageable. Once that is achieved, those nations, with tightened organizations built up around commercial principles, have a tendency to pressurize the nations that retain an agrarian mode of organization, such as Holland did to England, England to France, and the Western nations to Japan. The rising trend compels all nations in the world, working from their own geographical and historical limits in the background, to achieve a state of being mathematically manageable or at least sufficiently so to be able to cope with the new world situation. When private capital is utilized as the driving force to achieve the reorganization, we may consider the nation as in the fold of capitalism. On the other hand, if public finance plays a more important role, the nation can be recognized as having turned socialist.

The greatest difficulty that we encounter here is that to this day, no consensus has been reached to give the term "capitalism" a generally acceptable definition. Marx, who mentions capitalists, the capitalist era, and the capitalist mode of production, did not use the word capitalism. French historian Fernand Braudel suggests that Louis Blanc in the nineteenth century and Werner Sombart in the twentieth may have been the first writers to have promoted the term with its present-day usage.

After some discussion with British Sinologist Joseph Needham, I feel that from a technical point of view, capitalism represents a movement that has to promote the wide extension of credit, so that the idle capital can, through private loans, attain the maximum utilization. It also has to institutionalize impersonal management, so that the enterprise can be widened to exceed the supervising power of the owner himself. Moreover, it has to pool together the service facilities, so that the technological support can further extend business activities to a dimension unreachable by the individual firms if they have to provide those services themselves. At a glance, those are simple matters. But in reality, the three conditions build up gigantic networks of economic life until all citizens are involved, for which each nation has to go through a general reorganization to alter its dominant thought, jurisprudence, social structure, and social usage to provide the degree of interchangeability. Unfortunately, too many authors, before enlightening us with the detailed process of how this is done in each nation, first burden us with the argument whether capitalism is good or evil. Not fundamentally different from the traditional Chinese historians who write to praise or condemn, these authors, too, set for themselves a task of giving a technical problem moral interpretations.

With the abundance of published material on the subject, we have found that little is done in terms of chronological surveys that summarize how each nation solves the problem and creates the needed interchangeability. My own effort, presented in volume 4, number 2 of *The Chinese Intellectual*, attempts to stop the gap. Here I can only make a barebone summary of the essay, which is essentially an outline by itself.

The pioneers of capitalism in Western Europe were the free cities of Italy. In the contest for power between the empire and the papacy, those cities managed to remain autonomous. (But it is debatable that they ever qualified as modern states.) Among them the most prominent was Venice. Situated inside a lagoon, it enjoyed the unique benefit of being least affected by the affairs of the continent and its agricultural problems. Aside from ship construction, salt making, and glass and metal works, Venice did not prosper as a major manufacturing center either. The lack of fresh water dictated that it had to be a merchant republic. Its nobles had either reemerged as a plutocracy or been pensioned off. Its civil law was geared to commercial application. Its naval personnel were conscripted from the entire population, at one time close to 10 percent of the residents. Important trade was monopolized by the state. Ships moved in convoys. The organizational simplicity enabled Venice to appear as a large company, its citizenry being its shareholders. Even artisans and widows could also invest their small savings in the joint enterprises. The church's restriction against usury was simply disregarded. With all these, the city state entered the era of capitalism without any specific effort. Its defeat of Genoa in 1380, a dozen years after the founding of the Ming dynasty in China, confirmed its position as a major sea power and established a modern trend that small states may play disproportionately more influential roles in world affairs because of their organizational strength.

In the late sixteenth and early seventeenth centuries, when Venice was in decline, the Dutch Republic appeared as the leading capitalist power. Holland, one of the seven provinces that made up the federal republic, had two-thirds of its population and provided three-quarters of its revenue. Its weight enabled it to outshine the other units within the federation; often its name was taken for that of the entire nation, as it is still nowadays.

In the age when the contest for land power in Europe took place at the continental crossroads and the demonstration of naval strength was done in the Mediterranean, the Netherlands, left on the shores of the North Sea, attracted little attention. Many towns in the region became semi-autonomous in the absence of any powerful territorial lord. The Dutch people had no prior experience in organizing a national state of their own; yet political centralism was on the whole unknown to them. In the sixteenth century the Spaniards, raising the banner of Counter-Reformation, attempted to bring about drastic changes. They decided to establish new bishoprics in the territory, in the meanwhile setting up military tribunals and imposing heavy taxation to carry it out. The scheme provoked resistance in kind, and the Dutch Republic rose to answer this Habsburg challenge. A protracted war developed, and many entrepreneurs and artisans, in particular weavers and metal workers, were driven north to Holland. Amsterdam, already a seaport of significance, rose to become a center of money exchange. Agriculture in the Netherlands also favored dairy farming. All these conditions pointed to the natural outcome that the Dutch had to construct their new nation on the federal principle, to take commerce as an essential part of its organizational logic. Local autonomy was for the most part preserved. Calvinism settled the religious issue. Even the Dutch navy was made up of five separate colleges. Capitalism, therefore, was not less historically and environmentally determined than it was politically decided by resolution. Independence was declared in 1581, the ninth year of Wanli on the Chinese calendar. But the republic did not gain full recognition until the seventeenth century.

The lead of the Dutch Republic was overtaken by England. The latter, too, had to go through a long battle to become the foremost capitalist country in the world. In today's perspective, it is not too difficult to see that all the troubles England endured during a great part of the seventeenth century, internally and externally, were inseparable from its transition from a country entrenched behind agrarian organization to a streamlined state under the influence of modern commerce. In two areas the development became prominent. One was that after incessant crises in the sixteenth and seventeenth centuries, the pattern of landholding in England had become regularized. Another was that with an equal length of agitation, equity was finally accepted by the common law courts. Both contributed to the invisible power that made England mathematically manageable.

On the change of land tenure in the sixteenth and seventeenth centuries, research in the early part of the present century placed great emphasis on the issue of social justice when the real estate was transferred, evidently under Marxist influence in one way or another. Recent works, however, brought up the point that during the early part of the unsettled period a great many anomalies existed, and thus toward the end of the seventeenth century, while more concentration of ownership was part of the outcome, there was also a general improvement in land utilization as the holdings became more rationalized.[10] Historians on modern China can do well by looking closely into the unmanageable situation of land tenure in England during the late Tudor and early Stuart periods. For instance, the copyholders in this age, descending from villeinage, could not be said to hold title to the land, yet neither were they outright renters. The "entry fines" collected by the lords, in some instances tracing back to the manorial customs, showed a bewildering variety. Some of the landowners lost track of the properties in the field; there were cases when the chief tenants could not be located. The alienation of royal domains in the early seventeenth century was at one hundred years' purchase, suggesting the extent of irregularity involved. To put it bluntly, it took the civil war and restoration to clear up the internal ambiguity.

Common law was a product of medieval England. Bound by the precedents without free play, it worked well with an old-fashioned agrarian society. Only under the unbearable pressure of the seventeenth century did the courts of common law begin to accept equity, which represented a different approach to jurisprudence. The process was painfully slow. But what had started as a compromise in the course of time also accumulated a body of precedents of its own. With it the gap separating equity from law was narrowed. Agricultural management under the new ruling class came close to commercial practice, rendering the integration of the national economy possible. At the completion of the Glorious Revolution, the development was obvious. The date, 1689, was also the twenty-eighth year of Kangxi in China.

But as time went on, it became increasingly difficult to use the term capitalism to interpret the modernization process of all the nations in the world. Take the French Revolution for example: It eliminated the political power of the nobility and the clergy. It attempted to issue a national currency based on the credit of the entire country's landholding. It proceeded to redraw provincial boundaries by neatly separating its mountains and rivers. The works could also be said to have competed with the Code Napoleon. All these steps demonstrated a consistent effort at making the nation mathematically manageable. The adoption of capitalist measures in France undeniably had been easier after the revolution. But we would be overplaying the term capitalism, or, conversely, underrated the French Revolution, if we should ever say that from the storming of the Bastille to the Thermidorean Reaction, and from Condorcet to Robespierre, the French merely turned their country capitalistic. On the other hand, it would be premature to connect the revolution to the rise of socialism in France. More perplexities had yet to appear with the term. After World War II, Britain sometimes has demonstrated strong socialist tendencies, but on other occasions it remains uncompromisingly capitalistic. The United States, the most advanced nation in professing and practicing capitalism in the world, is not devoid of socialist inclinations in its various legislation and pronouncements. In the past, persons who discoursed on capitalism tended to expose its shortcomings. Since the cold war it has become fashionable to praise its ideal perfection.

Therefore, in interpreting China's reform today, we refrain from calling it a movement promoting capitalism. Rather, it signifies a conscious effort at merging Chinese history with Western civilization. (In the past there was only contact and clash, not a full-scale merger.) Its rationale arises from the fact that unless China becomes mathematically manageable, it can never break away from poverty and emptiness. This is far more than an economic reform. Nor is it a feudal system that China is trying to do away with. To be razed is the traditional bureaucratism, including the practice of erecting pyramids from the top downward. Although the work is merely getting organized at this late hour, it still has to start by securing the property rights of the individual; otherwise there will be no practical way to consolidate the infrastructure. While not going all the way to promote capitalism, China is no longer fastidious toward anything that is capitalistic. Many historical experiences of the capitalist forerunners will undoubtedly benefit the Chinese. The Dutch started with a federal form of government, so that the uneven economic accomplishments of several regions could be simultaneously preserved. England tried its best to solve problems through the judicial process, in view of the fact that executive orders and legislative bills making sweeping changes lack the deliberation of the court proceedings that give consideration to individual cases under particular circumstances, yet the accumulation of precedents could alter social customs and sometimes reconcile conflicting ideas. There is plenty for the Chinese to learn.

Not a Great Deal of Time Has Been Lost

When I read the works on Chinese history by writers of Chinese ancestry currently residing overseas, there are of course valid criticisms and constructive suggestions. Yet once in a while I run into complaints and condemnations. The main reason behind the indignant voice, I believe, is that those writers themselves have not visualized the magnitude and seriousness of the problems China has been facing.

Let me bring in another episode from my personal experience in 1941, when I served as an infantry platoon leader. The Fourteenth Division had been one of the best among the Nationalist battle formations. But because of the hostile environment of southern Yunnan, attrition and desertion had thinned the ranks to less than half of authorized strength. As we needed replacements, the Ministry of War in Chongqing obliged. It instructed a military personnel district in Hunan to furnish us with so many able-bodied men, called *zhuangding* in the military jargon. In reality, the conscription law of the Nationalist Government was proclaimed only a year before the war started, and it bore little connection with reality. Thus most of the installations and organizations of the so-called selective service existed only on paper. Nor were the supply agencies in place. As it happened, our divisional headquarters organized a "replacement escorting team" made up of officers and men called from the regiments and battalions. They marched to Guangxi, where they took the train to Hunan. When they detrained they were on their feet again before arriving at their destination. No *zhuangding* were awaiting them. Instead, the entire replacement escorting team was broken into squads and detachments. With the cooperation of the village leaders, the armed soldiers entered the hamlets and captured *zhuangding* on the spot. Those who were rounded up were detained in a Buddhist temple awaiting the completion of the whole order. The process dragged on, not for weeks but for months. While more men were turned in every day, some of those who had been in the compound might have run away, and the desertion affected even some of the armed guards who had been sent as escorts. About six months later the escorting team completed its mission and reported back to divisional headquarters. On paper, the military personnel district had delivered twenty-five hundred replacements to the Fourteenth Division. But the number could in no way be verified. Consideration must also be given to the fact that there had been no food service, living quarters, or medical care on the entire journey. No one could say for sure how many of the *zhuangding* deserted, fell ill on the way, died, or had been let go by the escorts. At the divisional headquarters, less than five hundred men were accounted for. A significant number of them were not even physically fit.

I must further point out that the burden of the war was for the most part on the agrarian population alone. The men seized from their homes, in the manner described above, were sent to the front with little training. Throughout the war the number ran into the millions. Deserters, if caught, were given hasty inquiries and often shot on the spot. Eyewitnesses like myself, students who had interrupted their education to see action, must have amounted to tens of thousands. What is mentioned here cannot be permanently held as a secret. I would not be surprised if such unpalatable details have already found their way into print.

As a historian, I would like to place the above piece of information, vital to our craft as it is, in front of the reader with a question: How should we handle it? Conceal it, or make accusations? Unable either to cover up or to place the responsibility on any particular individual, should I offer moral condemnation of some kind as a conclusion?

The last solution is in fact the traditional method of assuming the Natural Law is in our grasp. To make a moral judgment is, moreover, the easiest way to clear ourselves of guilt. Morality is the world's highest authority, and the last link in the chain of truth. Once it is cited, nothing is negotiable. The case has to be closed. With the above events

I can further say that I was not involved in the replacement escorting. Even though I served in the Nationalist Army, I was always a junior officer. Besides, except for a short period, I was always on staff duty. Once relieving myself of responsibility, I could also join the aforementioned writers in expressing my share of indignation.

But as a historian, I have neither the privilege nor the aptitude to conclude the case in such a manner. My suggestion is to lift the moral ceiling (see below) so that we can reexamine the issue as a technical problem. The way the *zhuangding* were seized in their homes in Chinese history could at least be traced to the Tang dynasty, as the poem "Shihao Village" attests. The execution of deserters after a brief inquiry goes even further back. In the *Book of Mencius,* there is a case dated about 300 B.C. One time Duke Mu of the Zhou complained to the Second Sage: "If I should start to execute them, there would be too many to be slaughtered." Our question is why the ruling class did not discontinue denying the governed their basic human rights during a war of national survival, by which the peasants were supposed to be emancipated. The final answer cannot run away from what has been repeated in this essay more than once: When taxation was placed squarely on the shoulders of the small self-cultivators, the scanty revenue was inadequate to support an efficient government. In those days China was still lingering on in a world several hundred years behind its time. The National Government, aside from putting up a modern facade on the Yangtze Delta, had no effective link to reach the inland peasants. Even in wartime emergency, there was no alternative but to resort to traditional bureaucratism. For this reason I have been constantly arguing that in order to understand modern China, the base line of history should be pushed back at least four hundred years.

China's reaction to the challenge of the West since the Opium War could not be summarily said to be tardy and ineffective. But owing to the tremendous differences in structure and anatomy, it would not be so easy for one side to discard whatever it had in order to take up things from the other side. The steps taken reflected a gradual enlargement of the scope of reform as more contact was made. To Qiying, Western civilization was completely worthless. Prince Gong recognized the necessity to make some adjustment to it. Zeng Guofan and Zuo Zongtang responded to the awakening by building up arsenals and dockyards, or by imitating the West to make the most of the materialistic benefit, inevitably concentrating on military applications. The Guangxu Emperor and Kang Youwei went another step further: they attempted to establish a constitutional monarchy. Given the ocean of difference between the two sides, it was not irrational that the reform had to come in progressive stages rather than one big jump. Later events further show that for China, a reform had to go all the way. To abolish the two-thousand-year-old monarchy was not enough. Parliamentarianism was to no avail. Yet neither could the military strongmen provide a breakthrough. From today's hindsight, leaders of the early republican era acted on wishful thinking. They thought that when a constitution was written and proclaimed, they could command a beast to turn into a bird. They kept an eye on the top, having no perception of what the bottom was like. In reality, the old system had been discredited and abandoned, but nothing new had been introduced to take its place. It was not a surprise that China entered the period of warlordism, since during the era of transition only military power in private hands had the temporary effect of holding things together. But such private military power would lose its influence, too, when it was extended over two or three provinces. Considering all the things that happened, personalities in the awkward age must appear clumsy and inept. Unlike ourselves, they did not have the benefit of history's depth, which would have empowered them to look back into the past to find the pertinent items to justify their own position.

The history of China in the twentieth century can irritate an impatient reader. I, for one, have had such an experience. But after reviewing the reconstruction that ran from the Northern Wei under the Tabas to the Sui and Tang, and the initial turmoil under James I to the final settlement under William and Mary, I have become convinced that for China, not a great deal of time has been lost. What made things look so chaotic and bad was the magnitude of the problem. Perhaps some readers are growing impatient as they compare China with the experiences of Japan and the United States.

They should be reminded that Japan, being an oceanic country, has a historical geography completely different from China's. For one thing, political centralism has never been environmentally required. Another favorable condition was that toward the latter part of the Tokugawa period, both the shogunate and the feudal fiefs were gradually putting their government finances on a commercial basis. Not anticipating a new world trend, the men who engineered the innovations and maneuvers were criticized by their contemporaries. The latter bemoaned the deviation from the traditional good government, as the unorthodox public finance was seen as nothing but a sign of decadence. The most ingenious organizer, Tanuma Okitsugu, received most of the condemnation.[11] The United States developed a virtually empty space in the era of technological advancement. Benefiting from the maneuverability of an immense territory, it still had to go through the growing pains of civil war and many other struggles. But the two cases cannot be compared with China's, whose overpopulation, land scarcity, and congestion of the internal problem with foreign pressure made the situation excruciatingly difficult. It was not a case in which the top leaders could always find the right solutions. When there were no institutional links to reach the bottom layer, peasants, thousands and millions of them, could only be maneuvered by the block. The unsatisfying situation was not to be helped with angry condemnations.

The May Fourth Movement, running from about 1917 to 1921, is an epoch-making event in that the Chinese intellectuals realized that if national affairs became troublesome, they themselves should take the responsibility to provide remedies. Reform, therefore, started from themselves. If we keep these suppositions in view, with the latest developments for added depth, it can be seen that the Kuomintang and Chiang Kai-shek provided New China with a superstructure, the Chinese Communist Party and Mao Zedong provided it with an infrastructure, and the present X-Y-Z leadership (Deng Xiaoping, Hu Yaobang, and Zhao Ziyang; coincidentally, these initials can also be used to apply to Li Xiannian, Chen Yun, and Peng Zhen) is fulfilling its historical mission by working on the institutional links from the top to the bottom. If we do not take this position, we will be at a loss to explain why China in the 1980s differs so much from what it was in the 1920s; nor will we have an answer as to where the new elements that had not existed before came from. Similarly, if we should continue to bemoan and condemn, soon we would not be able to give the May Fourth Movement an adequate interpretation, as it would inevitably appear to be absurd that while the leaders of the movement were all bright and dedicated, their followers and everything coming out of it were decadent and uninspiring.

If we are ever allowed to personify history, we shall see that "it" will not be moved by emotion, or make additions and subtractions to accommodate our likes and dislikes. Furthermore, its tools in shaping world affairs are limited. The kind of positivism derived from such thinking is close to what the Chinese Legalists championed, that heaven and earth would not exist for sages such as Yao and Shun, nor would they desist because of evil men like Jie and Zhou. The vision developed from this attitude makes it possible to see the long-term continuity of history, even though there are minor inconsistencies and fluctuations.

Rarely mentioned, the resistance against Japan from 1937 to 1945 was the largest-scale war China has ever fought; it was also the only war in a hundred years that concluded with a Chinese victory. (Duan Qirui, however, would count World War I.) Until the eve of the hostilities, the annual budget of the National Government amounted to 1.2 billion yuan,[12] at the then three-to-one ratio equivalent to some four hundred million dollars, or comparable to the budget of a second-class university in the United States today. Obviously, Chiang Kai-shek could not have maintained an army, navy, and air force and paid all the expenses of the governmental offices and educational institutions from this budget. What remains unsaid is that with the modern superstructure he had fabricated, he was ruling over an infrastructure that differed little from the days of the late Ming and early Qing, as I myself witnessed in Maguan County in Yunnan. Circumstances dictated that Chiang could only improvise. If there had been better ways, Chiang certainly would have abandoned his inferior approach, as he had no reason to sabotage his own career and deeds. As it happened, it was with his type of spirit—to swallow his pride and hold on—that the Kuomintang maintained recognition and survived the war. Chiang's organization, rhetorically committed to a state of ideal perfection, involved numerous threads of untruth and perversion. Not even emotionally appealing to us, we are, however, to this day unable to name an alternative, based on what we know about China some fifty years ago.

The heritage of this superstructure still exists in China. Many leaders of the People's Republic made their names during the war of resistance. To this day, the Chinese school system bears a deep imprint of the educational program of the Kuomintang. Even the People's Liberation Army is indebted to the Nationalist Army.

We will be even less inclined to praise or condemn when we review the deeds of the Chinese Communists and Mao Zedong if our vision of positivism continues to take hold. Indeed, the most crucial problem for China rested in the farming sector and the villages. The wealthy and large landlords never appeared as the major issue. Nor could they even organize a token resistance during the period of Mao's land reform. The most difficult to handle was the usury and indebtedness among the peasants themselves, whose exploitation extended to each other's neighbors and relatives. Mao's tactic started with the infiltration by the riffraff into the villages to agitate rebellion. Rallying the malcontents to their side, they seized control by violence. Only after the village had been secured would the better-educated Communists move in to start the campaign all over again. Some of the earlier rashness was rectified and disciplinary actions were meted out. Endless discussion ensued. The land was divided and redivided, until every factor was given consideration, based on fairness and practicality. During the process a Poor Peasants' League was organized for the village, which formed a nucleus around which a Peasants' Association was built up. The latter again provided the basis for the structure of a village congress. By then the membership of the local branch of the Chinese Communist Party was open for scrutiny by the villagers. Unless each member was "passed" by a majority vote during the hearing, he was barred from the party. Three rounds of such hearings were conducted to satisfy the grass-roots organizations. According to William Hinton's *Fanshen,* in 1947 partisan workers on land reform from four northern provinces gathered in the Taihang Mountains to coordinate their procedures. The meeting lasted for eighty-five days and was attended by seventeen hundred delegates (p. 263). All this was unprecedented. Mao Zedong never ceased talking on the subject of class struggle. He liked to make use of man's evil character to fulfill his revolutionary goal. His land reform could very well have taken three to five million lives. Unless the historian brings these up, his account is not genuine. Nevertheless, to complete his record, it must be mentioned that Mao provided China with a new infrastructure, the standard of which took the lowest element into account. The approach was completely opposite to the traditional way of erecting a pyramid upside down. With the preparation, later the nationalization of the entire agricultural land and the structuring of the people's communes met little resistance. Seen from today's vantage point, this is not an act of bringing communism instantly to China, but one of preparing the country with a level and unhampered foundation, with which it can be mathematically managed.

Even though the infrastructure is in place, in the absence of institutional links with the top it can be abused by the men in power. As the

"Cultural Revolution" showed, the whole nation could be maneuvered to act on technical nonsense. The reform of the present X-Y-Z leadership is designed to remedy this weakness. A commercialization of government finance on a large scale cannot do away with civic support on the second line and on the third line. Wang Anshi's failure to do so during the Song provided such a lesson for the millennium. The support only becomes effective when private property rights are secured. The Song practice involved a situation whereby "after silk fabrics were converted to money, the copper coins were again converted to wheat. When silk turned into money, the value doubled the original quota of silk fabrics. When the money was substituted with wheat, again the value of grain doubled the quota of coins. With increases handed out in such a fashion, the populace had no place to appeal to" (*Songshi,* Food and Money Monograph). The quotation in reality portrays a self-destructive mechanism within the system. For the Song administrators, however, consideration must be given to the fact that they might have been compelled to do so, for with many millions of peasants under their control, they did not have the technical capacity to keep the accounts in order. This is no longer the situation today, we hope.

When we broaden our vision, a paradoxical factor may help to explain why China held an edge over Europe during the first millennium yet was compared so unfavorably during the last several hundred years. One of the causes was that China would never allow *jianbin,* or the takeover of homesteads of the small cultivators by the large landlords. In contrast, Japan's daimyo appeared in a form of *jianbin.* Land changing hands in seventeenth-century England also constituted a form of *jianbin.* With a thin population over an immense territory, the United States never faced the necessity of *jianbin.* As late as 1862, the Homestead Act of the United States still made 160 acres of land available to an ordinary family at a nominal price. With such provisions, those nations enabled their citizenry to accumulate sufficient capital to support the commercially oriented public finance of the state. The recent conversion of the agricultural communes into a responsibility system by the People's Republic of China, in this particular connection, could also be regarded as a substitution for *jianbin.* While the takeover by the powerful landlords cannot be tolerated, technical concentration of landholding, its rational utilization, and the admission of private capital are the necessary steps to make forced savings from the agricultural sector possible. When those steps are taken, it is a sign that a historical breakthrough has taken place. With the news I feel confident that the Chinese revolution has successfully concluded and Chinese history is being merged with Western civilization. The change of atmosphere is also registered elsewhere. For instance, merely a dozen years ago the Central Intelligence Agency of the United States was less amicable in reporting on China. A journal like *The Chinese Intellectual* could not have existed then, not to mention the publication of Qian Jiaju's article, and my own essay would have been far more difficult to compose, if it had been possible at all.

A note must be inserted here that the economic development in Taiwan does not fall into the scope of my discussion so far. Under Japanese rule, Taiwan's economy was already in part commercialized, with rice, camphor, sugar, tea, and fruits earmarked for export, mainly to Japan. This was of a colonial character, of course. After the island was taken over by the Nationalist Government, the "Land to the Tillers Act" of 1953 became an important milestone, by which the landholding of each household was severely restricted. The excess was forcibly purchased by the government for redistribution to the tillers. But the price was set at two and a half years' yield. Thirty percent of the payment was made with the stocks of the enterprises taken over from the Japanese. In this way the agricultural surplus was compulsorily invested in industry and commerce. In the 1950s and 1960s, Taiwan under the National Government was a beneficiary of large-scale U.S. aid. The economic policy stayed away from the prestigious enterprises and concentrated on exporting the island's cheap labor, realized through labor-intensive products and articles that required secondary work. Under this direction the per capita income rose sharply in a short time. Only in the past few years has Taiwan, facing strong competition from other developing nations in Asia, seriously considered reorienting its economy to enter into high technology. With a foreign exchange reserve well over thirty billion U.S. dollars, an annual volume of foreign trade slightly above that of mainland China, and an urban population that accounts for more than 70 percent of the island's total, Taiwan has so far been making the most of its unusual situation.

The Moral Problem

My version of macro history, unavoidably with a heavy lining of positivism behind it, seems to have a serious shortcoming. It may imply that when anything happens, there must be background factors warranting it. Therefore, if an item makes connections with personalities and events before and after itself, it has already established its long-term rationality in history. Would not this have to mean that only survival counts, and morals and ethics are really irrelevant? But I would say that that is Social Darwinism, and not my purpose for writing this essay.

Macro history develops its emphasis on the collective wisdom, resolution, and morality of the masses. It gives consideration to the historical deeds of a nation or a people. Even though in this essay I mentioned historical personalities, I merely "borrowed" their life profiles to describe the direction of an incessant mass movement; no attempt was made to write their biographies. When I set my mind to present an outline of history to portray the merger of East and West, special caution must be exercised to avoid applying the particular moral concept as a universal standard. The case is similar to the question of how to look at Natural Law. We hope that we will be able to discover it as history gradually unveils itself. This is also close to *Tao* of the Taoist. When it is all-inclusive, no one is capable to give *Tao* a definition.

The diagram that follows illustrates my thought process. The solid portion of the curve stands for the written history of mankind. The skyward arrows represent our aspirations, moral concepts, and religious commitments. But in practice, none of these is entirely fulfilled. Our private aims, self-interests, and tendencies to err, which we have inherited from our forerunners, or what the Judeo-Christians call the original sin, will present a drag, which is represented by the shorter, centripetal arrows. Human history is the result of good and evil, the *yin* and the *yang*. Unable to separate ourselves completely from the past, our morning's work starts from the spot where our ancestors carried it to last night. In the meantime we have to remind ourselves that all the major events in the world happen only once. When we keep this thought in mind to look back on the curve to write history, we may escape from being lopsided.

When I say that the two great traditions begin to merge, it is similar to the case where two spacecraft rendezvous in the atmosphere. What makes it possible is that both are mathematically manageable and therefore can be maneuvered to make a contact. At this moment we can only overstretch a metaphor to explain what is taking place, as such a state of contact is merely being made, and it itself is historically unprecedented.

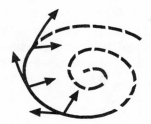

Macro history cannot substitute for historiography of other types, just as astronomy is not a replacement for bacteriology, and macroeconomics, built up from coarse concepts and presented as an outline, cannot be regarded as the sum total of all microeconomic studies. But at this moment it may fill an urgent need. It enables us to see the world in a new perspective. As my essay demonstrates, it brings us closer to the issue of survival.

Of course, survival is the main business of the historian. Only when the issue is given a narrow racial or national concern beforehand, such as that championed by Hitler, to stress that one of them has priority over all others will that appear to be objectionable. If, on the other hand, we read and write history with a primary interest in the survival of the entire human race, the approach already carries a moral platform, even though the word morality may not even be mentioned.

Natural scientists, when they extend their observation beyond what their naked eye can see and their unaided ears can hear, find themselves entering into a new area of experience. Likewise, when writers of history try to lift their moral ceiling and reconstruct the cause-and-effect relationship of major events beyond the one-hundred-year limit, or the maximum life span of the individual, they too arrive at new territory. This does not mean that we have to connive at tyranny and praise corruption. But rather, we may gain a fresh look at how things are developed, different from their images derived from conventional wisdom. Even though the reader may still disagree with the new findings, he can now at least understand why others could have drawn completely different conclusions from the same source materials.

If all I have said is true, that the purpose of the Chinese Revolution is no more than to follow a rising world trend, to substitute a mode of governance based on commercial principles for the older form of management based on agricultural production by the bulk of small self-cultivators so that the nation can be mathematically managed, and that the ultimate goal is not only to increase national wealth but to adapt the entire population to the living conditions of the modern world in order to survive, the movement indeed makes Chinese history merge with Western civilization. A question may arise: What will be the ultimate outcome of this merger?

At this point I must reaffirm my position: My area of study is history. Everything mentioned above is based on events that have already occurred. Only because of the unusual situation in China, the reorganization of the source material to bring it up to date, do I have the opportunity to make a large-scale maneuver on paper. In doing so I have made the most of macro history. But this does not mean that I shall extend my scheme beyond my area of specialization. Items about the origin of the human race, the story of genesis, and the destiny of the universe belong to anthropology, religion, and other areas of study. On the whole they are beyond what the present historical evidence can attest to with assurance. Therefore, in the diagram they are presented with dotted lines, to approximate what Immanuel Kant has said, that noumena differs from phenomena, or things in themselves are unknowable. On the practical side, we might be able to make a few short-range predictions. But again, we can never program the timing of the predicted factors, so that the prediction would also be hazardous. We can only assure the next generation that based on what we know, they should be able to survive. As to how to manage their world, we cannot be more specific than Thomas Jefferson. His motto was "Earth belongs to the living."

This essay carries one suggestion, however. If China makes it clear that its revolution over a century has been successfully concluded and that Chinese history is being merged with Western civilization, much inconsistency and misunderstanding can be avoided. For instance, in recent years China, while praising Mao Zedong Thought, has also condemned the Cultural Revolution, and never lets two or three months go without the government assuring the rest of the world that the country's open-door policy will continue. From the historian's point of view, the confusion could have been avoided altogether. China has endured a protracted battle in history. The account, when presented with full context and in its proper logical sequence, should help to clarify misunderstandings arising from ideological abstractions and win wide sympathy from the nations that are already mathematically managed and from those that are not. The reactions to the pressure of Western influence by many of the nations in the latter group to this day remind us of what China went through decades or a century ago, some of them in the stage of the Boxer Rebellion, others in a straddling position reminiscent of the "Chinese learning for the body and Western learning for the function" of the late Qing. Modern Chinese history provides no direct cure for the situation, but we can at least hope that the example-setting effect may somehow help to find ways to mitigate the agony during the transformation. In this way, for both its self-interest and world peace, China should be able to make a substantial contribution to lessening the tension of the rivalry of the superpowers.

Notes

Source: The Chinese Intellectual (New York) 9 (fall 1986) and Chinese Studies in History, XX:1 (fall 1986).

1. Herrlee G. Creel, The Origins of Statecraft in China (University of Chicago Press, 1970), vol. 1, p. 199n. Cf. Owen Lattimore, Inner Asian Frontiers of China (Oxford University Press, 1940), pp. 252–54, for the development of "marginal nomadism" to "full nomadism," and Cho-yün Hsü, Ancient China in Transition (Stanford University Press, 1965), p. 70, for cavalry in Warring States armies.

2. See Li Ch'ang-shu, Chou-li k'o-hsüeh-k'ao (1909) and Sven Broman, "Studies on the Chou Li," Bulletin of the Museum of Far Eastern Antiquities 33 (1961), pp. 1–89.

3. Max Weber, The Religion of China, trans. and ed. by Hans H. Gerth (New York, 1951), p. 37.

4. Arthur F. Wright, The Sui Dynasty, the Unification of China, A.D. 581–617 (New York, 1978) contains a considerable amount of material prior to the unification. The author's viewpoint is more or less ideologically oriented, however.

5. Denis C. Twitchett, Financial Administration under the T'ang Dynasty (Cambridge University Press, 1963), pp. 97, 112.

6. Mark Elvin's The Pattern of the Chinese Past (London, 1973) makes extensive use of secondary sources in Japanese to arrive at a synthesis. The volume contains misinterpretations, but the section dealing with the Five Dynasties period is by far the best.

7. See Gungwu Wang, Structure of Power in North China During the Five Dynasties (University of Malaya Press, 1963), which explains that consolidation on top enabled the Song to achieve reunification.

8. Madeleine Zelin, The Magistrate's Tael: Rationalizing Fiscal Reform in Eighteenth-Century Ch'ing China (University of California Press, 1984).

9. See Derk Bodde, "Feudalism in China," in Feudalism in History (Princeton University Press, 1956), pp. 49–92.

10. The two sides can be represented by R.H. Tawney, *The Agrarian Problem in the Sixteenth Century* (London, 1912) on one side, and volumes IV, V.1, and V.2 of *The Agrarian History of England and Wales,* ed. Joan Thirsk (Cambridge University Press, 1967 and 1985) on the other.

11. See John W. Hall, *Tanuma Okitsugu, 1719–1788: Forerunner of Modern Japan* (Harvard University Press, 1955).

12. See Arthur N. Young, *China's Nation-Building Effort, 1927–1937: The Financial and Economic Record* (Hoover Institution Press, 1971).

──── 5 ────

Capitalism and the Twenty-First Century

1. Capitalism

1.1 Lacks adequate definition

1.11 It seems that Louis Blanc first made use of the term. Afterward Pierre Proudhon and Werner Sombart also used it. Adam Smith never mentioned it. In the *Communist Manifesto* Marx referred to "the capitalist era." In *das Kapital* he brought up *Kapitalischer Grundlage* which means the "foundation of the capitalistic system." Recently some translators have rendered this phrase to read "capitalism." But never did Marx himself use the English word "capitalism" or the German word "Kapitalismus."

1.12 Blanc, Proudhon, and Sombart were not accommodating. When they mentioned capitalism, automatically it carried a tone of complaint and criticism.

1.13 A term coined in the nineteenth century and designated to summarize the development over several hundred years can hardly be fit to describe the situation nowadays.

1.14 Until the early part of the present century, it remained a "bad" designation. Capitalism was generally regarded to be responsible for the worldwide depression and the unemployment on a large scale. Only after the Cold War between the East and West did it gain respectability. It appears to be "good."

1.2 The three schools according to Dobb

1.21 In his book, *Studies in the Development of Capitalism*, Maurice Dobb, a lecturer of Cambridge University, divides the studies of capitalism into three schools. The first recognizes that when capital-ism takes hold, workers sell their labor power; they have no right to question the disposition of the manufactured goods. This is the Marxist school, to which Dobb admits that he himself belongs. The second school emphasizes the spirit of capitalism. While Max Weber upholds this spirit, Sombart derides it. They both belong to this school. The third school recognizes the technical aspects of capitalism. Capitalism is inseparable from large-scale and long-distance commerce. When capitalism is in ef-fect, wholesalers intervene in the affairs of retail trade.

1.3   Capitalism and China

1.31   We feel that regardless of their own merit, none of these explanations suit the Chinese situation well. While she never experi-enced the kind of sweeping commercial operations that characterized modern Western Europe, China nevertheless saw trade and commerce flourishing on a level exceeding that in Europe's inert Middle Ages. Chinese artisans had been separated from the merchandising of their wares long ago; this did not in one way or another affect the rise of capitalism. Weber believed that the self-denial ethics of Confucianism inhibited capitalism. That is not convincing either. Confucius taught Ran You how to manage the affairs of the Kingdom of Wei. His instruction comes in three steps: The first step is to augment the popu-lation; the second step is to *enrich* the people; the third step is to educate and discipline them. The Great Sage would only turn wealth and noble rank away when they were obtained by unrighteous ways and means. The third school is most prominently represented by Pro-fessor Fernand Braudel. But Braudel lacks system. In his discourse he does not separate East from West. While trying to substantiate his theory he mixes the ancient times with the present. In his confusion he mistakes Hunan for a coastal province. He asserts that between 1640 and 1680   (a period that falls into the reigns of Shunzhi and Kangxi of the Qing) China was conquered by the Mongols.

1.4   Our hypothesis

1.41   We use an inductive rather than deductive method; we put our emphasis on synthesis rather than analysis. For example, Marx indicates that the early accumulation of capital took advantage of slave trade and resorted to military conquests. It was so. But slavery was not a factor in Japan's case. Nor has the recent accumulation of capital by Taiwan involved military conquest. Therefore, we would not regard these as *common denominators* in the early accumulation of capital among all nations.

1.42   Our hypothesis: We recognize that the advent of capitalism is synchronized with a wide extension of credit, impersonal management, and the pooling of service facilities. So, capitalism stands as a kind of organization and a movement. All the three conditions hinge on trust; but trust cannot go very far without being sustained by law. Thus capitalism has to exist within each nation's boundaries. Its fulfillment is conditioned by the free and equitable interchangeability of services and goods (not only large-scale commerce). When a country fulfills these conditions, it becomes "mathematically manageable," which in turn dictates that capitalism become inseparable from money economy.

When this hypothesis is applied to what are generally regarded as "capitalistic" countries we find the aforementioned conditions all applicable.

2. Historical Development

2.1   Venice

2.11   When the Holy Roman Empire and the papacy competed for supremacy during Europe's Middle Ages, neither had total control of the Italian peninsula. Many free cities emerged. While all of them had the potential to turn capitalistic, it was Venice that came to the forefront.

Landholding in other places had a tendency to clash with the more volatile and mobile mercantile interests. In the background was also the confrontation between the pro-pope Guelphs and the pro-emperor Ghibellines. The political split interfered with the free and equitable exchange of economic factors. In some of these cities, the power of the guilds also obstructed the development of capitalism.

2.12   Venice, situated within a lagoon, was characteristically free from the clutch of landholding interests. Its wealth was initially developed from fishery and salt-making. Its salt water was not suitable for manufacture. All these simplified matters with regard to free and equitable exchange of services and goods. Its insulated position further made Venice aloof from the contest between the empire and the papacy. Its merchant marine was at once its navy. When a land force was needed, it chose to hire the *condottieri* rather than maintaining a standing army. The organization of the city state was thus streamlined; it more or less resembled a large corporation.

Before 1400, the peculiar constitution of Venice was already attracting attention. Many commercial laws and modern business techniques owe their origin to this city state.

2.2   *The Dutch Republic*

2.21   The Low Countries, including today's Holland, Belgium, and Luxembourg, were divided into seventeen dukedoms and marquisates in the sixteenth century; they had no experience of organizing national states. In reality, the whole region remained a private estate of the Spanish king.

2.22   In 1567 the lower nobility in this region rioted at dissatisfaction with the rituals proclaimed by the Catholic Church, at a time when the Spanish king tried to advance the doctrine of divine monarchy. Dutch nationalist feelings were fanned when the next year Madrid dispatched troops to suppress the rebellion, only to provoke a general resistance movement. The struggle started in 1560 was to drag on for over eighty years. Not until the Peace of Westphalia in 1648 did the independence of the Dutch Republic gain general recognition.

In the interim the Spaniards, in their effort to finance the war with local taxation, heightened the economic character of the proceedings. Leadership of the Resistance gradually fell into the hands of the burgomasters. Migration to the north increased; manufacturers as well as skilled laborers gathered around Amsterdam and its vicinities.

2.23   After the War of Independence, the new nation found itself secured by major rivers on several sides. It itself was disinterested in territorial expansion on the continent. The tradition of local autonomy was strong within the realm. This combination of circumstances induced the new republic to concentrate on trade, navigation, fishery, banking, and insurance. Tension existed between the maritime provinces and the inland sector; but federation eased much of the problem. The conditions sustaining capitalism cited above found themselves applicable in the Dutch Republic. Moreover, agriculture in the whole region gave preference to cattle-farming rather than cereal-production, making it easier to be teamed with commerce. Historically, agriculture in the Netherlands was never a significant factor weighing down on the advanced sectors of the national economy. Progresses made in industry and commerce, on the other hand, benefited agrarian production with modern techniques such as hydraulic control, artificial meadows, and wind mills.

2.3 England

2.31 In the seventeenth century, the major export item was wool (75 percent to 90 percent), a farm product. National affairs, therefore, had much to do with foreign trade and foreign policy. Frequent contact with the outside and increasing trade necessitated the growth of state functions. If this augmentation of function should be initiated and directed by the throne, it would strengthen an absolute monarchy. On the other hand, if this should be accomplished under the direction of a representative government, parliamentary supremacy would be the inevitable result, and judging from the conditions of those days, the outcome would benefit the mercantile interests.

But contemporaries had to act without the benefit of our vision of historical depth. The Stuart kings wished to strengthen themselves with the discipline of ecclesiastic authority and moreover endeavored to build a powerful navy with extra taxation. Those measures agitated widespread resistance. Pro and con, both sides cited precedents to sustain their argument. In reality, the situation had run beyond the sphere of past experience.

2.32 The country thus plunged into civil war, regicide, republicanism, and restoration. The controversy was not settled until the Glorious Revolution of 1688–89. Only then was the situation becoming clear.

2.33 The turmoil and violence made a general rationalization of landholding possible. Thereafter, agricultural land became more integrated and regularized, its utilization made more suitable for coexistence with a money economy. This facilitated further growth and development. Along with it, the admission of equity by the common law courts bridged the old and new, allowing a body of laws based on agrarian experience to readjust to modern business practices and making the interflow between agricultural wealth and commercial income easier.

2.34 Because the bottom structure had been tidied up, and a general atmosphere of free and equitable exchange prevailed, parliamentarianism became mature. In 1689, the Bill of Rights was proclaimed.

The authority of the throne was curbed and constitutional monarchy became a reality.

2.35   Capitalistic features of the settlement became more pronounced after the organization of the Bank of England in 1694. The Bank loaned to the government 1.2 million pounds. With this national debt the crown was no longer personally responsible for governmental finance. At the same time the arrangement opened the door to deficit financing. The Bank, receiving 8 percent annual interest for the loan, was also authorized to issue sealed bills of the same amount, which again could be loaned to the public for interest. With one pound serving the purpose of two, this new financial institution launched its career of credit inflation.

2.36   The example of England proved that a country with a substantial and strong agrarian background, once restructured, could be mathematically manageable; it could be governed by monetary policies. This is a superior organization. Many undertakings which could not have been attempted in the past now became feasible. In the eighteenth century, country banks mushroomed in rural areas, turnpikes appeared, and insurance business expanded. England began to apply the pressure of this superior organization to other nations which had yet to be similarly restructured.

2.37   Capitalist theoreticians such as James Harrington, John Locke, and David Riccardo all published in England. (Riccardo came from a Jewish family in Holland.)

2.4   Countries facing less resistance in restructuring

2.41   By the eighteenth century, the situation had become clear: the historical development of capitalism (differing from its ideological development) moved from small nations to large nations, from countries with no or little agrarian background to those of substantial agricultural wealth. The population of Venice around the fourteenth century was less than a hundred thousand. The Dutch Republic had a population of one and a half million in the sixteenth century. England saw her population grow from four million to six million when she went through the restructuring in the seventeenth century. In *das Kapital* Marx pointed out that early accumulated capital moved from Venice to Holland to England.

2.42   But the restructuring of these countries tipped the world's balance of power. The relative strength of these nations changed.

2.43   Later restructuring also became easier for maritime nations but more difficult for continental ones. Countries with a history of local autonomy handled the situation more swiftly than nations with tightly centralized controls.

2.44   The United States applied an already worked out system to what was basically an empty space. In many states there was never the division between the common law courts and equity courts. The merger of the two kinds of jurisprudence took place before its own inception. The opening of the inland sector of the United States took the capitalistic approach. Deficit financing worked its way out from east to west, from the Atlantic coast to the hinterland.

2.45   Germany, before unification in the nineteenth century, was divided into three hundred regional estates; they were principalities, bishoprics, and free cities. Therefore, the influence of local autonomy was strong; the Holy Roman Empire had little substance. Under Frederick the Great (toward the end of the eighteenth century) Prussia had already focused on state capital and foreign trade. The unification movement also proceeded by applying economic tools such as Zollverein (customs union) and railroad construction. Historians (see Bohme and Maehl) cite the success of Bismarck as capitalism saddling his horse.

2.46   Japan toward the end of the Tokugawa period (eighteenth and nineteenth centuries) was divided into 265 *han* (feudal fiefs). The lords, called *daimyo,* had exclusive power over finance and economy within each's domain. The agricultural surpluses were handled by merchant agents called *kuramoto;* those were sold only at Osaka and Edo (Tokyo). Therefore, the organization of a national market took place before the Meiji Restoration. The country was already approaching a mathematically manageable situation.

2.5   Countries facing difficulties restructuring

2.51   In the eighteenth century, France's centralization of power was superimposed on a bottom structure notably lacking cohesion. The intendants, appointed by the throne, had to coexist with local nobility and ecclesiastic authorities, whose estates appeared in a juxtaposed manner. The fragmented authorities could also overlap one another; there was no way to make the country mathematically manageable (except by revolution).

2.52   The revolution, therefore, had to be painful and thorough-going. The installation of a new system had to be preceded by a full-scaled demolition.

2.53   The new system broke away from the past. The top authority emerged with the Committee of Public Safety of the National Convention. Started by Danton, it was taken over by Robespierre. After the Thermidorean Reaction, this power fell into the hands of Sieyès and Barras, who later handed it to Napoleon.

2.54   The bottom structure of the nation was also realigned. When the confiscated land was auctioned, gone were the local influences tied to the nobility and the clergy. The new owners appeared as a new middle class. The geographical departments now attained a tidy outlook.

2.55   When the National Convention dispatched *agents national* and *representants en mission* to the provinces, at first to enforce the wage and price control (the Maximum), later to supervise the mobilization of foreign wars, a new system linking the top to the bottom came into existence. Many of those agents later became important in Napoleon's bureaucracy. The proclamation of Code Napoleon in the early nineteenth century could be considered to have given the revolution a final touch.

2.56   Recently, such prominent French historians as Lefebvre, Furet, and Soboul have not been hesitant to say that the French Revolution brought forth capitalism. Communism also emerged with the French Revolution, personified by Babeuf.

2.57   An objective observation would separate Marxist communism from the kind of communism practiced by the Russians and the Chinese.

2.58   Communism in Marx's mind, whether we consider it practical or not, will come as a higher stage of development after capitalism. It is unrelated to economically undeveloped countries. In *das Kapital* Marx mentioned China ten times (or nine times, depending how you divide the passages). On seven occasions he linked that country with India, both being colonies. In other instances, he pointed out the backwardness of China. Never did he suggest such a step as creating communism by bypassing capitalism. I am suggesting, therefore, that we call the kind of communism emerging in Russia and China "Wartime Communism."

3. Wartime Communism Can Imitate Capitalism

3.1   From the above examples it may appear that when a nation maintains an independent position toward outside influence and gets rid of all the factors obstructing free and equitable exchange of services and goods, that country will instantly become mathematically manageable. Actually it is not quite so. In Russia and China, continental influence is strong. Industry and commerce could not easily be established inland. To hastily turn hundreds of millions of peasants loose would create a problem of public safety.

3.2 Nor is primitive accumulation of capital in those countries easy. Marx enumerated the measures of the early accumulation of capital in the capitalistic countries; they involved slave trade, the utilization of slave labor, and the securing of war indemnities from defeated countries. Now these measures are no longer feasible. Nor are emigration (such as Germany, Norway, and Sweden) and floating prodigious loans in foreign countries simple matters. Wartime Communism becomes the last resort.

3.3 Peasants, nominally emancipated, could be enrolled into communes. Tsarist Russia organized communes as soon as the serfs were liberated in 1861. In the twentieth century both the Soviet Union and China followed this example. On the one hand, it solved the problems of population control and public safety; on the other, it facilitated the accumulation of capital. While capitalism moves toward free and equitable exchange of services and goods, Wartime Communism takes the road with collective and compulsory exchange. It disregards cost and profit in individual cases and abridges personal liberty as a whole. Only in wartime or shrouded in a wartime atmosphere could this mode proceed unrestrained. Both the Soviet Union and China isolated themselves from the rest of the world for decades while engaging in Wartime Communism. Their contact with the outside world was exceedingly limited.

3.4 From a technical point of view, Wartime Communism follows the lines of capitalism, with vital revisions. The extension of credit is limited to capital allocation under state control. As a result, a backward country can immediately enter into such areas as heavy industry and high technology (because they are linked with armament) without the normal decades of preparation. Bureaucratic assignments settle the problem with managerial personnel. Service support is handled with less regard to the field situation. When contending private parties are absent, numerous legal controversies disappear, as do issues of insurance and bankruptcy. Crude and unsophisticated human relations are outstanding features of Wartime Communism.

3.5   Wartime Communism created huge economic and management units. A collective farm in the Soviet Union could approach half a million acres. Hydraulic power stations and tractor stations were also noted for their mammoth size. We cannot brush aside their accomplishment. They empowered Stalin to defeat Hitler. Similarly the People's Republic of China, in its first thirty years, received a contribution from the Chinese peasants worth 600 billion yuan (between U.S. $200 to $300 billion). China's national and public capital owes everything to this compulsory saving.

3.6   But this is not a permanent solution. Without any sense of cost-consciousness and little regard to waste, both human and materialistic, it cannot go on forever. The entire setup cannot stand peaceful competition. Once the wartime atmosphere lifts, morale and organization collapse.

4. The Outlook for the Next Century

4.1   Among Communist countries, China was the first to abandon Wartime Communism. After their border clash of 1969, the Soviet Union intended to hit China with nuclear weapons, only to abandon the plan after the United States objected. The visits to Beijing by Kissinger and Nixon followed. The estrangement between the People's Republic and the West gradually dissipated. However, in 1978 Brezhnev contracted a military alliance with Vietnam, promising mutual assistance in case one of the powers should be at war with a third party, unmistakably with China in mind. The next spring Deng Xiaoping ordered the invasion of North Vietnam in order to fend off the threat of a two-front war. After the conclusion of that brief expedition, a wartime stance was no longer needed as far as China was concerned. Subsequently, the People's Liberation Army released one million men from its payroll. Wartime Communism could have been abandoned at this point. But the platform of "imminent war, large-scaled war, and nuclear war" was retained until 1985, when an enlarged plenary session of Beijing's Military Commission finally put it away for good.

4.2   With all this in view, we feel confident in concluding that the aim of China's protracted revolution over a hundred years is to replace her outdated agrarian social order with a modern constitution anchored in commerce, thus rendering the country mathematically manageable. To call the new structure capitalistic or socialistic is of less importance.

4.3   In fact, what was called by Marx "the capitalist era" or "*Kapitalischer Grundlage*" no longer exists today, at least not in the way he perceived it. In the *Communist Manifesto* Marx called for such remedies as the abolition of child labor, progressive taxation, and compulsory education—all of which have long been put into effect by and become the standard of modern Western nations. With the collapse of Wartime Communism, we need no longer feel anxious about the extreme left and the extreme right.

4.4   China, with the world's largest population and a vast inland territory, and burdened with a rigid cultural tradition, has managed to go through the metamorphosis in about a hundred years. This is epoch-making and encouraging. In my recent writings I have emphasized the superstructure of the new nation manufactured by Chiang Kai-shek and the Kuomintang, accomplished during the period from the Northern Expedition to the War of Resistance against Japan. Next is the new bottom structure created by Mao Zedong and the Chinese Communist Party, a product of the land reform. The urgent task still ahead is to provide institutional links between the top and bottom with laws and statutes. People in Hong Kong should have the opportunity to make a substantial contribution to it, because judiciary independence, installed by the British, will not go away after 1997, which should set a good example for China.

4.5   I am in favor of replacing outdated ideology with new historiography. The purpose is not to glorify our forerunners, but to lighten the burden of the next generation.

4.6   Please do not forget, even if China and Russia should become mathematically manageable overnight, half of the world's population is still not. They are still using religious dogma and traditional social norms to obstruct free and equitable exchange.

* * *

Minutes of the Discussion Session

Q What bottom line constitutes a "mathematically manageable" situation?

A I can answer that better by at first injecting a mathematically unmanageable situation. In general, it is a situation that cannot be monetarily managed, such as in China's Ming-Qing period, and today's rural areas of India, where castes and social classes supersede free and equitable exchange. When those obstacles are removed, the situation becomes mathematically manageable. It then can be put under monetary control.

Q Is China now becoming mathematically manageable?

A Now private capital in China is growing phenomenally. If this trend continues, China will become mathematically manageable.

Q It seems too idealistic to expect societies of different backgrounds to reach the same destiny. In your analysis of growing capitalism you have brought up a variety of backgrounds. Can the various nations arrive at the same destiny in the settlement?

A I think it is possible. Now the major problems in the world require the cooperation of many countries to find common solutions. They generally participate in free and equitable exchange. This will create a globe-wide mathematically manageable situation. Bargains will be made. When decisions are reached regardless of ideological orientations and the preferences of politicians, when both capitalism and socialism take mild approaches to problems, worldwide unity should be possible.

Q From your viewpoint, what is the difference between capitalism and socialism?

A There is no difference from a technical point of view. Both systems require wide extension of credit, impersonal management, and pooling of service facilities. Only when private capital carries more weight, when private capital plays a more important role in public life, is the system called capitalism. When public capital takes precedence, it is socialism. It is a matter of degree.

Socialist characteristics can also exist in a capitalistic system. In my home district in New York, my wife and I no longer have children attending schools, but a school tax of over a thousand dollars is assessed on our house so that children from families who own no real estate, one child or ten, can have an equal opportunity to attend school. This means that private property is not free from public obligations.

Q Will there be difficulties implementing the one-country two-systems formula? How will they be resolved?

A As it has not been tried out, I would say that there must be difficulties ahead. For one thing, there is a great confusion in political terminology, which requires clarification. Another thing we can help do is improve mutual trust. I understand, you people are afraid. But don't forget that the guys in Beijing are also afraid of you. Your demonstrations have attracted millions or hundreds of thousands of people, with everyone wearing a kamikaze turban, that is also threatening enough. (The audience laughs.) So, it is of vital importance to establish mutual trust.

Q How would "free and equitable exchange" go with "four things to be insisted on"? [The questioner was referring to Deng Xiaoping's statement that Marxism and Mao Zedong Thought must be retained etc.]

A About 20 percent of China's population remains illiterate. It takes time to reach the stage where the country witnesses free and equitable exchange in its full dimension. It is my personal opinion that the Chinese Communist Party could now discard the designation "Communist," and call itself "the People's Party" or something like that; that would be better for national unity in today's historical perspective. Personally, I have little faith in those outdated political slogans. But I do not wish to cause a problem or start a disturbance with my personal view.

Q Is it necessary for the socialist countries to accumulate capital before proceeding to reform and development?

A It is. Both the Soviet Union and China accumulated capital before reform. Only then could they have the capacity to handle technical problems. As I said, China received a contribution from the peasants amounting to 600 billion yuan. Without it, ideology alone would get nowhere.

Q In China today, some undertakings can now be abandoned; others need to be preserved. What needs to be retained?

A I believe that while imitating others China should continue to work on projects that may not pay off in the short term. Americans [the speaker at this point takes the position of a U.S. citizen] are preoccupied with projects which make quick profit, which may not be advantageous in the long run. I am speaking for capitalism, but in long-term perspective.

Source: A Lecture Delivered at the One-Country Two-Systems Economic Research Institute, Hong Kong, on April 23, 1992. An expanded version appears in book form. See *Tzu-pen chu-i yü nien-i shih-chi* (Lintang Publications, Taibei, 1991), and *Zibenzhuyiyu ershiyi shiji* (Sanlian Publications, Beijing, 1998)

—— 6 ——

Proposals for the Revision of Modern Chinese History

Ladies and gentlemen, when we are involved in a movement in progress, it is not unusual for us to lose the sensation of its velocity. The promotion of democracy and the setting up of a free press in Taiwan is a case in point. In 1984, several copies of the mainland edition of my book *1587, A Year of No Significance* made their way into Taiwan. Several young colleagues of mine from the Academia Sinica—Chang Pin-ts'un, Huang Ku'an-chung, and Shen Sung-ch'iao—wished to turn it into a Taiwan edition. But since the mainland edition of *1587* was typeset in the simplified script, its circulation in Taiwan was already considered to be offensive. The mentality under the martial law in those days was such that anything carrying a mainland imprint was by definition damaging or subversive to Taiwan. Even though this might not necessarily be the official policy, we had to be cautious. Very likely, gossip circulated by persons from questionable quarters would cause trouble. Fortunately, however, we had Mr. T'ao Hsi-sheng, who not only presided over the publication of a Taiwan edition of *1587*, but also graced it with an introduction. That was how the Taiwan edition managed to appear. When you compare our concern and uncertainty of those days—merely seven to eight years ago—with the wide range of opinions expressed by newspapers and journals nowadays, you realize that the difference between now and then is tremendous indeed.

I am indebted to my friends and senior colleagues at the Academia Sinica, without whose encouragement and assistance my concept of "macro history" might have not been able to claim a foothold in Taiwan. At the invitation of the Academy, I attended the Second International Conference on Sinology on the New Year's eve of 1986. My topic, "A Structural Approach to Modern Chinese History," could be regarded as unorthodox by the standard of those days. Furthermore, that trip enabled me to get in touch with senior members of this Institute, including Professors Lü Shih-ch'iang, Lü Shih-p'eng, and Chang P'eng-yüan.

I greatly benefited from this round of contact. The subsequent publication of my book *Broadening the Horizon of Chinese History* was assisted by Huang Chin-hsing, another friend from this Institute. Dr. Wu Ta-yu, president of the Academy, read both *1587* and *Broadening the Horizon* and four years ago granted me an interview. On that occasion he invited me to report to you my personal experience in studying history and conducting historical research over more than a decade. Of course, I relish this rare opportunity. Let me say thank you, Dr. Wu, and Dr. Ch'en San-chin, and my fellow historians. My thanks are also due to the two great newspaper chains in Taipei, *The China Times* and *The United Press*, and to Lü Hsüeh-hai and the Shehui University. If this presentation has any merit or usefulness at all, I must say that I owe it to the promotion and encouragement of all those mentioned and unmentioned. They have created this opportunity.

My concept of maintaining a macro perspective in reviewing modern Chinese history started late; it has been no more than a little over a decade. But as an eyewitness to the unfolding of historical events, I can say that my experience runs longer. It embraces several decades of my life. Broadly speaking, the origins of all the hazards and sufferings endured by my generation must in some way be traced to the greatest upheaval in history over a century. As for myself, I had the good fortune to be able to watch the proceedings from close range. When the war with Japan started, I went into the army. Subsequently, I served as a junior officer for over ten years. I wore straw sandals, ate dog meat, and learned to speak the kind of profanity prevailing among the soldiers. It enabled me to enrich myself with lessons not found in textbooks.

Take a fundamental issue for example: Before we were assigned to battle formations, we fancied that as graduates of the military academy, we should be able to establish the kind of leadership noted for the input of modern thought and technological knowledge of a new era. Only after being assigned as platoon leaders and company commanders did we realize that the ideal was nowhere close to the reality. The actual situation demanded us to line up with the soldiers and to be governed by their group psychology.

The cohesive power that held the troops together was not discipline, nor a sense of responsibility, but social values centered around such notions as "having face" and "losing face." When I served in the Fourteenth Division, there was a captain who kept insulting his men with caustic remarks. One day he would rebuke them: "Shame on you! Tung-t'ing Lake doesn't have a cover on it, why don't you guys all jump into it and drown yourselves?" Believe it or not, his soldiers bore such tongue-lashing remarkably well. But the captain himself, on the other hand, had to prove that he was truly rough-hewn, fulfilling the hero image in popular regard; in combat, for example, he dared to walk bravely toward the enemy line instead of crawling on the ground. The spirit was manifest even when we were in the India-Burma theater, where I still saw tank crews leaving turret covers open within enemy artillery range.

Ladies and gentlemen, here I do not say that this is the way it should be; I merely report what was and how it was. The point is that social power outbids personal influence and organizational principle. Many things happening in China seem to have been decided by a handful of persons at the top; often in reality those men have had to come to terms with the lower level, where hidden strength could be a surprise.

In subsequent years, my teaching career in the United States added a new dimension to my experience. I participated in research projects at Ivy League schools; but my teaching assignments were limited to the second or third-echelon universities. There was a benefit from serving in those institutions. Whether you were a specialist or not, the history departments in most of those schools would require you to handle at least one section of a basic course called *Introduction to Western Civilization*. The requirement forced me to attain a general level of familiarity with regard to the Reformation, the Renaissance, Dutch independence, the English Civil War, the French Revolution, etc. I presume that you all understand this: Having repeatedly gone through the subject matter, the instructor as a rule learns more than the students. At first, to be honest with you, I was not so happy about the arrangement. When you failed to qualify as a top-notch specialist, you turned into an all-around man. As time progressed, however, I began to realize that the assignment benefited me most by forcing on me a macro vision. When you have more opportunities to make comparisons and deductions, you gain a special kind of insight. The linear progression in Western history contrasts sharply with the dynastic cycles in

Chinese history. But this is not due entirely to historical development; in many respects the difference originated in historiography as well.

The errors committed by others may serve as warnings to ourselves. Currently, most historians in the United States give undue emphasis to analysis, paying little attention to synthesis. The deductive method overweighs the inductive method. The approach often ends with criticisms of specific individuals, and particular time segments or events, but gives little thought to the background structure and organization. History written in such a way tends to treat a gigantic topic with a petty vision and gauge a movement with a fixed frame of mind. Thousands of pages of complaints fail to establish the long-term rationality of history. Taking such a passive stance, those historians inevitably lose sight of the positive side of the story.

Almost a half century ago, on New Year's eve of 1944—this is still vivid in my memory—the Chinese troops fighting their way out from Yunnan and those fighting their way in from Burma were about to make contact near the national boundary. I was with the headquarters of the New Thirtieth Division, then stationed at a small Burmese village called Namhkam. With us there were several war correspondents. At supper, we squatted on the ground to eat boiled rice and sauerkraut. Next to me was Harold Isaacs, then representing *Newsweek.* When we started to chat, he told me pointblank in Chinese: *Chung-kuo lao-pai-hsin hao, cheng-fu li-ti-jen pu hao!* (Chinese people are good, those in the government are no good!) At that instant I felt that he was biased. All people were good, but after entering into the government they all turned no good. How could it be? What constituted good? What made it no good?—Those are the unanswered questions. That kind of observation, basically intuitive, was not supported by logic in its reasoning.

But Isaacs turned out to be a historian to be reckoned with. His book *The Tragedy of the Chinese Revolution* remains to this day a classic work.

You must remember General Stilwell. He quarreled with Generalissimo Chiang Kai-shek. Not too long after his recall from China, Stilwell died in the United States. His diary and letters were edited by Theodore White and subsequently released as the *Stilwell Papers.* There are sections in the volume showing the general's admiration and respect for the Chinese people. One day he saw a railroad car moving without a locomotive. It was pulled and pushed by scores of coolies alongside. At a distance, it looked like a centipede, with so many limbs crawling slowly. Stilwell put down what he saw in that day's entry; the theme was the great spirit of the Chinese people. So long as they maintained that spirit, the general decided, China would eventually prevail. The Chinese should feel gratified that the general felt that way. What remains unsaid, however, is who was behind the centipede. Who mobilized the manpower and the resources and directed the war against Japan, which lasted over eight years? Here once again intuition was running ahead by itself, unsupported by logic.

[After this address was published, the speaker discovered his own mistake: The source citing the above episode is Barbara Tuchman's *Stilwell and the American Experience in China*, not the *Stilwell Papers*.]

If you have some time, ladies and gentlemen, I suggest that you take a look at the *Stilwell Papers*. At places it discusses the corruption and mismanagement of the Kuomintang, with concrete evidence, in addition to testimonies provided by Chinese informers. White has blocked out the names of those people. My count shows that on fifteen occasions anonymous Chinese provided secret information to the American commander, exposing the cover-ups of their own government; whether this means that exactly fifteen persons were involved or not I do not know.

The fact is, in those days the Chinese government was in an awkward position; on a defensive position, it was unable to vindicate itself. Now, with the passing of time, we can bring everything into the open. Basically, it was unprecedented and virtually impossible for China to mobilize an army of three million to five million men to engage a formidable enemy on a battleground that extended to every corner of the country in a full-scale war that lasted over eight years. China was not prepared for it; she was not qualified to make such a gamble. From Ch'in-shih-huang-ti to the Hsüan-t'ung Emperor, no such undertaking had even been envisioned. Once the challenge was accepted, the power and function of the government must expand; they could not contract. Worse yet, Chinese society did not have the structural strength to go along; the demand was too much for its constitution. (Otherwise, the Japanese would not have been able to drive so deep into China's interior.)

What could China do? After the initial round of brave action, it was anything goes. Improvisation, evasion, circumvention, finesse, subterfuge, putting up a false front, self-inflicted wounds, and even self-deception, whichever enabled China to hold on one more day—no ruse was too vile, no sacrifice too dear. The torching of Changsha and the breaking of the dike on the Yellow River fit the pattern. No line was drawn between the legal and the illegal, not even what was rational and what was irrational. General Stilwell had not made the point clear: The feet of the centipede did not volunteer to push the railroad car to assert China's indomitable spirit; most of them were pressed into service.

When the society had not reached the level of attainment wherein matters related to mobilization could be mathematically managed, the irregularity and desperate measures could only be expected. To present a picture of good people vs. bad government, the observer only revealed that he himself had not come to terms with the core of the problem.

Those who furnished information privately to General Stilwell could be upheld as morally commendable. Even in wartime, they did not forgo their critical standard. Yet, viewed from a different angle, their deeds could also be condemned as being dastardly. Knowing that they were facing a formidable enemy, those who were captured risked being beheaded or turned into targets for bayonet practice; aware that their own leaders and colleagues were part of the problem, they tried desperately with whatever measure at their disposal, even to the point of trying to ingratiate themselves with foreigners by separating themselves from the common effort of their countrymen. They hardly deserved any sympathy. So, good or bad, it is a tricky question; it all depends on how you look at it.

At this point you may ask me: Isn't there any standard to go by? Is the right and wrong arbitrarily decided by every individual at his own whim?

Let me say this: The dilemma did not start with macro history. It is indeed a problem we are facing today. Those who write memoirs and compile historical works lack a general common understanding. This is a hazardous situation. In order to provide a remedy we must work together to broaden the field of observation and lengthen the depth of our study.

I can say that my whole life is entwined around this problem. In my early days, circumstances provided me with opportunities to observe the unfolding of events from a close range and at the lower level. The later half of my life has been devoted to finding explanations for those events, and to making comparisons with the histories of Japan and the Western world—those endeavors have provided me with a means of earning a living; they are the source of my food and clothing. Therefore, truly I have spent a considerable amount of time studying the entire development. Here is my conclusion:

What has taken place in China in the past one hundred and fifty years is a gigantic reorganization and restructuring process in human history. As such, it should not be gauged with an ordinary yardstick. At the very least, we should visualize this chapter of history as being of equal significance and of a similar dimension to the proceedings working toward China's split during the Wei-Chin Northern and Southern Court period until the reunification under the Sui and T'ang.

The fundamental cause behind such a major turnover is that the traditional society, founded on social values emerging from the simple tenets of man's position above woman, the aged over the young, and the superiority of the educated elite over the unlettered masses, was unable to survive the conditions of the modern world.

The major milestones of history during the late Ch'ing, including the Opium War, the Self-strengthening Movement, the Sino-Japanese War, and the Hundred Days Reform, should not be treated as separate episodes. They are links in a great and protracted mass movement. China's reaction heightened in response to the ever-increasing external pressure, until compulsively the country abandoned the particular type of monarchy that had existed for over two thousand years.

Warlordism in the early republican era was inevitable. Since the old system had already been dissolved, yet a new order still stood in the way of the future, during the interim only private military power could hold things together. Unfortunately, such power could hardly remain effective when extended over one or more provinces. The May Fourth Movement, arising in this transitional period, demonstrated the revolutionary character of the mass movement in the background. The leaders of the movement realized that revolutionary action started with a change of heart within themselves. Only when the educated elite went through such a process of self-renewal and soul-searching was Chinese history guaranteed of its continuing forward movement. Never again would it turn backward.

The story of establishing a new national and social order over the ruins of the old can be illustrated with the Chinese character *li* [立].

The dot and the horizontal stroke on the top stand for the new superstructure, erected by the effort of Chiang Kai-shek and the Nationalists. The organization of a new national army starting from the founding of the Whampoa Military Academy, the prosecution of the war against Japan, the abolition of unequal treaties, and the confirmation of China's position as an independent nation with territorial integrity completed the top of this character.

Under the leadership of Mao Zedong, the Chinese Communist Party worked for the renewal of the nation's bottom structure. The land reform and the rural reorganization provided this horizontal stroke at the bottom of the character. In Taiwan, the Land to the Tillers Act of 1953 had a similar effect.

The focusing on commercial expansion on both shores of the Formosan Strait at present aims not only at the improvement of the standard of living, but also at creating a plural society, in which institutional links function properly to correspond to the requirement between the top and bottom. In other words, they stand for the two vertical strokes in the middle of the character *li*.

Only a social structure based on a system of commercial principles can render all its components mathematically manageable. While everything within this organic body becomes institutionalized, China will be modernized as a result.

Since 1986, I have been trying to publicize this scenario, at first in newspapers, periodicals, and books, and recently with TV appearances. Most of the presentations are made in Chinese; on some occasions the message is delivered in English. I have disseminated the idea in New York, Taipei, and Hong Kong. The prologue of the latest edition of *1587* carrying the same general idea has appeared in Beijing. The overall reaction to my proposal adds to my fervent hope. Suffice it to say that nothing discouraging has blocked my path.

[After this address was delivered, the speaker's three-staged explanation of the Chinese Revolution also appeared in the August 1993 issue and the November 1994 issue of *Dushu*, Beijing.]

Of course, this does not mean that latter-day historians have to comply with my pattern. The most I can say is that, fortunately, living in the last decades of the twentieth century and witnessing the turmoils and conflicts of the past one hundred and fifty years being settled in front of our own eyes, we have the rare opportunity of executing a grand synthesis to close this chapter of history. The freedom of speech opening up in Taipei to the present extent is an indication that wartime conditions no longer exist, and, as an inference from it, China's revolution is coming to its fruitful conclusion. If my words cannot be accepted as final, at least I hope that you would consider taking them as a starting point for further investigation.

This year, on July 8, I published an article in the Literary Supplement of the *United Press*, I invited readers to revise my historiography, on the condition that it be revised forward, not backward. We have now secured freedom of speech. This right must be treasured. The practice of turning everything upside down in a complete reversal— make the white black and black white—is not a proper way of exercising this right. It is still turning the clock backward. Also, lately I have encountered critics saying that what I said about capitalism cannot be verified by Weber, or that it contradicts Marx. To be honest with you, that is the least of my concerns. That kind of review is retroactive.

The following are my suggestions for the future. If we can reach an agreement on the understanding that the convergence of historical causes and effects at this moment provides an opportune moment to sort things out, modern Chinese history can and should be revised. Now is the best time. From my point of view, the following steps can be taken:

First, *we need to gather more information from primary sources.*

My own knowledge of modern China comes in part from what I actually saw and heard. This kind of information is largely undocumented, because in the past, for many reasons, we could not or felt unwilling to disclose it. Yet often those missing links are of pivotal importance to our understanding of an era. For example:

I come from Changsha, Hunan. In the 1920s my father had a friend by the name of Li Tao-k'ai. Appointed magistrate of Chen-hsi County in the west part of the province, he abandoned his post without completing his tour of duty. He returned to Changsha with his family. Later I learned from my father that it so happened that a brigade commander in the area wanted Li's daughter for his concubine. Even the provincial authorities were unable to help. Unless he ran away, he could not have saved his daughter.

Another friend of my father's was Tso Kuo-yung, a descendant of General Tso Tsung-t'ang. In the 1930s he became the magistrate of the Liu-yang County. Once, in those days when banditry was commonplace, the county government arrested three suspects. Tso routinely tried the case and condemned all three to death. They were about to be beheaded. My mother, who was a visitor to the county seat, decided that among the three an old man, with his numb and frightened look, could not have committed the crime deserving the extreme penalty. She took the case and argued with my Uncle Tso the county magistrate. Indeed, she pleaded entirely on her impression of the man's countenance which is not to say that whatever evidence was presented at the trial was by any means more substantiated. As my mother became entangled in the argument Magistrate Tso told her contemptuously: "Such a wretched lot, live for what?" My mother countered him with: "You live for what?" Believe it or not, because of her persistence that old man was finally declared innocent and let go!

If I had not heard it from my own parents, surely I would not have believed that such a thing could happen in the twentieth century. Later, the study of history led me to go through the papers of Hai Jui of the Ming dynasty, in which there are expositions of the trial proceedings involving him as the country magistrate of Shun-an. Ch'ü T'ung-tsu's *Local Government under the Ch'ing* further impressed me that in reality the administration at the county level in China ran consistently through the Ming and Ch'ing periods and then the early republican era with few changes. My own research on taxation and governmental finance during the Ming brought me to the understanding that, with a few exceptions in the treaty ports, China's civil law, penal code, and local administration had to fall back on the background social conditions, and unless a thorough social reconstruction took place, which would usher in a breakthrough in taxation and public finance, the modernization of China would continue to remain empty talk. The two cases I here dig out from my memory are no more than evidence that traditional Chinese society, relying on the crude and simple tenets that men were above women, the aged over the young, and the educated elite superior to the unlettered masses to hold the primitive village structure together, was, as such, unable to face the changing conditions of the modern world. These two cases were not aberrations, I dare say. When you, ladies and gentlemen, come across Lu Hsün's short stories and Shen Ts'ung-wen's narratives, I wager that you will have a similar feeling.

The management of the armed forces during this difficult period is another area in which the true conditions have not yet been brought out into the open. On the eve of war with Japan, the Nationalist Government compiled an annual budget of ¥1.2 billion. Converted to U.S. dollars according to the exchange rate then, this sum was the equivalent of $400 million, an awfully small amount. It does not require a great deal of imagination to realize that utilizing this sum to support an army, a navy, and an air force, and to defray the expenses of construction and education, the administrators were in tight straights. After we were driven inland, the number of factories in the area controlled by the KMT army amounted to 6 percent of the national total, and electric power, 4 percent of the national total. How did we manage to survive? In 1941, I was a platoon leader. My monthly salary as a second lieutenant came to 42 yuan. At the same time, a restaurant charged 3 yuan for a bowl of noodle soup. The bandits in the high mountains offered to buy our light machine guns at ¥7,000 apiece, which was equivalent to forty years' pay of a first class private in my company.

Recently, I published a profile of General Ch'üeh Han-ch'ien, the commanding general of the Fourteenth Division, based largely on my own experience serving as a junior officer under him. Inevitably, the article touched on finance, which in reality, to make a long story short, involved lumpsum payments from the Ministry of War. The division commander nevertheless had to cover the difficulties arising from unfunded areas. The story involved anomalies arising from a mathematically unmanageable situation that could not be flattering to anyone, and I was afraid that the account could cause misunderstandings. Unexpectedly, after the story was published I received a warm letter from the late general's son, Mr. Ch'üeh Ting-cheng. He expressed his appreciation of my reporting which, from his point of view, had faithfully portrayed his father's character. The funds handled by the division had not always been allocated as directed. For that the commanding general took the responsibility. Nevertheless, the subordinates in distress were given relief. All these things went on according to the principle that woe and weal were to be shared and no one was to hold pecuniary gain as an end in itself.

Similar cases, I assume, must have happened everywhere. Yet today when we turn the pages of the accounts of those days, we encounter all kinds of accusations of incompetence and corruption. Actually when one corrupt official fattened himself, scores of others fulfilled their functions, unappreciated by the public. Please understand that the story of the KMT army is not only one of fighting against heavy odds, but also, it is one of seeking the means for survival. If you would take a few minutes to examine the following diagram, you would agree with me that blank charges of corruption and incompetence do not reach the level of understanding as illustrated. You would also realize that because of those charges, many true stories remain untold.

This goes back to my suggestion: We need to broaden the primary sources. Banishing old taboos and cover-ups, we will have the opportunity to produce a body of new memoirs and recollections. Within less than one hundred years, China's social restructuring takes the

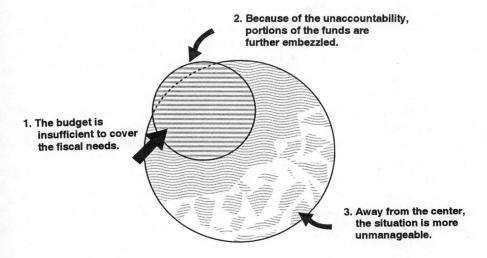

2. Because of the unaccountability, portions of the funds are further embezzled.

1. The budget is insufficient to cover the fiscal needs.

3. Away from the center, the situation is more unmanageable.

form of a thorough changeover that ordinarily would have marked a passage of at least three hundred years. Obviously, the task could not wait until all the tools were at hand, and for every step taken there had been a precedent. I will wager that as you, with courage and straightforwardness, deal with the new source material you will break away from yesterday's timidity and hesitation. With creative spirit, such new source materials should echo the heroism and gallantry that Ssu-ma Ch'ien wrote about eloquently.

Second, *in handling the material we should refrain from making hasty moral judgments.*

Under the "praise or condemnation" principle of traditional historiography, even today's writers feel compelled to turn the personalities they are studying into archetypes of good and evil: K'ang-hsi is a sagely sovereign; Wan-li is a ruler of debauchery. Chang Hsüeh-liang has character; Chiang Kai-shek doesn't.

This kind of categorization barely made sense in the old days, when the ethical standard, along with the social order, remained unchanged over a long period of time. Cast against today's background, when a revolution shakes everything loose to set up a new criterion, the practice is not only inappropriate, but also preposterous.

When Pan Ku compiled the *Han Shu* (History of the Farmer Han), he included in the work a table of 1,931 persons from the ancient times to his day, including legendary figures such as Nü Wo and You Ch'ao, the seventy-two celebrated disciples of Confucius, down to Chao Kao and Li Ssu. Everyone was given a character rating by historian Pan, ranging from the upper-upper down to the lower-lower. The only practical use of this table appears to be the breadth of vision of the author. Similarly, when our contemporaries cannot do away with their moral yardsticks, more likely it is their own field of vision that is being measured.

Professor Ch'ien Mu in *An Outline of Chinese History* indicated that during the period marking the end of the Eastern Han and the beginning of the Tripartite Disunion most prominent historical figures were concerned with moral integrity. Such concerns, he pointed out, were nevertheless inseparable from their own narrowness. At a time when the social order was dissolving and being reconstructed, those persons, confronting a situation to which they must react, yet the true nature of which they could hardly comprehend, fell back on the outdated moral standard for self-justification in denouncing their opponents. A similar situation took place in the early republican era of the twentieth century, when the warlords published circular telegrams to condemn their counterparts as infidels.

The practice of maintaining a rigid moral standard is by no means limited to contemporary Chinese historians. When the chair of the French Revolution was established at the Sorbonne, the first professor holding it, Alphonse Aulard, held that Danton was the hero and Robespierre the villain. His disciple Albert Mathiez turned virtue and evil inside out by portraying a venal and changeable Danton against a conscientious and steadfast Robespierre. Only with the approach of World War II did French historians free themselves from such good and evil archetypes, when Georges Lefebvre, also occupying the chair, declared that moralists praising heroic deeds and condemning cruelty missed the mark at supplying adequate explanations to the events.

When we urge that a hasty moral judgment not be made, it does not imply that we also banish morals altogether and remain scornful toward ethics. What is at issue here is that those elements stand for the highest authority on earth and the utmost truth. When they are invoked, there is no longer any room for argument; the debate is closed. We have seen histories compiled in which a narrow moral gauge cuts a great and gigantic story of human struggle into numerous segments to suggest that Yüan Shih-k'ai was wrong, Sun Yat-sen was wrong,

Chiang Kai-shek was wrong, and Mao Zedong was also wrong. And today Deng Xiaoping is again wrong. Whether the writers have been fair to those leaders or not, they had put a black hole in the history books to begin with.

I mentioned earlier that my comrades at arms wore straw sandals and ate dog meat. They wore rags to endure a war against a most ferocious enemy for eight years. Even though they did not by their own power defeat Japan on the battleground, they succeeded in dragging the enemy to his ruin. Not only is this case unprecedented in Chinese history, it is also exceptional in all annals of the world. The land reform immediately after exceeded the *chün-t'ien* (equal-field system) under the Sui and T'ang in scale and in thoroughness. All these are ignored [by the moralist historians].

At present, the promotion of commerce on both sides of the strait could completely change China's outlook in ten or twenty years, and enable her to become a world power in substance, compared with the colonial status or the position of a semicolony in the past. If historians turn their backs on all this, along with the hardships and distresses suffered by their countrymen at large, and in the sacrifices laid down by the martyrs, but instead only become concerned with such items as who had made a killing during this unusual period, and who had been wrongly persecuted in particular cases, all I can say is that they fit the description [by Mencius]: Their vision is sharp enough to see the tips of feathers; but they miss the sight of cartloads of firewood.

Joseph Schumpeter, historian of economic thought, declared that the ultimate function of historians is to present the proceedings of the past in order to rationalize the footsteps of the present. If writers of history turn out expositions to infer that you should not be standing where you are, or worse yet, after the wailing and moaning show no prospect for the future at all, it is the time to disregard them. There is the saying in the *Chuang-tzu:* Insects who complete their life cycles in the summer do not understand what ice is.

The Chiang Kai-shek Memorial marks its avenues of approach with signs which read "Greater Wisdom," "Greater Kindness," and "Greater Bravery." Clearly, the designer has not ignored traditional virtues. But the word *greater* means "exceptional." It involves a story that under extraordinary conditions unusual steps have been taken to cope with the unprecedented difficulties. That being the case, the historian, in reviewing those past deeds, should not lose sight of those unusual circumstances. The historical figures before us, under both internal and external pressure, often found there were few options open for them to do their jobs. Even though today I bring up my "Uncle Tso"—Tso Kuo-Yung, magistrate of Liu-yang County—it is not my purpose to criticize or condemn him. Knowing that unless he attended to the criminal cases with summary trials, he would not have been able to hold the district in peace and order for a single day. I couldn't imagine what it would be like if I were in his position. All I can say is that I take his case as an illustration of the social conditions in the early years of my own life time.

Third, *reviewing history with a macro perspective, we shall emphasize the impersonal factors.*

To sum up, China's protracted revolution pushed the society ahead three hundred years with an effort that has lasted for less than one hundred years. Its scope and time schedule could not have been engineered or even anticipated by any individual: yet, nor has it come about as a natural phenomenon. At the beginning, pioneers, compelled by circumstances, took whatever revolutionary action was feasible, and in doing so turned loose a number of social factors which had already been stirring. A large scale upheaval was thus set in motion; others plunged in, contributing to the mass movement. All this took a zigzag course, and combinations of forces and splits occurred; only toward the end of the entire proceedings did a rational solution to the problem appear.

What I have outlined as a three-staged settlement, involving the construction of the top, the reorganization of the bottom, and the establishing of the institutional links between top and bottom, are generally in parallel with the process of other nations that have gone through a similar metamorphosis. The details are outlined in my *Tzu-pen chu-i yü erh-shih-i-shih-chi* (Capitalism and the Coming of the Twenty-First Century).

The entire proceedings, indeed, reflect what Rousseau and Hegel designate as the outcome of the *General Will* [of the people or of the nation]. As such, it could not have been dictated by any individual. Often as it happened, leaders of the movement themselves turned out to be reluctant instruments of history.

An example is Chiang Kai-shek. He established the Nanking government and built up a new army and new ministries in line with the modern world. But lacking a similarly new and modern social structure behind them, the Generalissimo had to fill the vacuum, buttressing his own creation with personal striving and manipulations. While others accused him of being a dictator, he in his diary disclosed that he endured all kinds of agony and anxiety, not because he had to confront the enemy, but owing to the internal problems. If historians feel uncomfortable complimenting such a controversial personality, they can at least bring in impersonal background factors in their analysis.

The civil war of 1930 can be taken as an example. At the successful conclusion of the Northern Expedition, the proposal for an armed forces reduction led to a full-scale war. An anti-Chiang coalition enlisted Feng Yü-hsiang, Yen Hsi-shan, and Li Tsung-jen, who were joined by the Left Wing of the Kuomintang, headed by Wang Ching-wei, and the Right Wing, represented by the Western Hills Group. Altogether 1.4 million men were locked in battle for over a half year. At the high point the Feng Yü-hsiang group was able to fire twenty thousand rounds of artillery shells, the kind of fire power that the Chinese army was unable to produce several years later, when it engaged the Japanese. After the fighting Chiang admitted to foreign reporters that his forces suffered thirty thousand killed and sixty thousand wounded, while the Feng-Yen forces sustained a loss of a hundred and fifty thousand men (*The China Press*, Shanghai, October 13, 1930). The loss of lives and property damage for the general population were unreported. This happened only seven years before China's showdown with Japan. The atrocity and excessiveness of the internecine strife has been condemned by many writers.

It serves no specific purpose for historians to repeat the charges. From a professional perspective we need to discourse on why all this happened, as unusual a case as this is. Why were the million-plus soldiers willing to become cannon fodder, so many of them to perish without a protest? Why did the scores of generals and thousands of their subordinate officers, old and young, who could not as a group have been totally unconcerned with China's national interest, take the internal conflict in stride?

I do not suggest that in handling this theme of 1930 we must glorify the combatants and assert that indeed they had a cause nobler than was recognized. I do not even wish to say that the event had been totally inevitable. But since it happened, and the war was fought, it is encumbant on us to abandon such wishful thinking as to what ought to have happened and what ought not. We must, working from reality, establish under what conditions the war of 1930 took place.

First of all, the war does confirm man's dark side. I call it "man's nature" because it is not confined to the Chinese alone. During the English civil war, soon after the Cavaliers were defeated by the Roundheads, Cromwell's Independents lost no time to clash with the Parliamentarians affiliated with Presbyterians, which led to the second civil war. Japan, after the Meiji Restoration, saw the unhappy samurai pressing Saigo Takamori to lead them into an open rebellion. In those cases either the dissolution of a military establishment or the demobilization of an army, when not properly handled, once again turned loyalists into rebels. The fighting over China's Central Plains in 1930 came after the proposal of arms reduction. There was a similarity. It clashed with the professional soldiery.

But it also touched on regional interests. We should not forget that in the background what seemed to be the omnipotent power of China's imperial rule had actually been more phenomenal than real. The elaborate rituals performed in the court merely sustained the bureaucratic discipline. The punitive power of the throne, theoretically unlimited, could only be applied to individuals, and very selectively. As for armament, by tradition no defense installations of substance were established in the interior. And taxation aimed at minimum levies from a huge pool of self-cultivators. The proceeds were both small and inelastic. As a whole, the polity was noted for its passivity and quietism. An artificial balance held the vast territory together, with the economically advanced sectors restrained to keep pace with the less developed regions. Chiang's national government at Nanking, operating from the rich Yangtze Delta, intended to turn itself into a central authority in substance. It upset the tradition and custom. Not surprisingly, it met provincial resistance from every corner before its program went very far.

Strictly speaking, at this time the organization of a new state merely got started. Loyalty to the nation was still an abstract concept, while the status quo, and the fidelity in keeping up one's relationship with others were real and substantial. They affected the livelihood of every individual. The sense of comradeship and the superior-subordinate relationship in the armed forces were anchored on the latter's solid ground. Ladies and gentlemen, even numerous Americans until the Civil War—not much more than a hundred years ago—still projected patriotism as allegiance to the individual state, which took priority over the Union. May I remind you of my experience at joining the army, which I mentioned earlier—the cohesive power within the battle formation, as I discovered, did not co-exist with modern concepts of duties and responsibilities, but with traditional social values, among them personal loyalty and personal strength.

Up until the 1930s, China's literacy could be as low as 10 percent. The surplus population in the rural areas either entered into the various kinds of armed forces or turned into bandits; not too many outlets were provided by the society. This was a contributing cause of the civil war.

To pursue the topic of impersonal factors further, I wish to indicate that the fighting over the central plains in 1930 should not be given a totally negative rating. Before the war, the so-called national army was comprised of four army groups, not counting Chang Hsüeh-liang's Northeast Army. Some of those maintained their own foreign contacts. Feng Yü-hsiang's Second Army Group (the Northwest Army) was allied with the Soviet Union. The Northeast Army dealt directly with the Japanese. This was not permitted to happen again after the conclusion of this war.

Chiang Kai-shek's arms reduction program had called for limiting the national army to sixty-five divisions, with a maintenance cost not to exceed 40 percent of the national revenue. Had it carried, the troops would have to have been professionalized and upgraded for quality. Few had given thought to the fact that such an arrangement would not have been practical under the existing circumstances. Without the needed defense industry for its maintenance, or the social environment to assure adequate logistical support, such a lean army, although maybe more efficient by itself, would more than ever become a foreign body to the society, that is to say, it would stand little chance to succeed if it had to operate in the countryside over a sustained period of time.

The war of 1930 concluded with a partial fulfillment of Nanking's centralization. Chiang's base of operation in the lower Yangtze valley was secured. With it the government proceeded to abolish the *likin* (an inland transit tax and take up tariff autonomy. When Chang Hsüeh-liang's forces entered north China, he was made deputy commander-in-chief. All this effected a compromise. The territory actually placed under Nanking's control extended to the south of the Yellow River, roughly close to the 35th parallel. Nominally, the central government took over the taxation in four northern provinces. But a recent article by Ning Cheng-en gives evidence that in reality the special commissioner in charge of it was nominated by Chang Hsüeh-liang before being appointed by the Ministry of Finance (*Chuan-chi wen-hsüeh*,

No. 331, December 1989). The taxes on mines, excises on cotton yarns, tobacco, matches, etc., together with the proceeds from stamp taxes, were collected by this official. He delivered portions of them directly to several military leaders previously belonging to the Feng-Yen coalition who were now pledging their loyalty to the central government, yet in dealing with the latter still had to go through Chang Hsüeh-liang's intermediary.

Thereafter Feng Yü-hsiang never again was in a position to challenge the central leadership. His former subordinates such as Sung Che-yüan and Han Fu-ch'ü nevertheless maintained control over territories of provincial size. Nor had Yen Hsi-shan and Li Tsung-jen abandoned their former posts and autonomy. But their potential and influence were much reduced.

In this way a new balance of power took effect. The central government, in direct control of some thirty divisions of crack troops referred to by foreign observers as "Chiang's Own," subsidized the provincial armies who no longer appeared as rivals. Beyond those was still a third ring of battle formations which, while refraining from openly defying the central authority, were very much on their own. The total strength of the armed forces of various kinds was estimated to be 2.3 million men, having expanded from the 1.4 million before the Northern Expedition. Several years later, the Central Army further extended its influence in the southwest provinces while carrying out its annihilation campaign against the Communist forces. This new balance stood until the war with Japan.

We find the above proceedings in certain respects similar to the conditions of the unification under the T'ang and Sung. The necessary fluctuations suggest that technically, certain groundwork must be done, especially in the area of finance. The gradualism of the unfolding of events, having tested the patience of the contemporaries, cannot be eliminated from history. On the other hand, this round of development makes lots of sense when seen in the context of the subsequent war against Japan. China's social backwardness, combined with an abundance of manpower, had dictated a strategy of inviting the enemy into the quagmire and bogging him down with a protracted campaign, which could not have been executed by an army of quality but lacking in numbers and depth.

Chiang Kai-shek fabricated a new superstructure for China. Owing to geographical and historical factors, he could not at the same time impose quality controls to tidy up the bottom of his creation. To drive home the point I suggest that we give more emphasis to the impersonal factors.

Fourth, *maintaining a macro perspective, we must be prepared to differ from the vision of those who made history.*

The episode we have just discussed indicates that when facing a major turning point in history, there is a limit to what individuals can do. Chiang Kai-shek had a plan to reduce the Chinese army to a force of eight hundred thousand men, organized into sixty-five infantry divisions, eight cavalry brigades, sixteen artillery regiments, and eight regiments of engineers. It was never put into effect. Until the Sian Incident, he still hoped that the war against Japan could be put off for three to five years so that the build-up of the Chinese air force would have made a difference; nor was this aim achieved. In the end, war was triggered by time and circumstances against his wish.

You know what, ladies and gentlemen? When I keep on saying that Chiang created China's top structure and Mao rearranged the bottom structure, I cannot say that I am always free from self-doubt. It involves so much; and I am entirely on my own. However, last year I obtained a stack of source material from Mr. Chin Hsiao-yi, curator of the Palace Museum. Included in the material are excerpts from the Generalissimo's diary. One of the entries is of particular interest to me. Let me read it to you. These are his own words: *In making those decisions, often I found it necessary to prescribe the fiercest medicine that produces the most violent side effect. This is a gamble, the last resort, and our only chance.* (dated February 5, 1944)

He quoted *Li Chi* (The Book of Rituals). The passage confirms my thought that he proceeded to war without overall planning. Ordinary methods would not work. There was no logic to go by. He could only plunge in with his intuition and impulse.

This is by no means to downgrade the Generalissimo's accomplishment. In a broadcast last November at the CTS (television station), I mentioned that during the war I was a second lieutenant, at one time in command of thirty-six soldiers. The burden caused many sleepless nights on my part. I do not know how the Generalissimo dared to hold together millions of such soldiers and to engage Japan in war for eight years. I have to stretch my imagination far and wide to fathom his capacity and fortitude.

But both Chiang Kai-shek and Mao Zedong were active in the early part of the century; by the middle of the century they had already seen the high points of their career. Moreover, too close to the events, they could not have maintained an unswayed and unprepossessed vision such as ours. Compared with them, we have an advantage of several decades of added historical context to conduct in-depth studies, so that it is our privilege to produce an overall summary.

In the twentieth century, China has been facing a two-pronged problem. There is the immediate problem of survival. She needs to build up her modern armed forces to assert her independence, and to start with new fiscal and taxation systems to invite foreign assistance. Such tasks cannot wait. The resources are not there; there is little choice. As stated, the war on the central plains in 1930 was not an annihilation campaign. It was intended only to take over the opponents' potential. The reliance on the *pao-chia* (village self-governing units) system for conscription and service and supply again marked a compromise to make the most of the existing social order.

But there is another difficult job for China to perform. Unless the society is reconstructed, the country cannot provide itself with fresh vitality and energy. It cannot achieve self-reliance.

Even one of the Herculean jobs could have engaged any individual for a life time. Circumstances now dictate that neither can be postponed; they have to be taken up simultaneously. In the end two kinds of mass movement are incited. Technically they are in conflict; yet in terms of overall purpose they are mutually complementary. Two kinds of revolutionary theory are produced; their application leads to two types of organization and two sets of foreign policies. The campaigns of the KMT and CCP overlap each other yet they come out in a sequence. This explains why they had to battle each other and then become reconciled several times.

The way Chiang built up China's superstructure has been recognized by Mao. In *Strategic Problems of the Chinese Revolution* Mao Zedong mentions that the KMT "has reorganized its army—this differs from the armed forces of any historical dynasty"; "moreover, its total strength exceeds the quantity of the armed forces of any dynasty in Chinese history; it is also more numerous than the regular army of any nation." Inadvertently, with these few words Mao is giving his opponent Chiang Kai-shek a great compliment. Once such an army of unrivaled size is created, there must be a government managing it. This superstructure, even though it will not go by the world's standard, is an innovation, regardless. In this way Chiang Kai-shek has assured himself of a position in history with his creative work.

In 1987, the CCP published *The Annals of Major Events of the Chinese Communist Party*, with a first printing of fifty thousand copies. In the eight years of war against Japan, this book recounts, "The total deaths and wounded of the Chinese, civil and military, exceeded 21 million. The armed forces under the command of the CCP suffered more than six hundred thousand casualties. The number of deaths and wounded of the civil population in the Liberated Areas counted six million." While not specifically spelled out, the *Annals* admits that the total casualties of the KMT forces together with the population under their jurisdiction must have come close to fourteen million.

In the absence of a further sense of hostility between the two camps, we can now bring forth the true story for a general review. The success of the CCP came in part from its shrewd maneuver of taking the KMT's setup for cover. It did not organize a top structure of its own. Throughout the war it stayed away from large cities altogether. Urban culture was deliberately avoided. Large battle formations were coordinated with radios. In this way the partisans could concentrate on manufacturing a bottom structure for the new society. During the land reform some three million to five million lives were sacrificed, according to the specialists. Nevertheless, the new village order was constructed from the very bottom upward. As such, it was also unprecedented in Chinese history, and the design, aside from the method of executing it, merited originality.

Participants in the land reform movement disclosed that in each village the Poor Peasants League stood as the embryonic nucleus of the new order. It presided over the organization of the village Peasants Association, which in turn took charge of convoking the Village Congress. Membership of the CCP's local branch had to be reviewed by these three layers of organizations. Unless approved by all of them, a person found his status as a party member in jeopardy; very likely he would be sent to a reform school for rectification.

We realize that this happened more than forty years ago, and even in those days, manipulation of public opinion took place. But in the background until then the cell structure of rural China had never departed from being molded to run errands, and to take orders from government officials. Imperfect as it was, the new bottom structure from this point on separated itself from the traditional type. Today the agricultural

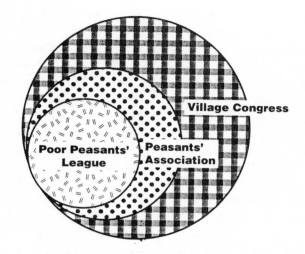

commutes are no longer operative. But when the current round of economic reform started to move, rural industries made the first stride, indicating that the vitality on the lower level had not dried up. Today the CCP has about 50 million members; of them perhaps 20 percent still remain illiterate. This stands for a formidable fact—that the party membership is a profile of the nation. I do not take seriously the news circulated by those who have recently come out from the mainland that the leadership of the Chinese Communist Party is on the brink of collapse.

What we can feel assured of is that, in the long run, the mass movement represented by the CCP, with its accompanying social conditions, cannot be a direct move toward what Marx and Engels designated as communism. Liu Shao-ch'i has said that communism represents the idealist high point of mankind. For China, it wouldn't make sense after basically realigning agricultural production, and barely moving toward the organization of industry and commerce, to consider freezing the division of labor at the present level. We can, however, characterize the general activities of mainland China from 1949 to 1979—altogether thirty years—as *wartime communism*. In these three decades the nation insulated itself from outside contact, waged foreign wars in all directions, and decreed that its citizens be clad in drab blue garments and eat at common kitchens. It achieved one thing: Accumulation of national capital. According to a general estimate made by an agency under the State Council, during those years the state purchased foodstuffs from the countryside at low prices, and at the same time distributed them to the urban population also at low prices to keep wages low. In this way the accumulated capital exceeded ¥600 billion.

[During the presentation the speaker indicated that he could not cite the source offhand; he advised the audience to refer to his publications. The item appears in the *Newsletter* of the Institute for Rural Development of the Development Research Center, under the State Council of the PRC, Supplement, No. 21 (December 1986), p. 5.]

Because of this, China can proceed with the present economic expansion without foreign subsidy. Whether the current program should be called capitalism or socialism is not a vital concern of ours. Not being ideologists, we are not so concerned with nomenclature. A modern economy is hinged on these three conditions: One, wide extension of credit; the capital is always put to work. Two, impersonal management; talent must be utilized and the business administration is unencumbered by ownership. And, three, pooling of service facilities; this involves transportation, communication, insurance, legal services, etc. We can see that currently the CCP is striving to achieve these. So long as they are at it, what they carry on as the *Four Points That Must Be Insisted On* does not bother me. As historians, we are primarily interested in history's continuity and fullness; this may have to differ from the logic of those who are involved with making history.

[After the presentation of this address, the speaker has modified his position considerably on this point. Now he believes that the CCP may have to drop the word *Communism*.]

Writing a biography differs from compiling a history. Chiang Kaishek, Mao Zedong, and Deng Xiaoping may have remained adversaries to one another personally. Yet in developing history's continuity and fullness we see them in a relay movement. It must be so. Otherwise, would not China in the 1990s remain exactly what she used to be in the 1920s, or even be moving backward?

As said, in developing this thesis I cannot always feel free of self-doubt. But let me quote a historical personality of stature. The following comes from his own writing: *Where there is failure, there must be success. Where there is success, there must also be failure. Today's bad cause might produce a felicitous effect tomorrow. On the other hand, what we hold as bad consequences at present could have gener-*

ated from the sources that at one time we would have regarded as benign. Adapting such a view, we will see all things roving in an eternal contradiction. No end result is absolutely good.

The author of this passage sees a changing history over time. It is close to what the Leftist writers refer to as dialectical materialism. Ladies and gentlemen, can you imagine who wrote these words? The answer is Chiang Kai-shek. The passage comes from his diary, dated May 31, 1944.

You see, at least in this instance we all agree: Historiography varies with our frame of reference.

This about concludes what I want to say. I still remember my first trip to Taipei, in 1985, after an absence of thirty-five years. On that trip I met a colleague who challenged me: "Well, the way you talk, you know all the causes and consequences. Won't that allow you alone to do all the writing and publication? My specialty is the Sino-Japanese War of 1904 1905. If I listen to you, would I let you talk me out of a job?"

"Absolutely not," I responded to him. How could I? All I am calling attention to is a time element in historiography. At this crucial turning point of historical development, there is an unprecedented opportunity for a synthesis. I call my craft *macro history*; it is an imitation. Economists lay down a few general principles about market mechanisms and the circulation of money and call the body of knowledge macro-economics. It is superficial; it does not go into the details. Such a preliminary study needs to be verified by research with a micro vision. Marco-economics cannot deal with employment; it does not handle price indices; nor does it conduct a survey to test the consumers' psychology. Hopefully, my general outline of history will provide a starting point for high school students and at most, a reader for freshmen in colleges. It is to be revised with further analysis.

Even if any young scholar should adapt to my vision in toto, all he needs to bear in mind is that behind him there is a violent historical background that heaven and earth change places. From 1949 to the early 1950s, some two million people migrated from the mainland to Taiwan. This alone is unprecedented in history.

I repeat, we have gone through a difficult time reminiscent of the Wei-Chin Northern and Southern Court period; in front of us is a period of Renaissance and reconstruction, similar to the rise of the Sui and T'ang. For historians, this is a golden opportunity. We should not let our unhappy encounters in personal experience block the view of this great period. That is why I suggest introducing *macro history*.

Thank you, ladies and gentlemen.

Source: Address to the Modern History Institute, Academia Sinica, on November 5, 1992; translated from the *Newsletter for Modern Chinese History*, no. 15 (March 1993), published by the Modern History Institute, Academia Sinica, Taipei.

——— 7 ———

A New Direction for Modern Chinese Historiography

Abstract

1. A hundred years ago Chang Chih-tung announced: "Chinese studies to build up the foundation; Western learning to provide its usefulness."

2. In terms of modern historiography, the above order can now be reversed.

3. What happened in China during the past century seems to be chaotic and irrational. But if we link the theories of the following Western thinkers together, we can see them develop into a definite pattern. China has gone through a round of bodily restructuring. Since this is beyond her own historical experience, an explanation has to draw axioms from the sources.

4. I suggest that we look into the following:

> Jean Bodin [1530–96] (for his discourse on the process of converting a dynastic state to a national state)
>
> Niccolo Machiavelli [1469–1527] (the paramount importance of public interest, especially in a critical time for survival)
>
> Thomas Hobbes [1588–1679] (the need of an omnipotent authority to create order from lawlessness)
>
> John Locke [1632–1704] (labor theory of value, the principle of tacit consent, the right to emigrate by dissidents)
>
> Karl Marx [1818–83] (his theory critically reviewed by Joseph Schumpeter and Joan Robinson)

Adam Smith [1723–90] (the importance of free trade, the utilization of commerce to establish a governing system)

Jean Jacques Rousseau [1712–78] (freedom in the context of public well-being, the idea of the general will)

G.W.F. Hegel [1770–1831] (general will further sharpened, logic of historical development beyond individual's personal intention, that a constitution can be discovered but not manufactured)

5. Armed with the above notions, we shall see that when China entered the twentieth century she was still a dynastic state rather than a national state. Her top structure relied on the omnipotent power and the mystic quality of the throne. Remaining on the bottom were many hundreds of millions of small, individual self-cultivators, from whom the bulk of the taxes was collected. In between the top and the bottom was the civil service bureaucracy; the criteria for admission to its membership were limited to literary skill and a pledge to the traditional code of personal ethics.

None of the above survived the protracted revolution. The monarchy was terminated in 1912 with little difficulty. The bureaucracy had been undermined even earlier: with the abolition of the civil service examination in 1905 it had already lost its raison d'être. Finally, the pattern of landholding also had to go. The small parcels of land simply would not permit the accumulation of capital, regardless of whether there was a tenancy problem or not.

These conditions explain the country's violent upheavals in the past century. The restructuring was preceded by a total demolition. Its immediate effect fell into Hobbes's description of "everyone against everyone."

6. In retrospect, the period of warlordism and anarchy was inevitable. The entire country had lost its balance; no adequate laws were applicable. The early constitutions were destined to fail because they were hastily manufactured and bore no connections with the Chinese society which they had the ambition to govern.

7. Leviathans appeared. Chiang Kai-shek and the Kuomintang (KMT) created a new superstructure for China, manifested in a national army, a legal tender, a conscription law, and a modern form of a central government that was recognized by foreign powers. Calling Chiang corrupt and incompetent, the critics have ignored a basic fact: All Chiang possessed was a facade; he did not have the needed social forces in support.

Mao and the Chinese Communist Party (CCP) were neither Communists in a Marxist sense nor merely land reformers. They uprooted China's bottom structure and started things anew. The justification was survival. Only during the period of land reform did the field workers discover that land scarcity and overpopulation had reached such a stage that drastic measures had to be taken.

Chiang and Mao were personal enemies. But in the long-term development of Chinese history they also formed a partnership of a kind. The mass movements led by the KMT and CCP, while overlapping in certain time periods, in fact carried out a relay that changed China's destiny.

The positive effects must be taken into account. Even during the period of the Cultural Revolution when the entire Chinese population were clad in blue and ate at communal kitchens, an accumulation of national capital of ¥600 billion was realized. This provided a base for Deng Xiaoping's economic reform.

In Taiwan, Chiang and his followers carried forth the "Land to the Tillers Act" of 1953. With massive American economic aid, this milder program made it possible to achieve a breakthrough without following the atrocious road taken on the mainland.

8. Now that the deeds have been made irreversible, the historian is left no choice but to present the facts in their natural sequence without overt praise or condemnation. He must nevertheless stress:

While wartime communism has taken place, the word "communism" is a misnomer in connection with the proceedings described above. Ultimately, the long-term rationality of the CCP's program is to establish the interchangeability of all the components within China's bottom strata, using the labor theory of value as a tool.

Accepting the arbitration of history, we believe that for all these there is a general will behind the proceedings.

Its purpose is to render the country mathematically manageable. New laws have yet to be enacted that will enable the country to be fully monetarily managed. Whether the program is called capitalist or socialist is relative, and, ultimately, it will be decided by economic realities.

Broadly speaking, the restructuring follows Western precedents. It should enable China to coexist with the rest of the world.

9. In the days ahead, the quintessence of traditional Chinese culture should have its place in the functioning of the newly restructured coun-

try and society. For that I would like to particularly suggest that the following items of China's cultural heritage be given emphasis in the curricula of grade schools and high schools:

- humanism
- the tenet of self-restraint and mutual deference, and, family cohesion, thenceforth from nationalism to cosmopolitanism.

Source: "Western Studies to Build up the Foundation; Traditional Chinese Studies to Provide Its Usefulness." This is an outline of a paper presented at the National Museum of History in Taipei, December 12, 1995. An expanded version appears as *Xinshidai di lishiguan* (Commercial Press, Taipei, Hong Kong, Singapore, Kuala Lampur, and Los Angeles, 1998).

8

A Second Look at the Year-End Revenue Data in *Ming Taizong Shilu*

Part One

The *Veritable Records of the Ming Dynasty* is a collection of official papers of considerable comprehensiveness. The current photolithographic edition issued by the Academia Sinica contains 133 volumes, plus another fifty volumes of correctanea and appendices. The combined contents amount to about one-third of the newly issued *Twenty-four Dynastic Histories*. In the West, only the *Calendar of State Papers* of England, generally falling into the same time period and of a similar bulkiness, can be considered to be in a comparable range.

But the *Veritable Records,* aside from reproducing important decrees, edicts, memorials, and petitions in full or in excerpts, also carries dialogues between emperors and courtiers, descriptions of palatial life and ceremonies, brief descriptions of battles that involved the imperial army, and notes of unusual astronomical phenomena and weather conditions, not all of which are found in similar Western chronicles.

In the *Veritable Records,* national financial data, however, appear irregularly. The figures usually appear within the related documents. An outstanding exception is the Year-end Revenue Summaries of the Yongle Period.

The Yongle Emperor, or Taizong of the Ming, reigned for twenty-two years from 1403 to 1424. The complete annual summaries are preserved intact in the *Veritable Records*.

Each summary starts with population and household figures, then carries land tax in kind—stated in the number of piculs of grain—followed by cloth, cotton, cotton wadding, silk floss, and paper currency paid in the number of *quan*. The list continues with gold, silver, copper, iron, lead, cinnabar, and cowrie shells. Two important commodities, salt and tea, come up next. The income from military farming, also stated in piculs of grain, is separated from the regular land taxes. Concluding the summary is the number of horses owned by the government.

After 1409, the grain delivered in Beijing is quoted as a separate item. After 1515, copper coins in the number of *quan* is added. The Yongle Emperor seized a northern portion of today's Vietnam and annexed it as a Chinese province called Jiaozhi. Its tributes in terms of silk fabrics, varnish, sapanwood, kingfisher feathers, and paper fans regularly appear on the list starting in 1416. There are cases when an item or two is missing from the list in a particular year. But on the whole the summary is maintained with remarkable regularity. No such summary ever appeared in the *Veritable Records* before the Yongle period; nor was it continued thereafter.

Taxation and governmental finance can be studied as a cross-section of the country and society under examination, since its narration inevitably touches on the superstructure: in other words, it is directly connected to the regime's capacity and its policy orientations. Following the data downward, the examiner furthermore sees the general conditions of the populace. Moreover, tax collection and fiscal management are themselves essential institutional links between high and low, top and bottom. Traditional Chinese historiography rarely presents such a full-dimensioned set of data. If we take the numbers seriously and scrutinize them with lateral information found elsewhere, we may be able to attain a general view of the earlier years of the Ming dynasty; moreover, the findings can lead to the appreciation of certain social and economic features of traditional China not too far removed from the present.

In this study seven items are sorted out for examination.

1. Grain in National Land Tax Quota

During the Ming dynasty, land tax was apportioned to the provinces, prefectures, and counties on a permanent basis; but adjustments were made from time to time. The amount was payable in husked rice or winter wheat depending on the produce in each locale. The unit was the "picul," a dry capacity measurement of about 107.4 liters. The reign of Yongle, falling into the early and unsettled phase of the dynasty, saw some significant readjustments that affected the national total. The following chart is a graphic presentation of the figures listed in the *Veritable Records.*

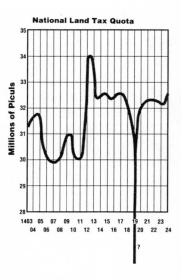

National Land Tax Quota

As a whole, the annual proceeds fluctuated between about 30 million and 32.5 million piculs. An incredible exception is the case of 1419, when the national total fell below 23 million piculs. A check of the contemporary hand-copies of the *Veritable Records* further discloses that one copy specifies the total to be 22,248,673 piculs and another 22,428,673 piculs. The discrepancy occurs as the third and fourth digits are reversed, but the unusual low remains.

Since the grain quota represented the dominant portion of state revenue, a sudden drop of close to one-third of the annual total and the subsequent prompt recovery the next year would be inconceivable. Scholars suspected that there had been a clerical mistake which made the first digit, supposed to be "three," appear as "two"; all this could have been caused by omitting only one stroke of the Chinese character for "three." And it was quite possible due to the deteriorated conditions of the original document, that had confused the copier. When a group of Japanese scholars compiled the *Annotated Food and Money Monograph of the Ming Dynasty History* (*Minshi Shokkashi Yakuchū*) under the editorship of Dr. Wada Sei, they simply restated the 1419 figures to be 32,248,673 piculs without further explanation, a correction that has since then been accepted by learned circles.[1]

As for the lesser ups and downs on the curve, apparently they actually happened. During the reign of Yongle partial readjustments of the land tax quota took place often. For instance, between 1405 and 1406, the emperor had on several occasions written off the assessments on households who had either died out or absconded, affecting a total cultivated acreage of 7,345,097 *mou.* (A *mou* is close to one-sixth of an acre.)[2] Such write-offs offsetting augmentations explain the fluctuations on the curve, usually within 3 percent of the annual average.

The origin of the drastic surge, culminating in an all-time high in excess of 34 million piculs in 1412, can be traced to the annexation of Jiaozhi. In 1408, the emperor is known to have instructed Huang Fu, the civil governor of the new province, to fix the tax quotas for its counties and prefectures.[3] The extraction of foodstuffs was one of the reasons that led to the general uprising of the Vietnamese, however. In 1413 Yongle retreated, circulating a general order in the territory to effect "lightened taxation and reduced corvee labor."[4] The steep rise and significant drop that followed it on the national record must have reflected the doing and undoing, then and there.

In history, Yongle was a vigorous and despotic monarch. No emperor of the Ming dynasty could ever again match his vitality and arbitrariness. Riding on the early surge of imperial power, he ordered the invasion of Vietnam, personally led the expeditions to the Mongolian desert, constructed the city of Beijing, executed the modern Grand Canal, and dispatched the eunuch admiral Zheng He on six overseas missions. All these projects incurred exorbitant expenses. Yongle's excessiveness was such that when his Minister of Revenue, Xia Yuanji, petitioned against an expedition to Mongolia on account of logistical difficulties, he threw Xia into prison. The hapless minister did not regain his freedom until Yongle's death in 1424.[5] Nor was the emperor always bound by his own law. By Ming statute, artisans were liable to be called for thirty days' unpaid service during the year. Records show that during the Yongle period the construction of the palace in Beijing retained those workers over years.[6]

But the reign of Yongle ended with revolt in Vietnam and a general refusal to pay land taxes in the Yangtze Delta. His grandson, the Xuande Emperor (reigned 1425–1435), had to order a drastic retrenchment to pacify the realm. The province of Jiaozhi was abandoned, and a permanent reduction of the tax quota in the lower Yangtze region took effect. With such curtailments, the national quota of some 32 million piculs was brought down to close to 27 million piculs. Thereafter no noticeable increase or decrease was ever again registered; there were only small and slow erosions. The *Da-Ming huidian* lists 26,782,259 piculs in 1502 and 26,638,412 piculs in 1578;[7] this general level was to remain the rule for the rest of the dynasty.

Yet the quota was neither the sum total paid by the taxpaying public nor the aggregate amount checked in at imperial granaries. In practice, the provincial and prefectural assessments were broken down into a dozen or so consignments, some with long-distance delivery obligations, freight, projected losses in handling, and additional service charges being borne by the taxpayers; others briefly commuted to silver payments, often at a rate below the food cost at the point of origin. My calculation shows that "one picul of tax grain" in assessment in South Zhili in the late sixteenth century could cost the taxpayers from 0.26 taels of silver to 1.91 taels, depending on which consignment it fell into.[8] Such variations gave the central government as well as provincial administrators the flexibility to deal with different classes of taxpayers and changing situations in the locales. But as a whole, we can assume that the total value of the land tax was restricted at a relatively rigid level, once the Xuande Emperor's concession was made. In traditional China, when taxes were assessed on every individual peasant household, with progressive taxation most difficult to manage and tax exemption for the poor not feasible at all, a general tax increase after each dynasty's middle period was virtually unenforceable. What benefit derived from additional acreage under cultivation and increased productivity had been canceled out by population growth, with a generally low standard of living continuing to prevail,[9] and with the few affluent households having purchased ranks to gain tax-exempt status.[10] In the early seventeenth century, in order to meet Nurhaci's challenge in Manchuria, the Ming court finally decided to mobilize the empire's financial sinews. The tax increases were gingerly ordered, with a minimum extra added each time. Yet the move wrecked the entire system. Payment arrearage quickly shot up. In 1632, arrears that constituted 50 percent or more of the receivables were reported in 340 counties, more than a quarter of the empire's fiscal districts. Moreover, 134 of those counties had not delivered anything to the central government at all.[11]

Thus, the land tax data on hand can be utilized for studies in connection with the rise and fall of the Ming, and dynastic cycles in general, rather than restricted to the annual comparisons of the years of the Yongle reign alone.

2. Grain Received in Beijing

The grain checked in Beijing, called "tributary grain" by Western scholars, was derived exclusively from the land tax quota discussed

above. It also came mainly from the
Yangtze Valley and was transported on
the Grand Canal. It was of vital importance to both the Ming and Qing dynasties. During the Opium War of
1840–42, when the British employed
the strategy of threatening this item of
supply by arriving at the southern ter-
minus of the canal, the Manchu resistance quickly ceased.

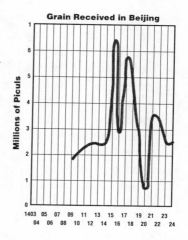

The annual statistics in the *Veritable
Records* start recording this item in
1409. Until 1414 the range of the annual
delivery is narrow, moving between 2
million to 2.5 million piculs. Much wider
fluctuations are recorded thereafter. The 1415 figure is in excess of 6
million piculs; that of 1417 is in excess of 5 million piculs. However,
in 1420 an unusual low is reported; it is below 1 million piculs.

Despite these variations, the figures are considered to be reliable.
The grain was transported to Beijing prior to 1415 via the sea route.
The convoy, with a fixed number of ships of uniform capacity, was apt
to repeatedly arrive at approximately the same results. After 1415 the
shipment went through the Grand Canal, which, newly constructed,
was still awaiting completion. The army transportation corps handled
the grain supply by relay, designating Huaian, Xuzhou, Jining, and
Linqing as intermediate stations, where depots and warehouses were
set up. Therefore, the collection of tributary grain as a part of the land
tax and its distribution in the north ran continuously; no longer was it
an annual operation.[12] There were cases in which a year's worth of
grain unloaded in Beijing was significantly less than other years' as the
shipment was partially in deposit at intermediate points. On the lunar
New Year's Day of 1421, Yongle formally transferred his capital to
Beijing. There is reason to believe that the granary reserves built up in
prior years were sufficient to meet the demand that year, at a time
when the riverboats as well as the transportation personnel were hauling items of higher priority for the upcoming event.

The deliveries from 1415 to 1425, while showing variations from
year to year, nevertheless averaged 3.2 million piculs annually, which
is consistent with the background conditions. The grain received in

Beijing was distributed to families of government officials, the capital garrison, and artisans on duty in lieu of a food subsidy. It started at an annual total of 2 million piculs, then it expanded slowly but steadily, until an imperial decree in 1472 fixed its yearly volume to be 4 million piculs.[13]

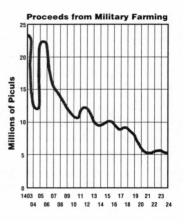

The numbers and figures related to the tribute grain were not liable to be falsified on account of their close connection with palace operations. By tradition, the Ming government assigned an official with the title of vice-minister of revenue to superintend the cluster of granaries around Beijing.[14] All personnel on duty with the transportation corps who handled the grain in transit, down to sergeants and lieutenants, were held personally accountable for the consignments in their custody. There are scattered documents indicating that some of them sold their children to make up for the losses en route rather than facing the severe penalty.[15]

3. Proceeds from Military Farming

This item, unlike the first two, cannot be verified for its accuracy. It started in 1403 at some 23 million piculs, a level that was almost comparable with the total proceeds from the land tax. Yet, with a drastic dip and a quick recovery the next year, it slid downward steadily with only minor retrievals on the way, until it came close to 5 million piculs. The figure was omitted from the report of 1424, the last year of Yongle's reign.

The military farming program in Ming times had never been soundly organized as an institution. Laws were proclaimed in the early years of the dynasty that frontier troops should utilize the wasteland around their barracks to produce their own food, and in inland districts each hereditary military family was supposed to receive a land grant of 50 *mou* and turn in 24 piculs of grain annually.[16] All evidence points to the fact that the proclamation was more an ideal rather than a reality. No central agency was ever established for the program; no fiscal officer was designated to be responsible for the operation. A Ming source points out that in the early years of the dynasty Sichuan Province listed 65,954,500 *mou* of land as being under military farming, yet the total number of troops within the province was 14,822 men. Had the military farming program been put into effect as directed, it would have required every soldier to till 4,500 *mou* (approximately 750 acres) of land.[17]

No explanation is ever given to the above Yongle figures. An educated guess is that initially, under pressure from the throne, all commanders were forced to give some targeted numbers, those being a promise rather than an accomplishment. As Yongle continually mobilized the troops for his northern and southern expeditions, those commanders were only too happy to mark down or to cancel their estimates, thus resulting in the steep slide of the curve. But even with the reduction, the remaining figures were of little practical value. That is why at the end of the reign the compilers of the *Veritable Records* chose to omit the item from the annals altogether.

Yet, the dynasty's dictum that the military should produce its own food was never formally rescinded, causing irksome problems for the latter-day administrators. When in 1570 Pang Shangpeng was commissioned to inspect military farming among the frontier army posts, he reported the conditions in Liaodong as: "After incessant fighting and famine, land records have vanished. Cultivated acreage is now divided among the hereditary military families not on active duty. The military farming program is virtually abandoned." His impression of the Dadong area was: "There are figures according to the books, but not the persons who deliver the proceeds." Upon stopover in Gansu he confessed his inability "to unsnare the accounts so artfully manipulated."[18] Nevertheless, these reports were filed in the Longqing period, when the Ming court still routinely kept on record an annual total of 3.7 million piculs as proceeds from military farming. By then no one dared to puncture the myth of a self-supporting army that had been built up since the reigns of the founding emperors.

4. Salt Revenue

This item started in the vicinity of 1.3 million *yin* at the beginning of the Yongle period, showed an increase to over 1.4 million *yin,* and finally went down to below 1.1 million *yin*. The figure for 1411 is missing.

As a whole this set of figures can be regarded as reliable. The fluctuation could have actually happened. The *yin* was an official license authorizing the circulation and sale of a fixed amount of salt, a commodity always under governmental monopoly, in Ming and Qing times as well as during the republican era. While "lesser *yin*" were issued, the standard *yin* covered 400 catties of salt (a catty is about one and a quarter pounds), a quantity roughly sufficient for the annual consumption of 40 adults. The 1.3

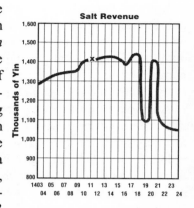

to 1.4 million *yin* should be adequate for some 60 million persons, children included; that was also the census figure of the early Ming dynasty.

The disposal of the salt followed a peculiar barter method called *kaizhong*. At first, private salt traders had to deliver food and animal fodder to the frontier army posts, who in return issued to them "granary receipts." While negotiable, those receipts were not promissory notes for salt valid everywhere. Each of them authorized the bearer to go to a particular producing area to receive the commodity. The *yin* was furthermore controlled by the Nanjing office of the Ministry of Revenue, which specified the route of transit and final destination of each parcel of cargo accompanying a particular license, thus assuring timely and even distribution of this daily necessity to the empire's vast realm and its entire population.[19] So many bureaucratic departments and agencies were involved in the operation that it was virtually impossible to manipulate the numbers locally.

Abuse of the system happened, in later periods, when the government oversold the annual crop and was unable to make the promised deliveries. To meet certain emergency needs, it also divided the same commodity into several categories, for spot and future deliveries at differentiated prices. But the compromising of the system did not take place until the middle of the fifteenth century.[20] An exception during the Yongle period was that on account of the military exigency in Vietnam some quantities of salt produced in Zhejiang had been switched out from the regular distribution to meet the demand there,[21] which may explain the dip in the curve. There is no evidence that either the production or the sale had been curtailed.

5. Income in Silver

Throughout the Yongle period silver remained domestically demonetized for the purpose of promoting the government paper currency. This, however, did not prevent the throne from assessing annual "commissary silver" from chieftains of minority groups on the Yunnan border. Quantities of silver were also obtained from government mining, which operated under a quota system. Supervisors and foremen had to guarantee the projected amounts of production, calculated from the size of the labor force under their command.

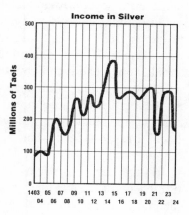

Silver was used for jewelry production. The precious metal was also cast into official seals and silver frames to encase patents and nobility title certificates. A significant amount was taken overseas for purchasing curios. From time to time, silver was awarded to foreign tributary missions. At Xuande's accession, one million taels of silver was distributed to court officials and their families as general awards.[22] But with all these, the precious metal was prized for its ceremonial function rather than its monetary value. The amount handled by the court in the fifteenth century was relatively small. It was not to be compared with the situation in the sixteenth century, when silver of many million taels regularly passed through state treasuries.

6. Income in Paper Currency

Government notes, declared to be the legal tender during the early Ming, were issued in huge quantities in the late fourteenth and early fifteenth centuries. Based on sixty-nine entries in the *Veritable Records,* I have calculated that in the year 1390 alone, the dynastic founder Zhu Yuanzhang circulated 95 million *quan* of paper currency as general awards to his officials and military personnel, and for famine relief and for grain purchase from the open market.[23] In that same year, however, the government income in paper currency amounted to only some 20 million *quan.*[24] Thus in that one year alone the quantity of paper currency in circulation was inflated by an amount close to two and half years' proceeds from the land tax if the official rate (one *quan* for one picul of grain) should apply, and it still counted as close to a half year's total from that source if the market value of those notes (about four *quan* for the picul) held steady. Apparently, fiscal irresponsibility had started before Yongle's reign.

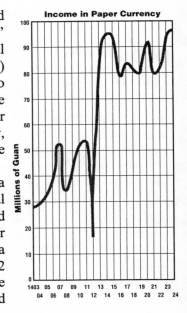

In this chart the year of 1412 marked a turning point. Before that year, the annual income in paper currency rarely exceeded 50 million *quan;* thereafter it hovered over 80 million *quan,* at times pushing toward a hundred million. In between, the year 1412 itself marked an abysmal drop on the curve. So far we have been unable to find the cause leading to this break.

But we know that currency inflation continued during Yongle's reign. The court initiated several schemes to check it without success. In 1407 the portions of land tax covering summer crops were made payable exclusively in paper currency. After 1413 the commutation of punishment to fines widened the acceptance of those government notes. The most ambitious program was the attempted salt rationing, enacted in 1404. It was supposed to cover the entire population and all the payments had to be in paper currency.[25] None of those devices brought forth noticeable results. No salt was ever rationed; yet the scheme, having once received the approval from the throne, could not be abrogated. Thenceforth "the payment for rationed salt" became a nuisance tax for the duration of the dynasty. Further devaluation of the paper currency made the total amount so infinitesimally small that most counties decided to let the district's land tax quota absorb it.

In 1425, or immediately after the reign of Yongle, it took forty to seventy *quan* of paper currency to purchase a picul of rice.[26] The close to one million *quan* of government notes annually turned in to the state treasury was therefore not a significant factor in public finance.

7. Horses Delivered

In this chart, the figure for 1407 is missing. That for 1419 is known to be in error. After a correction in the addenda to the *Veritable Records,* it still shows as a dip on the curve. But otherwise the progressive rise of the number of horses under imperial control is steep and uninterrupted. In fact, it starts with 37,993 horses in 1403 and ends with 1,736,618 in 1424. Over the twenty-two year period, the increase is 45.8 fold.

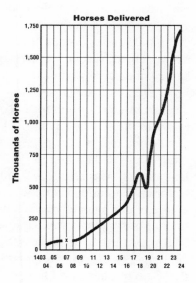

It is suspected that these numbers are not produced from head-counting, but mathematically arrived at from a projected rate of fecundity. The breakdown of the annual figures shows an increase of 20 percent in 1421, 10 percent in 1422, 33 percent in 1423, and another 10 percent in 1424. Nor could this rate of proliferation be adequately supported by private and public stable services.

In early Ming times, the procurement of horses went on briskly. Through purchase and through submission as tribute, horses came to government stables from Yunnan, Guizhou, Korea, Manchuria, and Samarkand. After retaining a number for its own use, the government farmed out the rest to civilian households for upkeep. In North Zhili, Henan, and Shandong, a number of counties and prefectures were designated as "stable service districts," where every five able-bodied males had the service obligation to take care of one stud; the government in turn remitted a half of their taxes to defray the cost. Quotas for yearlings were assigned. Whenever the quota was not met or a stud died, by law the custodial household had to make it up from its own purse.[27] Until the end of the fifteenth century, the officially prescribed rate of fecundity was two yearlings for each stud in a three-year cycle. Lu Rong, author of *Shuyuan zaji,* indicated that in his capacity as an imperial censor supervising the branding of government horses in 1477, he witnessed many animal custodians forced into financial ruin by making up the losses.[28] The numbers noted in Yongle's account as "horses delivered" seem to be closely related to this practice.

In 1425, after Yongle died, the declaration at the new emperor's enthronement carried this passage: "Wherever there are cases that persons, under civil or military registration, on account of shortages in horse breeding, are pressed by government to sell or place their wives, concubines, and children as collateral to raise loans, we hereby demand that relief be given, and the offices concerned upon receiving this decree redeem the persons thus separated from their families, and return them to their homes."[29] It is extremely doubtful that the benevolent tone of the message was subsequently carried out in full. From the historian's point of view the message nevertheless provides additional evidence that the above account of "horses delivered" is derived from a series of simple multiplications.

It may further be noted that the problem with yearlings and studs continued to distress the population in north China for a good part of the sixteenth century. Only in 1568, as a major reform, did the court finally order the discontinuation of the arrangement; yet it took another dozen years to have the directive carried out in full. The sale of government studs, by then a hundred thousand in all, was completed in 1581. Thereafter horses were procured through purchase.[30]

I first ran into this series of numbers almost thirty years ago. Preparing a book on the fiscal administration of the Ming dynasty, I planned to introduce these figures along with the graphs in the opening chapter of that volume. What better way to acquaint readers with the characteristic and capacities of the financial establishment under examination? But my academic adviser was against it. All scholarly works start with nomenclatures and organizational charts; they are supposed to furnish definitions and clarify operating procedures. The form precedes the substance. I argued that if I could have created such a neat picture with Ming governmental finance, I would have become a fiscal reformer of the first class; there would have been no need to strive to become a financial historian. This said, however, in the end I had to abide by the wish of my adviser, who represented not only scholarly expertise but also financial backing of the research project.

But my argument was not entirely lost. Originally the book was intended to cover the entire duration of the Ming dynasty. As a compromise, its focus narrowed to the sixteenth century only. Both the author and his readers were thus relieved from much of the myth of an ideal perfection regularly credited to the founding of a dynasty; the new format offered an opportunity to deal directly with how it actually worked. The office titles were announced, their functions prescribed; but as soon as the formality was served the writing moved to describe the operations in the field, with full dimension of their arbitrariness and eccentricities. My only regret was that the aforementioned Yongle figures and charts, for me a rare piece of information, had to be altogether discarded.

Then, there came a second chance. Soon after my book was published, a group of authors, scientists, and educators in Shanghai planned a *festschrift* volume to honor Dr. Joseph Needham's eightieth birthday, and I was asked to contribute a chapter. It occurred to me that the particularities involved in the collecting of revenue and the accompanying moral justification well fit what Needham called "bureaucratism," to be distinguished from feudalism in Western history, about which hitherto many Maoist writers had been hopelessly confused.

My chapter, entitled "Administrative Statistics in *Ming T'ai-tsung Shih-lu,*" points out that Chinese official bureaucratism is noted for the following features: (1) its claim to fully grasp the Natural Law, therefore, the undebatable nature of the high points of its political philosophy; (2) its adhesion to the Chinese monarchy; (3) myth and make-believe as a part of its discipline; (4) the suppressed truth found in the lower echelons which could have challenged the assumptions on the top; and (5), its exclusiveness. In sum, it featured a particular form of management, wherein the semantic integrity and assumed perfection of the literati reigned, and it was not answerable to any outside power or influence.

I mentioned that the Yongle Emperor, née Zhu Di, was a tyrant by nature and by deeds. Yet his courtiers honored him with the posthumous title: *Our Cultured Emperor Who Has Embodied Heaven and Magnified the Truth, Heightened Enlightenment and Widened Our Destiny, Combined Saintly Valor with Divine Accomplishment, and Served with Pure Kindness as Well as Absolute Filial Piety.* Taken with the financial management discussed earlier, this practice amply illustrates the character of traditional bureaucratism. Its reliance on idealism to the extreme has nothing in common with the practicality of Western feudalism.

This was the first piece of writing I ever published on mainland

China since its reopening to the outside world. The *festschrift* volume carries the title *Explorations in Science and Technology in China*, put out by Guji (Ancient Classics) Publications in Shanghai (1982), subsequently it was also included in the *Fang-k'uan li-shi ti shih-chi'eh* (Yungchen Publications, Taipei, 1988). An English translation appears in *Ming Studies* (Minneapolis, 1982).

Historiography, nevertheless, is a craft of timeliness. That chapter has been in print for fifteen years. Today "feudalism" is no longer such an omnipresent trap to Chinese or Western scholars. On the other hand, economic breakthrough in China is now gaining momentum, the background and nature of which is urgently in need of historical explanation. I am convinced that the Yongle revenue data and the accompanying factors can be more advantageously redeployed to serve that purpose. Cast in the background, they help to explain why China endured a prolonged period of stagnancy prior to the violent restructuring in the twentieth century, and in the discourse the long-term rationality of the present movement may emerge.

If we indeed were to have an opportunity to launch a fiscal reform in Ming times, we could at first diagnose its management as revealed by the data during the reign of Yongle as lack of system. There was no central treasury in the capital city. The collection of goods and monetary items proceeded from contradictory principles; they were handled by separate departments. Above all, the many items of income were not matched by a list of major expenditures.

On the list, cloth, silk, and cotton waddings could have either been assessed as regular land tax collected from the producing areas or accepted as substitutes for the grain quota payable by the districts.[31] Strictly speaking, grain delivered in Beijing should have been counted as an item of expenditure rather than income, since the quantity was derived from the land tax proper, not from a separate levy. Moreover, once it reached Beijing, the whole amount was earmarked for distribution. Gold was another item used to substitute for tax grain. Its total amount was small. Even though it grew from 50 taels in 1403 to 5,340 taels in 1423,[32] that still amounted to no more than a speck within the revenue of the empire, hardly worth citing. Industrial metals including copper, iron, and lead, on the other hand, were extracted from mines privately operated but under governmental supervision; their collection was a function of the Ministry of Works.[33] Likewise, government horses were under the jurisdiction of the Ministry of War; even its cash account was out of reach of the Ministry of Revenue. The inclusion of paper currency to the list further threw the picture into confusion. The notes were issued by the government without backing; therefore, each bill returned signified the cancellation of credit to that amount. When the summer tax of 1407 was made payable in those paper notes, for instance, it must have resulted in a corresponding reduction of the grain quota collected in that year. As we shall spell out below, bronze coins were not an item of significance in the national account.

Cowie shells were circulated only in Yunnan, their value being negligible. They, therefore, hardly deserved national listing. The kingfisher feathers and paper fans submitted by Jiaozhi, while adding color to the palace pageantry, hardly contributed anything substantial to the national economy. The proceeds from military farming and the number of government horses, projected from expectations, should never have been jumbled together to confuse the quantities of articles derived from actual counting.

From today's point of view, all such inconsistencies and irregularities could have been cured easily. What the Ming administrators badly needed was a sound monetary system, against which all the articles could have been reevaluated and restated. A number of items could have then been dropped from the general list. When the remaining articles were rendered mathematically manageable, their calculation would have a common denominator to go by. The trend of increase or decrease, the surpluses and shortages, could then be seen at a glance. Such a suggestion, however, would not have served the purpose of the Ming administration.

Reviewing the list of dozens of articles once more, we can say that the concept of balancing expenditure with income may never have been given consideration by the contemporary administrators. All the receivables signified the assessed obligations of imperial subjects to the sovereign. One item, when handled by two separate parties, had to be counted twice. For instance, certain taxpayers were required to deliver their tax grain on the waterfront of the Yangtze River; but it was the army's transportation corps that was obligated to haul it up the Grand Canal to Beijing. So that the same picul of grain became statutorily different when it changed hands; a shortage in one category was not to be confused with that of the other. Disbursement of the revenue, on the other hand, was an imperial prerogative, which could be executed in an *ad hoc* manner. An example was the supply train of Yongle's 1422 expedition: It was made up of 117,573 wagons hauled by 340,000 mules, on which 370,000 piculs of grain was loaded. Added to them were 235,146 drivers and attendants. The column was moreover escorted by 1,000 cavalrymen plus 5,000 foot soldiers.[34] The procurement of draft animals affected several provinces. It is apparent that these forces were hastily assembled at imperial direction. While there is no solid evidence of forced purchases, the handing out of paper currency in large amounts points in that direction. The reader may remember that it was due to his petition against this campaign that Minister of Revenue Xia Yuanji was imprisoned for over two years.

As a whole, we do not see any concerted effort by the Ming dynasty to establish what we would call a sound monetary system. As noted above, gold and silver entered state coffers only in unimpressive quantities. The precious metals were turned into jewelry and utensils, official seals and frames of important documents and patents. Even when handed out as awards, they carried more ceremonial significance than monetary value. The bronze coins circulated in Ming times were the traditional *wuzhuqian*, about the size of the American nickel but less thick and with square holes in them. The Song dynasty had minted such coins in enormous quantities. Several hundred million had been put into circulation annually. From the late eleventh century to the early twelfth, the yearly output exceeded three billion.[35] It has been estimated that the total amount of the bronze coins minted during the entire 276–year span of the Ming dynasty was roughly equivalent to two years' worth of the Song in its heyday.[36]

That the Ming administrators took a dim view of these bronze coins can also be observed from the Yongle annual data. The listing of those coins started in 1415, with an inconsequential 3,000 *quan*. For reasons unspecified, the amount from 1418 to 1424 was routinely registered as 3,106 *quan* every year for seven consecutive years, without variation.[37] Throughout the Ming period, these metal coins never carried any significant weight in taxation or governmental finance. They could never rival, for example, tea or horses for importance in the ledgers.

The paper currency was not redeemable. Except on rare occasions when the government allowed the notes to be accepted as payments to itself, for specific items and within particular time periods, they lacked the power of legal tender. Thus by circulating paper notes, the imperial government again exercised a prerogative without incurring any obligation to itself.

All told, in devising this entire fiscal setup, the Ming court shunned any attempt to promote the national economy. Its primary concern was to secure its own power base. As a result, the sharp rises and sudden drops on the curves plotted from the Yongle fiscal data are, without exception, for incidental and administrative reasons; sheer economic influence did not come into the picture.

There were even instances when the statutory provisions worked against social trends. In the fourteenth and fifteenth centuries, the caste system had little chance to survive in China's mobile society. Regardless, the imperial government decreed that the households serving the army, and performing saltern and artisan duties, answer service calls of their vocational specialities in perpetuity.[38] This impractical approach caused great difficulties at administration in later periods and constituted the chief reason for the decline of the military establishment.

Also, it may further be observed that in the absence of law or any lateral authority to scrutinize the operation, the entire fiscal setup functioned only under pressure from the top, and thus its efficiency was low. The populace had no resort but to hope that officialdom would practice enlightened despotism, failing which, when driven to desperation, it turned to rebellion, as did people in Jiaozhi, or staged group resistance, as did taxpayers on the Yangtze. On the other hand, the administration, not answerable to the governed, empowered tyrants like Yongle to produce great wonders in his lifetime. The delayed consequences had to be borne by his successors.

Yet, when those deeds are reviewed against the entire length of Chinese history, we will see that Yongle's style of management is linked to China's development in very recent days. This we shall take up in the second portion of this article.

Part Two

In part one of this article we stressed that the annual fiscal data found in the *Ming Taizong shilu,* when studied along with the surrounding conditions of financial management of the early Ming dynasty, reveal that the whole design placed a great emphasis on political control, at the expense of economic considerations. In actuality, such lopsided attention was consistent with the entire imperial period. Although differences in degree existed between and among the dynasties, management did not vary a great deal in substance. Furthermore, nor did Western Europe of the Yongle Emperor's time fare any better. With exceptions of certain free cities in Italy, where administrations might have run ahead, rational management of public finance in the West is a recent development, mainly within the past three hundred years. We, therefore, may comfortably take the fiscal management of the early Ming as a good starting point in seeking to explain why it was inevitable that China had to lag behind the West during the subsequent centuries.

Owing to the demand for water control and famine relief, in addition to devising preventive measures against the nomadic peoples on the northern frontier who occasionally mounted large-scale cavalry charges against her sedentary population, China had in the very early years organized a huge bureaucracy managing the affairs of tens of millions of peasants. Such an order could be said at the outset to contradict the principles of economic expansion. For instance, since the numbers counted, the government did its utmost to promote the small self-cultivators as the chief component of its taxpaying population and the pool of conscripted soldiery. Their scale of production was small, incapable of yielding sufficient surplus for large-scaled exchange. The disputes and clashes of interests among the governed were often of such a petty nature that the officials were inclined to dismiss them out of hand, which in turn was not conducive to the development of jurisprudence. Moreover, the limited resources of the peasantry made an elaborate court system out of the question. A long-term consequence was that the bureaucrats were more inclined to handle public affairs in an *ad hoc* manner with their common-sense mentality rather than involving themselves with massive technicalities. Decorum and rhetorical balance took precedence over mathematics and methodology. The concept of the inviolability of private property, running counter to their humanism and sense of fair play, was often ignored.

In other words, modern economics takes charge of unbalanced situations; the Chinese literary-bureaucrats were more inclined to manufacture artificially balanced situations beforehand. As for the coinage of money, the Chinese bureaucracy contemplated facilitating only primitive transactions among peasants, not providing means for commercial operations of a significant magnitude.

Throughout Chinese history there have been attempts to improve the livelihood of the populace by monetary approaches. Usually they failed for lack of commercial capital and large-scale business expertise. Even at the dawn of the Christian era, the usurper-reformer Wang Mang deplored that at one time during the Han the land tax had been reduced to one-thirtieth of the crop, yet in his time prime producers were surrendering a hefty 50 percent of their produce as rents. He reasoned that the self-cultivators must have been "cheated and swindled out of their possessions by the roguish wealthy." As if taking common ground with medieval Europeans, he counted usury as the sole cause of such an unhappy event,[39] and it could be cured by an all-embracing monetary system. In his design, gold, silver, tortoise shells and cowrie shells, and metal and cloth money (this was before paper was invented) were classified into twenty-eight denominations, all made interchangeable according to a complicated conversion schedule.[40] With this scheme, Wang was confident that all business transactions would be under his scrutiny and the abuse of usury would be forever interdicted.

Wang Mang failed to see that money by itself could not produce miracles. Interest rates, like prices, could only be driven lower when there was sufficient capital to go around. Draft animals, seeds, and surplus food in the planting season must be made available to sustain his reform. As it happened, before any benefit of Wang's device came about the populace had already been confused by his conversion formula.

Thereafter no dynasty lacked fiscal and taxation reforms. A common failure arose from the fact that no program, regardless how well intentioned, was able to achieve universal coverage. Working against the general trend of the time, it could only be partially scrutinized. Official operators, keeping business in their hands, took possession of public transportation, monopolized river and canal channels, commandeered porters, and made forced purchases by paying below-market prices. In a word, they could never fully deny themselves the convenience that as imperial commissioners, they were entitled to such prerogatives, derived, in a sense, from the dictum that the emperor owned all under heaven.

Thus before the reform showed any substantial benefit, it broke the symmetry and balance that the bureaucracy strove to maintain. There were cases in which astounding achievements were made in the short term; as a rule, however, the effort could not be sustained. Not infrequently, the reformers themselves were later impeached or even forfeited their lives. Sang Hongyang of the Han; Yuwen Rong, Wei Jian,

Yang Shengjin, Wang Hong, and Liu Yan of the Tang; Cai Jing and Jia Sidao of the Song; and Ahmed, Lu Shirong, and Sang of the Yuan made the list.

But at this point we must point out that this is more than a simple case of official corruption. When the poetic-minded bureaucrats were appointed to manage the affairs of a multitude of peasants with primitive technical support, and lacking, furthermore, the effective surveillance of an independent judiciary, the result was that even the primary data could not be seriously scrutinized. In the area of finance and taxation, Edwin O. Reischauer and Wang Yuqian had pointed a finger at the powerful and rich, who shifted their tax liabilities to the poor and inarticulate. In reality, the latter group was by no means any easier to handle. In the Food and Money Monograph of the *Suishu* we encounter a passage indicating that in the sixth century in Yangdi Prefecture the inhabitants of several tens of thousands of households all registered themselves as bachelors, as the current tax laws permitted them, as such, to pay half taxes.[41] When the falsification of records started from the bottom, the most incorruptible administrators on the top remained helpless.

What took place in the sixth century also happened in later ages. Within that millennium, the greatest fiscal reformer was undoubtedly Wang Anshi. His "New Policy" started from a general land survey. Monetary payments replaced most taxes in kind. "Green-crop Money," a low-interest public loan, was made generally available to the agricultural population. Surplus materials in the hands of the government were sold to merchants; at the same time purchases were made for articles not in stock. The theory was that the economy, with such stimuli, would widen its amplitude. The increased production and volume of commerce would therefore end with more receipts in the state coffer even when tax rates remained unchanged. But this was to apply a convincing theory of the twentieth century to the rural community of eleventh-century China.

The program was bound to fail because it could never be carried out with precision in all individual cases. As for Green-crop Money, "the rich were reluctant to borrow, only the destitute desired it." An operating procedure was worked out "to enroll the rich and poor into mixed groups, with all the households within each taking collective responsibility, and the wealthiest among them serving as group captains."[42] This description portrays a multitude of peasants, destitute and illiter-

ate, and unable to place their landholdings as collateral for the borrowed financing. In the meantime there were neither banks nor an
adequate judiciary system to service the program. The terms "wealthy
households" and "group responsibility" suggest political pressure applied from the top. Under the circumstances, it is difficult to distinguish *ad hoc* requisition from legitimate taxation. Worse yet, the
selling and buying by the government turned into "a form of confiscation by the *yamen* authorities."[43]

Wang Anshi's failed reform in the eleventh century was followed
by Cai Jing's design and economic expansion program in the twelfth
century. Again, the inability to guarantee fair and free exchange in
individual cases ended with a mathematically unmanageable situation
in the hands of the government officials. About fixing prices, the Food
and Money Monograph of the *Songshi* complains: "After silk fabrics
were commuted to copper cash, the latter was again converted to winter wheat. The bronze coins doubled the cost of the silk; and the wheat
again doubled the value in copper cash. Against such stepped up increases, the ordinary people had no place to appeal to."[44] The same
source discloses that from Wang Anshi to Cai Jing, there were eleven
methods by which the government could purchase foodstuffs from the
public, involving leveling, persuasion, price control, etc.[45] The expose
suggests quotas assigned by the top echelon which were never met,
new categories responding to fresh demands, and both the functionaries and the tax-paying population constantly on the run with the unend-
ing fiscal obligations.

The targeted increase in revenue only ended with currency inflation,
made worse in this age with the advent of paper currency and negotiable notes. The trend carried on during the Southern Song, the Liao, the
Jin, and the Mongolian dynasty of the Yuan.[46] Cast against such a
background, the founding of the Ming dynasty under Zhu Yuanzhang
in 1368 and his campaign to restore old values, accompanied by an
announced program of fiscal retrenchment, could be reckoned as a
reaction to the economic expansion traced back to the days of Wang
Anshi.[47] On the whole the financial tightening was a success in the
short term. (He also issued paper money. But the Ming notes came to
total disuse in the fifteenth century, with no enduring effect on the
dynasty.) But the damage that Zhu Yuanzhang has done to China
comes from the other extreme: His policies worked awkwardly against
the growth and expansion soon to be engineered by Western Europe.

Yet, at this point we could also admit that practical solutions were indeed few, when the nation had to employ brigades of scholar-officials to administer the affairs of multi-millions of peasants in a pre-industrial age.

Another way of summarizing Zhu Yuanzhang's policy is that he avoided the use of money wherever and whenever possible. Having striven to reach a general equilibrium throughout his realm, he made it a point to prevent the amassing of wealth in private or public hands. As a general rule, he demanded that the populace answer service calls in person, including those already commuted to monetary payments since the days of Wang Anshi. The land tax as a whole was collected in kind. The proceeds in parcels were delivered by taxpayers organized into teams, laterally to government offices and army units, thus omitting the intermediate vaults and depots. Even furniture and stationery needed by the governmental offices, as well as bows and arrows for the army, were requisitioned from the population, with quotas assigned to the local districts.[48]

As a whole, Zhu Di or the Yongle Emperor inherited this system. Aside from the tributary grain in transit on the Grand Canal, which partially consolidated the delivery, he generally followed the managerial procedure, left by his father. The omission of a central treasury, the demonetized precious metals, the official monopoly of salt and tea, the listing of mineral products and horses as items of income, along with kingfisher feathers and paper fans, the registration of artisan, saltern and hereditary military households aside from the general population, and the principle that the army units produce at least a part of their own food all came from the design of the dynastic founder.

Yongle's extravagance and extraschedule extractions were either discontinued or significantly curbed by his successors, the Hongxi and the Xuande emperors; but the general pattern of fiscal and taxation management remained as before. Even in the sixteenth century when taxes and service obligations were largely commuted to silver payments, the administration followed the design put in place at the founding of the dynasty. A central treasury was still missing. Tax payments, which previously had been delivered in foodstuffs by the local districts laterally to various agencies, were now delivered in silver, still in small parcels, by counties and prefectures directly and separately to those units. One revenue-collecting agency could furnish supplies to a dozen or so disbursing agencies; one disbursing agency could also be serviced by a score of revenue-collecting agencies. In 1592, Shen Bang, the magistrate of Wanping County, whose office was situated in Beijing, indicated that he had to make annual deliveries to twenty-seven places, yet the amount involved totaled less than two thousand taels of silver.[49]

That is not the end yet. In 1644, the Qing dynasty of the Manchus replaced the Ming. The same style of fiscal management continued.[50] Therefore, until the dawn of the present century, China's Ministry of Revenue remained a huge accounting office. Only under extraordinary conditions was it ever an operating agency. The tributary grain was still hauled on the Grand Canal. No operating budget was ever compiled for public finance; nor was there a central treasury. Lateral transactions between and among governmental offices, featuring numerous short, crisscrossing supply lines, prevailed.[51] Unminted silver and metal ingots were handled by official circles as well as by private parties. Only in 1882 did Jilin Province start to coin silver dollars, followed by Guangdong five years later.[52] Those coins, circulated in restricted areas, were by no means legal tender. More critical to the situation, until then China still had no adequate legislation governing the use of money appropriate for modern life, private or public.

Peng Xinwei, in his book *A Monetary History of China* (*Zhongguo huobishi*), declares that in the world there have been only two kinds of independent "monetary cultures," namely, that of China and that of Greece. From the latter the Western Europe type emerged. Its tradition started with coins minted with precious metals of limited quantities which did not penetrate deep into the general public.[53] The Chinese system, on the other hand, was built up from the *wuzhuqian,* minted with bronze, and in circulation since the First Emperor of the Qin in the B.C. era. It was issued in larger quantities and made a deep penetration with its users. It is paradoxical that China's monetary economy ultimately lagged behind that of Western Europe.

This reaffirms our thought that money by itself will not create miracles. It becomes a significant factor because laws are enacted to sustain its function; yet legislation prevails only when social conditions render it operative. In the narratives above we encountered a situation in China in which within a sizable district, practically all the heads of households declared themselves to be bachelors, meaning that the basic statistical data were of a dubious quality. The practice of lining up individuals together to assume group responsibility, on the other hand, reveals that the rights and obligations of the individual could not be clearly defined and safeguarded. It leads to the conclusion that peasants, millions of them, could only be maneuvered in blocks. That *ad hoc* requisition was made indistinguishable from legitimate taxation indicates that property rights were never seriously regarded. All these conditions created a "mathematically unmanageable" situation. Since the government itself could not put things in order, it would be unrealistic to expect the officials to guarantee fair and free exchange of services and goods among the citizenry. Free exchange would inevitably touch on questions of inheritance, bankruptcy, tort, embezzlement, fraud, and deceit, and further extend to issues of partnership, patents, bottomry, salvage claims, insurance, respondentia bonds, etc. The tendency leading toward mercantile practices was not only beyond the capability of the old-fashioned bureaucrats but also repugnant to their cultural heritage.

Making a comparison over a wide span of history, when we take up the subject of money, we must pay attention to "monetary culture," which links currency with law, politics, social conditions and habits, and dominant thought and religion.

Returning to the subject of the financial accounts compiled in the *Ming Taizong shilu* for the reign of Yongle, we can say that data as such have only relative value. The whole compilation reflects China's monetary culture—as a whole, the figures cannot be trusted for accuracy. The articles were collected and assembled under different circumstances. A general rule to go by is that the farther away from the center the item was processed, the less reliable the figures are. Under similar circumstances, sometimes numbers were supplied for the sole purpose of satisfying bureaucratic rhetoric.

The Yongle annual report involved as few as eighteen articles or as many as twenty-five. Never were the quantities audited with equal vigor; nor was a general audit feasible. Even setting aside other reasons, this factor of varied degrees of statistical fidelity alone would have made it impossible to restate the total value in monetary terms.

But Zhu Di was a vigorous monarch. His reign followed that of the dynastic founder, barely interrupted by the insignificant Zhu Yunwen. Only under Yongle did the Ming bureaucracy reach a high degree of maturity, which made the compilation of the aforementioned list possible. All things considered, we can say that the list on hand reflected the managerial capacity of the Ming-Qing Empire at its inceptive stage, an era when China's organizational power still showed its supremacy over the mosaic that was Europe, but soon to be overtaken by the latter.

In comparison with the parallel development of the West, we can say the following about the polity under examination:

(1) It derived its strength from ideological commitment.

There are only three basic methods for governing a large number of people. The first is military conquest, followed by the exercise of police power. The second is spiritual guidance. Religious faith, political ideology, and revolutionary zeal could all be considered in this cataegory. The third is economic coordination. When a national economic framework is set up, individuals can be encouraged to pursue their self-interest within; the teamwork creates order and discipline. While combinations of these methods may appear, often we see within a particular case one element dominating.

In the past it was the fashion for Chinese historians to call the Ming-Qing Empire a feudal state. This is unrealistic. Feudalism features a warrior tradition. By subinfeudation, the knights become masters of villas. This is a far cry from the Chinese style of management wherein the emperor ruled over the entire populace through a civil bureaucracy. The mainstay of the traditional Chinese state is religious belief.

There is a general misconception that the Chinese do not take religion seriously. No religious war was ever fought in Chinese history. Only occasionally did issues of faith become causes of controversy within the imperial court. The Jiajing Emperor of the Ming professed Daoism; Wanli became a Buddhist worshiper. Shunzhi of the Qing straddled the border between Buddhist faith and Catholicism. Their personal preferences on ecclesiastic matters in no way disturbed the nation.

But we can also use the word religion in its broader and somewhat looser sense. In medieval Europe, Tawney has pointed out, economy was treated as a hierarchy of values, on the very top of which was religion.[54] Its corollary was that spiritual pursuit was the utmost purpose of material life. That being the case, religion must have been perceived as being diffused in politics, and inseparable from an individual's social and economic well-being. Within the Christian church of seventeenth century England, especially during and prior to the Civil War, sectarian clashes, manifested in disputes over church organization and liturgy, could trace their origins to changing economic life and social values, which were by then very much influenced by the rising mercantile interests.[55]

When cast in a similar light, religion is regarded as a higher purpose in everyday life, the religious influence in the traditional Chinese polity becomes transparent.

The Chinese regarded their emperor as the "Son of Heaven," his decrees as "sacred edicts." Executive, legislative, and judiciary powers were concentrated in his own hands, and he had unchecked prerogative but no mandatory legal obligations appropriate to it. He remained responsible only to heaven and constantly carried on his function through ceremonies. All this made capital out of religion.

Indeed, imperial government was always, to larger or lesser degrees, restrained by humanism. Yet the final decision handed out by the court was as indisputable as natural law. With such absolutism the bureaucrats proceeded to compile fiscal data to safeguard their own rhetoric at the expense of factual truth. The Ming exceeded previous dynasties on this count, culminating at the superhuman title that the court posthumously bestowed on the Yongie Emperor. In reality, the claim of infallibility sealed his deeds and pronouncements against review or criticism for as long as the dynasty lasted.

This single factor could impede the development of a modern money economy, not to mention an economic system known as capitalism, because, vital to such development and organization is the fair and free exchange of services and goods, which must sustain an objective standard of its own. When laws congenial to a trading community are enacted, justice starts from the free conscience of the believer. Matters concerning bankruptcy and breach of contract have to proceed from property rights and custom; they cannot be overburdened with ecclesiastic dogmas and episcopal commands. On the eve of the English Civil War John Bates, a commoner merchant, dared to sue the king for illegal collection of "ship money." This would have been inconceivable in a country where the sovereign was held to be as solemn and inviolable as a demigod, such as he was under the Ming or Qing. The argument resonates with our previous observation that in order to examine money's function in a specific society, one must at first scrutinize the monetary culture of that society. In that sense ideology and religion loom large against the background of traditional China.

(2) It functioned with dynastic cycles.

All dynasties in Chinese history came about as a result of military conquest. (That also happened in many other countries. But after the War of the Roses, the dynasties of England came about through a succession arrangement. The last Tudor queen arranged the orderly ascension of the first Stuart king. William and Mary as co-sovereigns were invited by London politicians and merchants. And the Havoverian takeover was preceded by an act passed in Parliament.) The strength of the sword backed up dynastic founders as law-givers. Their orders were more likely to be carried out in full and their reforms to be closer to reality. This happened to Zhu Yuanzhang, the founder of the Ming, and to Zhu Di, the Yongle emperor, who had also waged a four-year war to wrestle the throne from his nephew Zhu Yunwen.

Much has been said about Yongle's atrocity and ruthlessness in requisitioning material and labor. On second thought, however, we must also recognize the fact that without either large-scale commerce or a dynamic modern economy in which investment could be made, the emperor could not make better use of the surplus of his realm but to spend it on construction and on military campaigns in order to set the tone of his empire and maximize its dimensions. The mobilization inevitably involved some extent of squeeze. His case typifies China's dilemma where the political centralization went ahead too early to have room for a Renaissance or a Reformation. Once the pattern was set, dynasties had to be made and unmade to absorb the effect of the changing circumstances instead of riding on them for linear progress.

During the middle period of the dynasty, the increased population and more developed water transportation added splendor to the inland ports. But the structure of the *yamen* made it impossible for it to adapt to the style of commercial operation; nor dared the merchants attempt to overextend themselves to challenge the existing order of things.[56] The overwhelmingly large portions of state income still came from farmland, where horizontal assessment continued, omitting any feature of progressive taxation or tax exemptions for the most destitute.

The peasants, habitually dividing their small holdings for inheritance, created an ever-worsening state of parcelization of land; moreover they frequently mortgaged their minimal holdings to their neighbors and relatives. In a typical county, such marginal landowners counted more than one hundred thousand. To chastise the tax delinquents, the magistrate arrested them and flogged them. But in the end the unpaid taxes after a certain deadline had to be remitted in the benevolent name of the emperor. The officials were aware of the fact that unless the previous arrearages were written off, the collection for the next year would be even more difficult.

The practice created a vicious cycle. In the end even those who were able to pay also kept their payments in arrears, anticipating a general amnesty that would inevitably wipe out their own delinquency.[57] In this way public finance became a chain whose strength would be tested at its weakest link.

In Part One we alluded to some difficulties in tax collection even during the Yongle period. Zhu Di's son Zhu Gaozhi and grandson Zhu Zhanji ordered tax reductions on humanitarian grounds. But on the other hand, state institutions of the dynasty had been set up with fixed incomes and expenditures. It was most difficult to tap the untaxed resources thereafter.

The incursion of Japanese pirates on the east coast in the mid-sixteenth century compelled the affected districts to order tax increases to meet the emergency. About the same time, the general conversion of payments from taxes in kind to silver provided an opportunity to let certain increases ride over. When Zhang Juzheng became grand secretary (in effect, prime minister) in the 1570s, he tightened fiscal discipline and gave the Ming a needed "restoration" typical of China's dynastic histories. But soon after his methodical effort, governmental finance of the Ming was once again on the downward slope until the fall of the dynasty.[58]

Grain in land tax quota, the benchmark of the empire's financial strength, remained at some 31 million piculs at Yongle's death. It came down to 26 million piculs in the sixteenth century.[59] In the early seventeenth century the dynasty was fighting for its life; yet attempts to increase taxes stalled. Before more income turned up in state coffers, the strain and stress caused by the ordered increases had already wrecked the fiscal machinery, resulting in more and larger payment arrerages, as mentioned in Part One. By the turn of the century the population of the empire had increased to close to 150 million from some 60 million at the founding of the Ming.[60] As the standard of living of the populace could not be lifted, the more mouths to be fed became an extra burden and the dynasty had to succumb with it.

The dynastic cycle also applied in the Qing. With their military prowess, the Manchus made some sweeping reforms of the tax administration on their takeover. Exemptions were drastically curbed; delinquents were prosecuted with vigor. Thousands of north Chinese farmers were relocated, to make room for the Manchu bannermen who restored the military colony system and grew their own food. At the same time the large amount of silver that the Ming court used to cart to the northern frontier was now rerouted to the south to assure prompt circulation within China proper. A reign of terror involving literary inquisition and the decree that all men shave their foreheads to the pate on the pain of death carried the message that imperial edicts were not to be treated lightly. Everything worked, at least for several decades. The seventeenth century passed without a hitch. The eighteenth still saw the Qing maintaining a formidable front worthy of the name celestial empire. But recently, two scholars from the West, on a closer examination of the records, came to the realization that by then decline had already set in. What seemed to be increases of the land tax receipts were actually less than the effect of price inflation, and the cure provided by the most energetic emperor of the age had only certain cosmetic effects but no enduring value.[61] The dynasty went on at a weakened pace.

In the nineteenth century the Qing fought domestic rebellion and foreign incursions. Yet a "restoration" again came into the picture. The Taiping rebels were suppressed, a universal surtax on goods in transit, called *likin*, was imposed, which enabled the dynasty to finance a new regional army to fend off the immediate crisis. But, whether from this point on Chinese history should be considered to follow the old track or not, the Qing dynasty of the Manchus collapsed in the early twentieth century to complete its cycle, together with the imperial period.

But unlike the dynastic cycles of the Han and Tang which ran their course as the local governments managed to detach themselves from the center, or those of the middle period of the Song, Liao, Jin, and Yuan, where currency inflation was their main cause of failure, those of the Ming and Qing, among other causes of failure, came about because these dynasties saddled themselves with an inelastic system of governmental finance, thus denying themselves the needed renewable capability that came together with the qualitative improvement of the national economy.

(3) In this context in terms of managerial capability China seems to have lost its competitive position vis-à-vis the West within the transitional period between the Ming and Qing.

Before we probe this hypothesis further, let us first quote Adam Smith. In *The Wealth of Nations,* he had this to say:

> China has been long one of the richest, that is, one of the most fertile, best cultivated, most industrious, and most populous countries in the

world. It seems, however, to have been long stationary. Marco Polo, who visited it more than five hundred years ago, describes its cultivation, industry, and populousness, almost in the same terms in which they are described by travelers in the present times. It had perhaps, even long before his time, acquired that full complement of riches which the nature of its laws and institutions permits it to acquire.[62]

Smith's treatise was published in 1776. On his last expedition to the Mongolian desert the Yongle Emperor Zhu Di died at Yumuchuan in 1424. There is an interval of about three and a half centuries in between the two dates.

When Yongle died, England and France were still locked together in the Hundred Years' War. Only after this protracted struggle did the two begin to organize themselves into modern national states, with the necessary ingredients including national armies, boundaries, and public finance. In the days of Yongle, field armies in Western Europe still lived off the country. They could not have compiled financial lists comparable to those of the Ming emperor. Moreover, another hundred years later, during the heyday of the Tudors, England was no more methodically managed than the Ming dynasty. But when Adam Smith penned the above passage, he spoke with such a tone of confidence that clearly the West had already overtaken China in accumulating wealth and in devising schemes to manage it. The related historical context seems to suggest that it was within about a hundred years prior to 1776, coincidently the date of the Declaration of Independence of the United States, that China lost her lead. Whether this is the case, and if it is why and whether we can sustain it with further evidence or not—these questions we shall take up in the concluding part of this article.

Part Three

As mentioned earlier, the year-end revenue data found in the *Ming Taizong shilu* is a peculiar work of the Chinese bureaucracy. The numbers vary in their reliability, some precisely accurate and others absurdly impossible. Only the compilers would regard them with good faith, as if those figures would indeed shine with the enlightened administration under a sage ruler. The single-mindedness reflects a form of religious devotion.

This said, however, we cannot find a comparable set of numbers in Western sources within the same time span. The closest to it perhaps is the list of annual income under Henry VIII of England (r. 1509–1547), about one hundred years after Yongle. Henry carried out the Reformation in England and confiscated monastery properties. With Thomas Cromwell as his chief adviser, his "chamber system" achieved preliminary consolidation of royal revenues, which made it possible, at a later date, to deliver all proceeds to the Exchequer. This marked the beginning of an epoch-making effort.

Henry's annual income can be put together in the following table, with the numbers found in specialists' studies:

Table 1

The Annual Income of Henry VIII During the Last Decade of His Reign[63]

Delivered at:	
Court of Augmentations (average)	£120,000
Court of First Fruits and Tenths (maximum)	£ 78,000
(the low)	£ 30,000
Court of Survey	£ 38,000
Court of Wards	£ 4,400
Duchy of Lancaster	£ 11,000
Total ordinary revenue	£250,000
Receivables from:	
Parliamentary subsidies	£ 81,000
Profit from the mint	£138,000
Customs	£32,000 to £42,000
Purveyance	£ 60,000
Total extraordinary revenue	£300,000

Compared with the Yongle data, the Henry figures can all be stated in pound sterling. There is no grain in piculs, no silk in taels, no salt, no horses, no cowrie shells. But on the other hand these numbers are not official figures entered in the books, but data compiled by historians, who have to make estimates and do the rounding. The Tudors, like China's Ming dynasty, did not establish a central treasury. The chamber system made each chamber independent of others; they derived their receivables separately and often disbursed them separately. At times the king also called for cash deposits from one or more chambers and disposed of the sums as he saw fit.[64] Under the circumstances, it would have been impossible to compile an annual budget.

When the Tudors reigned, the feudal system had already collapsed; but many usages and practices of past centuries lingered on. Among other rules, tradition held that in peacetime the king must live on his own. That is, being the largest landowner, he possessed about one-sixth of England; he should derive sufficient income from his own estates, along with other customary revenues which were also considered to be indisputably his, to rule and govern without encumbering his barons and royal subjects further. Only in wartime or any emergency situation would he call Parliament, whose authorized taxation was called "subsidies."

In 1534, Henry VIII repudiated papal supremacy and established himself as Supreme Head of the Church of England. The Court of Augmentations was created to take charge of the confiscated monastery properties. Its revenue was comprised of both the rents and proceeds from the sale of land. First Fruits and Tenths were collected from the upper clergy, who, similar to vassals within the feudal system, used to present one-tenth of their annual income to the pope as a one-time gift upon receiving the benefices and thereafter one-tenth of their annual income. Now the revenue was transferred to the church's Supreme Head. The Court of Survey mainly dealt with the king's own domains. Since the collapse of the manorial system, landholding in England had been in disorder and confusion. There were cases that the tenants-in-chief could not be located, and field conditions could not be checked against the records. This happened not only during Henry's reign. At least until the time of Elizabeth I (r. 1558–1603) the derangement lingered on.[65] The Court of Survey had been created to tidy things up and at the same time to recover some of the revenue owed the crown.

By feudal tradition, when the vassal died, the lord had the obligation to appoint a guardian for the heir until he or she reached maturity. At the same time, this trustee could manage the estate for personal profit. At the time of the Tudors, wardship became lucrative. Often it was offered for a price just as other revenues were contracted to tax farmers. These circumstances necessitated a special office for the business thus generated. In 1546, wardship grossed £12,346, a sizable income.[66]

The Duchy of Lancaster marked in part the origin from which the Tudors claimed the English throne. Its internal management differed from other domains. It also justified the care by a special chamber.

The above ordinary income, almost exclusively from land, reached

£250,000 annually. But before Thomas Cromwell, all royal income including customs duty grossed only £100,000.[67] Clearly, the confiscation of monastery properties and the fiscal revamping under Cromwell turned a new leaf in the history of crown finance.

The item of "subsidies" hereby listed also came from land, the only item akin to a "land tax" in the modern sense, distinguished from the revenues derived by the king himself as a large landowner. For eight years from 1540 to 1547, Parliament granted the king altogether £650,000, averaging £81,000 a year.[68] The large landowners who refused to pay were either tossed in jail or sent to the battlefront as common soldiers.[69]

Profit from minting money derived from the debasement of coinage. From May 1544 (still in Henry's reign) to January 1551 (son Edward VI had ascended) this item netted £900,000.[70] Averaged for six years, the annual income from this source amounted to £138,000, larger than any other item in the above table. But the debasement of coinage meant price inflation. In the long run it was not beneficial to the king, who had to purchase his war supplies.

English customs revenue in this age was a very complicated matter. Customs duties, according to the articles, were divided into "great" and "petty" customs. Imports were separated from exports, and French wine alone stood as a separate category. All this was necessary because of tradition and because they were farmed to different tax farmers. So long as the items followed precedents, the collection was legitimate. The controversy came from a subsidy item called "tonnage and poundage." Its collection also followed precedent; but in the past when Parliament authorized its collection it carried the condition that along with duties on wool and cowhides the proceeds must be used for coastal defense. Moreover, when Parliament made the subsidy available it had either limited the imposition to three years or termed it collectible for the king's life.[71] The parliamentarians therefore jealously regarded the right to grant this item essential to their control of the purse. Customs duties were in general small during the Tudor period. But in the seventeenth century when the volume increased under the Stuarts, the collection of tonnage and poundage sparkled a major controversy between the king and Parliament.

At first glance, purveyance seems to be an item of expenditure rather than income. The king's court always remained a ground of feasts and festivals. The lavish banquets consumed chickens and cattle by the thousands. Beer and wine flowed freely. The supplies, together with the wagons transporting them, were purveyed. The quantities were farmed to the shires and townships by justices of peace, as far away as Wales. Henry VIII spent £20,000 annually on this item; Elizabeth I doubled the amount. But more than purchase, the cost of the purvey material was unitarily decided by the purveyor. In the early years of the seventeenth century, Francis Bacon disclosed that the price paid by the court in general consisted of only a quarter of the market value.[72] The hidden requisition during Henry's reign therefore had a value of £60,000 annually.

When all the above items are counted, Henry's ordinary annual income should have been in the vicinity of £250,000. With extraordinary items added, it went to £550,000.

Other income is omitted from the above listing. Tax receipts at Calais (in France) and Ireland were spent locally. Bills of attainder were accompanied by the confiscation of the properties of the offenders. Praemunire means disrespect of the crown; it resulted in a stiff fine. Together with fines on the clergy, those items might be significant but uncertain. Royal borrowings from merchants in Germany and Flanders played a significant role in governmental finance in this age. Nevertheless they should not be allowed to confuse revenues.

Henry's major financial problem came from military expenditure. From 1540 to 1550 (the last eight years of his own reign plus the first three years of Edward's), England spent £2,134,000 in waging wars against Scotland and France.[73] A specialist concludes that if that had not been the case, the king should have had an annual surplus of £60,000.[74] The writer goes on to lay charges against the king: "Henry had squandered his resources. He left to his son a debt of £100,000 fl. in Flanders, an empty treasury, a debased currency, depleted estates and charges vastly increased by the necessity of maintaining a postwar establishment in France and against Scotland."[75]

With the long historical context of 450 years subsequent to Henry's time and with surrounding events in view, we are not, however, altogether anxious to embrace the above criticism. The adventures of Henry VIII marked only the beginning of a colossal organizational change that was demanded of the entire Western civilization. Europeans were at first faced with the choice in the sixteenth century: Should there be an ineffective universal empire or would individual states in a competitive stance working toward a balance of power be a better alternative? Could the universal church continue to take hold? When the several states, secularized and structured on a nationalist basis and rivaling one another, emerged to become the answer, they began to secure their boundaries and make their territories compact. Only then did England become aware that continental bridgeheads had to be abandoned; union with Scotland had to be pushed through in one way or another. Even Oliver Cromwell's onslaught on Ireland could be said to have come from this impulse. But all this had to be tried and tested in the field. We cannot see how the intervening steps, wasteful as they may seem to us, could have been altogether avoided.

Development in the seventeenth century was further tied to episcopal discipline versus parliamentary supremacy. In retrospect, efficiency was a deciding factor of paramount importance. At a time when governmental functions had to expand, its finances might have to take general participation and public supervision into account and the entire polity had better be remodeled on republican and mercantile lines. But this was far from clear until the eighteenth century and even later. And we ourselves had to turn the pages of Machiavelli, Bodin, Harrington, Hobbes, Locke, Smith, Hegel, and Marx to become familiar with the proceedings of how a medieval society worked its way toward the modern age. For most of the time impersonal factors took command. Men of historical fame merely acted as agents. Their exertion brought the forces to bear.

Henry VIII in his youthful years fancied being elected Holy Roman Emperor. Next he wished to have Cardinal Wolsey installed as pope. Only when frustrated on both counts did he break with Rome on the issue of marriage nullification and work in earnest for an independent England. In reviewing his governmental finance, we can do better by focusing our attention on the fact that he had taken a step toward turning England from a dynastic state to a national state, even though it was still only a preliminary step. Only in this light can we make a relevant comparison between his financial establishment with those of China's under the Ming and Qing.

With all items stated in pound sterling, Henry's finances outwardly seem to have reached the stage of being fully "mathematically managed," that is, all items of income and expenditure are collected and disbursed and can be audited in accordance with a set of laws governing the legal tender, so that the moneyed items remain interchangeable, and consequently,

government finance merges with civilian economy and becomes a component of primary importance. This was far from the case, however.

We cannot even say that Henry's "system" was superior or inferior
to Yongle's. Both sides derived the lion's share of their income from
land. On paper, the Chinese had a well-established system of taxation;
its broad and uniform coverage seemed to be streamlined. Its weakness
was embedded in the fact that the whole concept of taxing the individual self-cultivators ran ahead of its time. Lacking adequate technical
and legal support, the program was always corrupted beforehand. The
inadequacy had to be covered with bureaucratic connivance. A tax
base built up from the mass of the peasantry moreover restricted any
future maneuverability.

On the other hand, Henry barely managed to integrate the various
kinds of revenue into his own hands; he still suffered from the feudal
fragmentation of authority. The same revenue from land had to be
divided into rents, dues, tithes, wardship, and subsidies. Those categories traced their origins to the different concepts of ownership (in reality, "seizin," or right to possession) entangled with a bewildering
assortment of rights and reciprocal obligations that had been built from
the bottom up, so that, obsolete as they were, they could not be simply
swept away. Such being the infrastructure of the rural economy, the
collection of customs duties followed the same pattern. Nor would a
money economy or a market economy progress very far, so long as
those conditions prevailed. Purveyance remained necessary because
the market mechanism to supply the needed articles in quantity was not
yet in place.[76]

Stressing China's monolithic tax structure, we must point out that
landed properties under direct imperial control or carved out as
princely estates under the Ming and Qing were negligible in number
and never came close to being a significant factor interfering with
governmental finance.[77] As for off-schedule extraction, both Yongle
and Henry resorted to it with mixed results.[78] The only difference
rested in the fact that in England rights to private property could be
occasionally raided but not ignored completely. When pressed, Henry
had to resort to private borrowing and the pawning of the crown jew-
els. The Chinese emperor, acting under the pretense that he personally
owned what was within the Four Seas, acted with no such scruples.
Yet in practice he was also restricted by his own institutional capability. In the seventeenth century when the tax collectors failed to deliver,

and there was nothing to be borrowed, the dynasty had to fall with its failed finance.[79]

In terms of total revenue in monetary value, a quick comparison can be made by converting the figures into net worth of silver. Since in Henry's last years the pound contained only four ounces of silver[80] (here we follow Peng Xinwei's calculation formula), his annual income of £550,000 could be restated as worth 2,200,000 ounces of silver. A similar calculation of Yongle's revenue would be difficult, as the accounts contained a large number of commodities collected in wide areas, not to mention off-schedule impositions. But in the late sixteenth century when the use of silver was widespread in China, and tax revenue had been much more regularized, the net worth of the Ming empire's annual income could be estimated as follows:

Table 2

The Annual Revenue of the Ming Empire
(Circa 1570–1580)[81]

Land taxes, as delivered to the county government, including service charges	taels 25,000,000
Salt gabelle.	taels 2,000,000
Miscellaneous, including business taxes, income from mining, and administrative income, etc.	taels 3,780,000
Total	taels 30,780,000

A tael weighs about 1.3 ounces. The above total therefore has a value of close to 40 million ounces of silver. The amount clearly dwarfed Henry VIII's £550,000, calculated to be worth 2.2 million ounces, only some twenty years earlier.

We realize that this is a wild comparison. Prices varied. Population figures and territorial sizes were different. The resources mobilized by Henry were almost all spent by him—the local government incurred very few expenses—while the revenue of the Chinese empire was depleted all the way up by three tiers of bureaucratic management before being delivered to the center. But our purpose is to fix the date when England overtook China in national wealth and fiscal administrative ability (see below). Suffice it to say that this did not happen during Henry's reign.

Nor did it happen during those of the next three Tudor monarchs, Edward (r. 1547–1553), Mary (r. 1553–1558), and Elizabeth (r. 1558–1603).

Running into deficit, King Henry had started to sell off the monastic properties that he had taken over from the church. This was followed without interruption by his heirs for several decades. Especially during Elizabeth's reign, England faced several serious crises, including the Spanish Armada. Even more calculating, she is known to have disposed of estates which had produced an annual income of £24,808 for £813,332.[82] The accession of James I (r. 1603–1625) saw the crown lands seriously depleted; yet further sales were necessitated by royal indebtedness until, in 1628, "the crown lands ceased to be an important part of royal income, where a century before the crown had been the principal landowner in the country."[83]

In the past, historians deplored the fact that the Tudor and Stuart royal houses, too anxious for cash, had sold monastic and crown lands at giveaway prices. The thoughtless act weakened the monarchy. A new school of British scholars in recent decades, however, has looked at the matter differently. While there were cases of corruption and giveaway in the sales, the fundamental problem in disposing of the estates in question arose from the fact that they were entangled with possession and rental problems deeply embedded in the feudal past. It had been a medieval tradition that the lands could not be sold. But in practice customary laws could be bypassed and money changing hands with the estates had been going on for centuries.[84] There was the problem with the villeins, who, following their ancestors, had been working on the same plots of land for a long time. Yet it was unclear whether they were self-cultivators or renters. Some of them paid a stiff entry fine but only token annual rent. From 1500 to 1600, farm prices in general increased fourfold. Yet on some lands the rents could not be readjusted. There were cases in which the properties were hidden and the tenants-in-chief could not be located. Conducted in a hurry, the sales were moreover poorly organized and short of funds for proper management.[85]

Given these conditions, the sales in reality offered an opportunity for individual buyers to clear away the ambiguities and put the acreages to more efficient use. At the same time, elimination of the king as a large landowner simplified the tax administration; the classification of land revenue into several categories could be avoided.

The civil war that tormented England for a large part of the 1640s could in a similar manner be seen as a part of the integrating and rationalizing process. Landed properties had been confiscated, sequestered, and auctioned during the turmoil, and in many cases redeemed by the former owners. The turnabout also called for more investment in ownership and thus strengthened the estates, although there was little justice in the individual cases.

Together with the enclosure acts, this movement of settling problems of landownership was a long-term process. So far as I know, therefore, no single treatise covered all the details. (Since the original problem is said to be troublesome, it is unlikely that it can be adequately documented.) But we have sufficient lateral evidence to testify that after a century's turmoil, a settlement was in sight. At first, in the early seventeenth century, villeins disappeared. By the middle of the century, cases calling for entry fines became rare; annual rents had become the norm. Freeholders began to assume their present status; they no longer paid rents. From the end of the civil war to restoration, that is, from 1648 to 1660, litigations on landownership rising from disputes over customary law were no longer so often heard. The cavaliers who had lost their landed properties during the war were, with few exceptions, able to borrow money for their redemption. From this point on toward the early eighteenth century, large landowners gained ascendancy. Farms less than 300 acres diminished in number, while those over 10,000 acres increased. The common method of expansion was the gradual takeover of the parcels and plots on the fringes of one's own compact holding. It was an age, as a contemporary saw it, of "opportunity for the capable, loss for the incapable."[86]

While all this was going on, more enclosure acts were passed. The terrain gradually took the shape of the checkerboard pattern that has since then defined the rural landscape of England. The absorption of commercial capital by the farm belt also made it possible to build many turnpikes and to allow country banks to mushroom in the early eighteenth century.

The sale of monastic and royal lands was not the sole factor making the gradual transformation possible; but it was, initially, the most significant factor in setting the entire sequence of events in motion.

Nevertheless, the movement was so slow and gradual that even researchers nowadays need time to grasp the causes and effects along with the background factors. They were less clear to contemporaries.

And dynastic rulers had no inkling of how to take advantage of the situation. In Mary's time faced with dwindling income from land, the court shifted its attention to customs revenues.[87] Otherwise, lacking institutional reform, it would go deeper into indebtedness. The shrewdness and improvisation of Elizabeth made little difference. The trend was carried on until the arrival of the Stuarts. Royal revenue in the early seventeenth century appears as follows:

Table 3

Royal Revenue under the Early Stuarts[88]

	1610	1614	1619	1623	1635
Customs and imposition	£247,810	£242,788	£284,900	£323,042	£328,126
Land and feudal revenue	£144,154	£130,474	£157,744	£170,608	£192,340
Tenth and First Fruit	£ 16,000	£ 16,000	£ 18,072	£ 18,137	£ 19,359
Star Chamber fines	—	£ 1,000	£ 14,000	£ 14,000	£ 3,964
Recusancy fines	£ 9,000	£ 6,000	£ 6,300	£ 5,000	£ 13,408
Miscellaneous	£ 44,561	£ 25,634	£ 19,568	£ 21,716	£ 30,852
Composition of purveyance	—	—	—	—	£ 30,330
Total	£461,525	£421,896	£487,984	£589,903	£618,379

In the above table revenues from customs counted for more than half the total, while those from land in general were about a third, and the remaining one-sixth had much to do with the church and clergy. In the face of still growing demand for funds, it seems quite logical that the Stuart kings had to clash with their subjects over the collection of customs duty and over their attempt to govern with ecclesiastic discipline.

Tracing the causes of the English civil war and revolution, one school of thought puts emphasis on religion. The first two Stuart kings, James I (r. 1603–1625) and Charles I (r. 1625–1649), cherished church discipline. Their sense of good kingship went hand to hand with stalwart bishops, which in turn ran counter to the popular demand for freedom of conscience. The next two kings after the restoration, Charles II (r. 1660–1685) and James II (1684–1688), embraced Catholicism; they wished to line up a French style of government, which also agitated the public.

Another school of thought stresses economic influence. Since the sale of monastic properties by the Tudors, the center of gravity of England had moved in favor of the rising gentry. The conflict of interest reflected the new rich asserting itself.

In reality, the two schools of thought are not so unconnected to each other as they may at first seem to be. Within the historical context of the seventeenth century, religious emphasis had strong socioeconomic implications. As happened elsewhere, in the course of major reconstructions of society, the preliminary steps are always stirred up by ideology. When even the revolutionaries are unsure about their own objectives (this happened to Cromwell, too), symbolism and abstraction best serve the purpose at this early stage. But once the deeds are done and the revolutionary zeal already expended, the economic character of the new order becomes evident and the cause-and-effect relationship within the entire sequence of events is no longer puzzling.

We have admitted that in China, when the emperor was regarded as Son of Heaven, the notion immediately carried a corollary that he owned all that was within the Four Seas. If James I's vision that "kings are breathing images of God on earth" should take hold, there would be no telling how far the royal prerogative in England would go along the same line. In fact, in 1637, when the Court of Exchequer decided in favor of Charles regarding the collecting of ship money, the opinions expressed by several judges already inflated the king's prerogative "beyond all expectation or limit," and, should it have been fully realized, it would have created a situation in which "no man were left with anything that he might call his own."[89] No wonder that in the subsequent showdown the renunciation of Arminianism had to accompany the refusal to pay tonnage and poundage. One grievance led to another, and the irreconcilable positions moved toward armed conflict. War by itself rarely solves problems. For England during the mid-seventeenth century, the rationalization of landownership outlined above was still in progress; the enactment of new laws rendering all economic components interchangeable had not yet been given serious consideration. Oliver Cromwell (effective head of government, Commonwealth and Protectorate, 1649–1658), even in victory, found his own position not fundamentally different from that of his predecessor Charles, whom he had sent to the scaffold. He too had to dissolve Parliament; he even installed a government by major generals. He too, forced loans from the East India Company and borrowed from

London's goldsmiths. When his son Richard (Protector, 1658–60) took over, annual government finance appeared as follows:[90]

	England	Scotland	Ireland	Total
Revenue	£1,517,000	£144,000	£208,000	£1,869,000
Expenditure	£1,548,000	£307,000	£346,000	£2,201,000
Deficit	£ 31,000	£163,000	£138,000	£ 332,000

Unknown to contemporaries, government indebtedness in this age could no longer be avoided. Call it capitalism if you wish, a rapidly expanding economy requires deficit financing, in private as well as in public sectors. The wide extension of credit, impersonal management, and pooling of service facilities, including legal services, call for the interchangeability of all the economic components in order to maximize the utilization of the nation's resources. The other side of the coin is that unless the men in charge were hard pressed and debt-laden, they would not strive to seek breakthroughs.

For England, the breakthrough finally came in 1689. William and Mary (reigned, 1689–1702), although legitimate heirs of the Stuarts, were invited over to be co-sovereigns by the politicians and merchants of London. Thus as king and queen they were elected. The Bill of Rights established parliamentary supremacy in principle. But it was the founding of the Bank of England in 1694 that settled the issues of taxation and governmental finance on a long-term basis. The bank loaned to the government £1,200,000 at an annual interest of 8 percent, guaranteed by customs revenue and excise on alcoholic beverages. So long as the annual interest was paid, the principal could remain in the books. There were 1,267 shareholders of the bank, headed by the king and queen themselves.[91] Clear for all to see, William and Mary separated themselves as individuals from the throne that they occupied, which means that from then on the king or queen was no longer personally responsible for national finance. Parliament had taken over.

The Glorious Revolution (1688–1689) was glorious because it succeeded with virtually no bloodletting. It went this way because the slow and gradual background work of rationalizing and integrating landownership, after going through ups and downs for decades, now began to bear fruit. Another determining factor, also accomplished with little fanfare, was the major progress made in judicial proceedings. Ever since the sixteenth century, a certain ineffectiveness in the nation's court system was evident. The common law, basically a legal instrument of the agrarian society and of the medieval age, inflexibly demanded that all events follow precedents. What had not been done before could not be attempted later. With legal process moving at a snail's pace, no provision was made for the changing circumstances of the age. Only as a relief, Tudor and Stuart prerogative courts had occasionally applied the principle of equity in some of the trial cases. The progress was interrupted by Parliament, which abolished those courts before the civil war. After restoration, the chancery once again took up the task in earnest. Soon the application of equity also created a body of precedents of its own. The time was ripe for a merger. In 1689, Sir John Holt became chief justice on King's Bench; he directed that thenceforth cases involving commercial interests be handled according to prevalent mercantile practice.[92]

Little noticed, when England moved toward the closing of the seventeenth century, it was no longer the same nation which had one foot in the medieval age and the other in the world of dynastic states. Now there was a new superstructure in parliamentary supremacy. There was a new bottom structure in the integrated land tenure. And there was a new set of institutional links between the top and bottom in renewed jurisprudence and in the fresh arrangement for public finance. The country could now be mathematically managed, all economic components were fully interchangeable between the private and public sectors and between the agrarian hinterland and the maritime coastal regions. In short, a nation with a substantial agricultural base could now be administered as if it were a city state.

Perhaps this success is less publicized than it deserves because it is mixed up with the advent of capitalism. The ideological emphasis obscures its broad coverage. But Joan Robinson, a scholar quite sympathetic with China's effort at renewing itself, argues that even in volume three of Marx's *das Kapital* the apostle of class struggle himself has pointed out that when the volume of production increases, the capitalists are in a state of competition, and profit must fall. It could not be otherwise.[93]

For England, the immediate benefit of the mathematically manageable situation was that it had rendered all items in the books clear and comprehensible. The land tax of 1692, without the service of tax farmers, produced £2 million at the Exchequer, which alone was unprecedented.[94]

Why had tax farmers been indispensable in the past? The ambiguities on the bottom level, including land tenure, debt obligations, etc., could not be unsnarled; and the responsibilities and functions on the top also remained uncertain. Legislation had not been brought up to date. Tax farmers, aware of all the anomalies, especially within their own areas of specialty, knew how to manipulate and bargain to fulfill the tax target with a profit for themselves.

Aside from lending to the state, the Bank of England lost no time in turning itself into an instrument for deficit financing to serve the general public. Recognizing the credit of £1.2 million that the bank had extended to itself, Parliament in addition authorized it to issue sealed bills in the same amount, which could also be loaned to private parties at interest. In this way one pound became two pounds. Credit inflation soon engulfed the country. Bad consequences such as that involving the South Sea Bubble had yet to happen, but, as a whole, many undertakings which could not have been attempted before could now be launched. The national expenditure of England jumped from £5 million in 1702 to £8 million in 1714. Within the same dozen years her national debt accumulated from £13 million to £36 million.[95] With her resources more efficiently husbanded at home and her overseas influence expanding steadily, she felt confident regardless.

The year 1714 was the fifty-third year of the reign of the Kangxi Emperor. A Qing historian estimates China's state revenue by then as follows:

Table 4

The Annual Revenue of the Qing Empire
(circa 1712–1722)[96]

Customs revenue, salt gabelle, and miscellaneous	taels 6,370,000
Land tax, poll tax, after local expenses	taels 23,000,000
Total	taels 29,370,000

Since one tael weighs about 1.3 ounces, the sum has a value close to 38 million ounces of silver, in the range of the annual expenditure of

England in 1714, again calculated at 4 ounces of silver to the pound, to be 32 million ounces. But by then England had a population of only 6 million, against China's 150 million.[97] We can say for sure that it was in the late years of the Stuarts, or the early period of the Qing, when the dynasty still maintained its high point of power, that China lost its lead in organizational capability and in the ability of developing national wealth to the West, in this case represented by Britain.

We have come a long way to assess the fiscal accounts of Yongle. In this present connection the numbers and figures by themselves are of no great value to us. But put together, they help to explain how the Ming Empire was managed in its early days. The significance of this set of data in modern Chinese history rests in the fact that with little revision the same style of management represented by those numbers held out until the early days of the twentieth century. Cromwell defeated King Charles at Marston Moor in 1644, the year of dynastic change in China. But we know that thereafter the Chinese virtually retained their state institutions intact. Thus, while Smith's speculation that China had been stationary over 500 years might have been exaggerated, an inevitable consequence is that China's national economy grew only with currency inflation and population size, but no qualitative, substantive changes.

The English experience enables us to see that what is referred to as the rise of capitalism does not come about merely from manipulation by moneybags. State institutions have to be committed. Public finance, embracing fiscal and taxation policies, has a great deal to do with the mobilization of a nation's resources. Especially in the developing of the service sector of the economy, jurisprudence holds a commanding position. Ultimately, though, a primary source of wealth comes from the agricultural sector; for that, landownership has to be integrated and made profitable. The process is so all-embracing that ideology and religion, positively or negatively, will be involved. Perhaps, after all, it should better be known as a change of monetary culture.

Regardless of how and why China fell behind, history proves that she must catch up. As Albert Feuerwerker pointed out forty years ago, China's failure to force savings from the agricultural sector of the national economy paralyzed her modernization effort. Until the last days of the nineteenth century, the entire revenue of the state amounted to only 89 million taels of silver. The sum had yet to service both the central and local government. China's defeat by foreign powers further siphoned away resources to war indemnities, comparing miserably with Japan's ascendancy.[98]

Following the long string of events, land reform and the subsequent Cultural Revolution in the present century, therefore, might have been bitter pills that China had to swallow. We know now that during those decades when the entire nation was clad in blue and ate at communal kitchens, it did amass substantial savings. According to a research institute under Beijing's State Council, the contribution from the agricultural sector alone amounted to ¥600 billion (1985 prices).[99] Beyond our power of praising and condemning, we only hope that with all these and the current economic reform Chinese history has finally rid itself of its dynastic cycle, and the state apparatus of its religious tone in governance.

Notes

Source: Part of this article, in Chinese, appear in *Explorations in Science and Technology in China* (Ouji Publications, Shanghai, 1982) and *Fang-k'uan Li-shi ti shih-chieh* (Yungchen Publications, Taipei, 1988).

Part One

1. Wada Sei, *Minshi Shokkashi Yakuchū* (Tokyo, 1957), p. 145.
2. *Taizong shilu,* pp. 0689, 0895–96.
3. Ibid., p. 1043.
4. Ibid., pp. 1693–94.
5. *Mingshi* (Zhonghua shuju reprint, Beijing, 1974), ch. 149, p. 4153.
6. *Taizong shilu,* pp. 1435, 2070.
7. *Da-Ming huidian* (Dongnan shubaoshe reprint, Taipei), ch. 24, p. 14; ch. 25, p. 12.
8. Ray Huang, *Taxation and Governmental Finance in Sixteenth Century Ming China* (Cambridge: Cambridge University Press, 1974), p. 101.
9. The low wage in China was mentioned by Adam Smith in the eighteenth century and by Karl Marx in the nineteenth century. See Smith, *An Inquiry into the Nature and Causes of the Wealth of Nations* (Everyman's Library), vol. 1, p. 63, and Marx, *Capital: A Critique of Political Economy,* vol. 1, trans. by Ben Hawkes (New York: Vintage Books, 1977), p. 749n.
10. Toward the end of the dynasty, a wealthy county usually had about one thousand persons receiving tax and service exemptions. See Huang, *Taxation and Governmental Finance,* pp. 246, 357n.
11. Ibid., pp. 308, 365n.
12. *Mingshi,* ch. 79, pp. 1916–17.
13. Ibid., ch. 79, p. 1918.

14. Ibid., ch. 72, p. 1745.

15. Huang, *Taxation and Governmental Finance*, p. 55; *Mingshi*, ch. 79, p. 1919. For the hardship of soldiers on transportation duty, see my doctoral dissertation, "The Grand Canal During the Ming Dynasty, 1368–1644" (University of Michigan, 1964), pp. 86–90.

16. *Mingshi*, ch. 77, p. 1884.

17. Sun Chengze, *Chungming mengyu lu* (Longmen Shuju reprint, Hong Kong), ch. 36, p. 3.

18. Xu Fuyuan, et al., eds., *Huang-Ming jingshi wenbian* (Xuesheng Shuju reprint, Taipei), ch. 368, pp. 21, 24; ch. 359, p. 3; ch. 360, p. 10.

19. Huang, *Taxation and Governmental Finance*, pp. 189–95.

20. Ibid., p. 203.

21. *Taizong shilu*, pp. 0176–77, 0249–50, 0280, 0590, 0622–23.

22. *Xuanzong shilu*, p. 0095.

23. These sixty-nine entries are found in *Taizong shilu*, pp. 2981–3078.

24. The exact amount is 20,382,990 *quan*. See *Taizong shilu*, p. 3079.

25. About rationed salt, see *Taizong shilu*, pp. 0509, 0589–90; Wada Sei, *Minshi Shokkashi Yakuchū*, p. 608; and Huang, *Taxation and Governmental Finance*, pp. 138–39, 247.

26. *Xuanzong shilu*, p. 0175.

27. *Taizong shilu*, p. 1667; *Da-Ming huidian*, ch. 151, p. 6.

28. Lu Rong, *Shuyuan zaji* (*Jilu huibian* ed.), ch. 181, pp. 25–26.

29. *Renzong shilu*, p. 0015.

30. *Mingshi*, ch. 92, p. 2274; Sun, *Chungming mengyu lu*, ch. 53, pp. 4–6; Huang, *Taxation and Governmental Finance*, pp. 104–5.

31. *Mingshi*, ch. 78, p. 1895; Huang, *Taxation and Governmental Finance*, pp. 136–37.

32. *Taizong shilu*, pp. 0488, 2421.

33. Huang, *Taxation and Governmental Finance*, pp. 227, 240–43. Based on *Mingshi*, ch. 81, pp. 1973–74, and *Da-Ming huidian*, ch. 194, p. 76, and several local gazetteers.

34. *Taizong shilu*, pp. 2308–9.

35. Peng Xinwei, *Zhongguo huobishi* (Shanghai, 1954), p. 281.

36. Quan Hansheng, *Zhongguo jinjishi luncong* (Hong Kong, 1972), p. 384; Huang, *Taxation and Governmental Finance*, p. 317.

37. *Taizong shilu*, pp. 1908, 1974, 2052, 2117, 2245, 2300, 2364, 2421; *Renzong shilu*, p. 0194.

38. *Mingshi*, ch. 78, p. 1906.

Part Two

39. *Hanshu* (Zhonghua shuju reprint, Beijing, 1960), ch. 99b, p. 4111.

40. Ibid., ch. 24, pp. 1777–78.

41. *Suishu* (Zhonghua shuju reprint, Beijing, 1973), ch. 24, p. 676.

42. *Songshi* (Zhonghua shuju reprint, Beijing, 1977), ch. 176, p. 4281.

43. Ibid., ch. 186, p. 4550.

44. Ibid., ch. 174, p. 4213.

45. Ibid., ch. 175, p. 4243.

46. Quan, *Zhongguo jinjishi luncong,* pp. 235, 325.

47. *Taizong shilu,* pp. 2681–82, 4143.

48. Huang, *Taxation and Governmental Finance,* pp. 34–35. This is based on local gazetteers. Among them the 1578 edition of *Jinhua fuzhi* and Shen Bang, *Wanshu zaji* (reprint, Beijing, 1961) give detailed descriptions.

49. Ibid., pp. 45–50.

50. Huang, *Taxation and Governmental Finance,* p. 322.

51. Chen Gonglu, *Zhongguo jindaishi* (Taipei, 1965), pp. 238–39, 665–66, 687–89; E-tu Zen Sun, "The Board of Revenue in Nineteenth Century China," *Harvard Journal of Asiatic Studies,* 24 (1962–63).

52. Peng, *Zhongguo huobishi,* p. 508.

53. Ibid., pp. 493, 502.

54. R.H. Tawney, *Religion and the Rise of Capitalism* (Pelican ed., 1977), p. 158.

55. Huang Renyu, *Zibenzhuyi yu ershiyi shiji* (Taipei, 1991), p. 143.

56. Ping-ti Ho, "The Salt Merchants of Yangchou: A Study of Commercial Capitalism in Eighteenth Century China," in *Harvard Journal of Asiatic Studies* 17:1–2 explains how the rich merchants squandered their fortunes away. They could not and did not try to work for unlimited capital accumulation.

57. Huang, *Taxation and Governmental Finance,* p. 150.

58. Ibid., pp. 294–301.

59. *Da-Ming huidian,* ch. 24, pp. 14–16; ch. 25, pp. 1–3. The exact amounts are 26,782,259 piculs for 1502 and 26,638,412 piculs for 1578.

60. Chinese population is based on Ping-ti Ho, *Studies on the Population of China: 1368–1953* (Cambridge, MA: Harvard University Press, 1959), p. 264.

61. Yeh-ch'ien Wang, *Land Tax in Imperial China: 1750–1911* (Harvard University Press, 1973) and Madeleine Zelin, *The Magistrate's Tael: Rationalizing Fiscal Reform in Eighteenth-Century Ch'ing China* (Berkeley: University of California Press, 1984).

62. Smith, *Wealth of Nations,* vol. 1, p. 63.

Part Three

63. Joan Thirsk, ed., *The Agrarian History of England and Wales, vol. IV, 1500–1640* (Cambridge University Press, 1967), pp. 262–63; Frederick C. Dietz, *English Government Finance, vol. I, 1485–1558* (London, 1964), pp. 138–41, 156–57, 162, 177.

64. Dietz, *English Government Finance,* vol. 1, p. 142.

65. Thirsk, *Agrarian History,* vol. IV, pp. 265–67.

66. Dietz, *English Government Finance,* vol. 1, pp. 30–31; Godfrey Davies, *The Early Stuarts, 1603–1660* (Oxford: Oxford University Press, 1937), pp. 4–5.

67. Dietz, *English Government Finance,* vol. 1, p. 138.

68. Ibid., p. 159.

69. Ibid., p. 166.

70. Ibid., p. 177.

71. Ibid., p. 11.

72. Thirsk, *Agrarian History,* vol. IV, pp. 516–19; L.A. Clarkson, *Pre-Industrial Economy of England* (New York, 1972), pp. 161–62; Davies, *The Early Stuarts,* p. 4; Dietz, *English Government Finance,* p. 424.

73. Ibid., p. 147.
74. Ibid., p. 142.
75. Ibid., p. 158.
76. Allegra Woodworth, "Purveyance for the Royal Household in the Reign of Elizabeth," *American Philosophical Society NS,* xxxv, 1946, pp. 3 sq.
77. Ray Huang, *1587, A Year of No Significance* (Yale University Press, 1981), p. 77; Huang, *Taxation and Governmental Finance,* appendix A, p. 325.
78. Dietz, *English Government Finance,* vol. 1, pp. 165–66.
79. Huang, *Taxation and Governmental Finance,* pp. 308, 365n.
80. Dietz, *English Government Finance,* vol. 1, p. 176.
81. Huang, *Taxation and Governmental Finance,* pp. 175, 216, 263.
82. Thirsk, *Agrarian History,* vol. IV, p. 268; Dietz, *English Government Finance,* vol. 1, p. 298.
83. Thirsk, *Agrarian History,* vol. IV, p. 272; Dietz, *English Government Finance,* vol. 1, p. 301.
84. Theodore Plucknett, *A Concise History of the Common Law,* 5th ed. (London, 1956), pp. 159, 539.
85. Thirsk, *Agrarian History,* vol. IV, pp. 265–76.
86. Ibid., vol. IV, pp. 302–5, 684–85; vol. 5, pt. 2, pp. 144–45, 153, 163, 198–99.
87. Dietz, *English Government Finance,* vol. 2, pp. 306–7.
88. Samuel Gardiner, *History of England from the Accession of James to the Outbreak of the Civil War, 1603–1642* (reprint, New York, 1965), vol. 10, p. 222.
89. Maurice Ashley, *England in the Seventeenth Century* (Pelican ed.), p. 68.
90. Godfrey Davies, *The Restoration of Charles II, 1658–1660* (San Marino, CA, 1955), p. 70.
91. John Giuseppi, *The Bank of England: A History of Its Foundation in 1694* (reprint, Chicago, 1956), p. 12.
92. Plucknett, *Concise History of the Common Law,* p. 246.
93. Joan Robinson, *An Essay on Marxian Economics,* 2d ed. (London, 1967), pp. viii–ix, xv, 15.
94. J.S. Bromley, ed., *Cambridge Modern History,* vol. 6 (Cambridge: Cambridge University Press, 1970), pp. 285–86; G.N. Clark, *The Later Stuarts, 1660–1714* (Oxford: Oxford University Press, 1940), p. 169.
95. Giuseppi, *Bank of England,* p. 35; P.G.M. Dickson, *The Financial Revolution of England: A Study of the Development of Public Credit, 1688–1756* (London, 1967), pp. 42–46.
96. Xiao Yishan, *Qingdai tongshi* (reprint, Taipei, 1972), vol. 2, p. 1254; Zelin, *The Magistrate's Tael,* pp. 1n, 312.
97. The Chinese population immediately after 1700 remained in the vicinity of 150 million. Ho, *Studies on the Population of China,* p. 270.
98. Albert Feuerwerker, *China's Early Industrialization: Shen Hsuan-huai and Mandarin Enterprise* (Cambridge, MA: Harvard University Press, 1958), pp. 42, 247.
99. Rural Research Institute, *Development Research Bulletin,* supplement no. 21 (December 1986), p. 5.

Index

With his books appearing in six languages and selling more than a million copies, **Ray Huang** is undoubtedly one of the most popular writers in Chinese history. In January 1999 alone, four of his books were on the best-seller list in Beijing. While his works are popular, his research is assiduous and his thinking startlingly original.

He has contributed to the *Cambridge History of China* and the *Ming Biographical Dictionary*; soon a chapter he co-authored with the late Joseph Needham will appear in a new issue of *Science and Civilisation in China*. He is the author of *1587: A Year of No Significance*. His articles and book reviews have been published in the *Journal of Asian Studies*, *Oriens Extremus*, and the *Pacific Historical Review*.

Broadening the Horizons of Chinese History stands on the middle ground between his more erudite works and his popular titles. While rich with insight into modern Chinese history, the exposition nevertheless reaches out to specialists and general readers alike. This volume may also be regarded as a sourcebook for and teacher's guide to Mr. Huang's succinct and popular *China: A Macro History*.

Ray Huang served in the Chinese Nationalist Army as a junior officer for ten years. He received his Ph.D. in history from the University of Michigan.